Slinging Doughnuts for the Boys

Elizabeth A. Richardson, American Red Cross Volunteer, 1944. *Courtesy Anne Bodle Schuknecht.*

Slinging Doughnuts for the Boys

AN AMERICAN WOMAN IN WORLD WAR II

James H. Madison

INDIANA UNIVERSITY PRESS

BLOOMINGTON AND INDIANAPOLIS

This book is a publication of

Indiana University Press
601 North Morton Street
Bloomington, IN 47404-3797 USA

http://iupress.indiana.edu

Telephone orders   800-842-6796
Fax orders   812-855-7931
Orders by e-mail   iuporder@indiana.edu

*The paper used in this publication meets the minimum require-
ments of American National Standard for
Information Sciences—Permanence of Paper for
Printed Library Materials, ANSI Z39.48-1984.*

MANUFACTURED IN THE UNITED STATES OF AMERICA

Library of Congress Cataloging-in-Publication Data

Madison, James H.
Slinging doughnuts for the boys : an American woman in
World War II / James H. Madison.
p. cm.
Includes bibliographical references and index.
ISBN 978-0-253-35047-3 (cl : alk. paper)   1. Richard-
son, Elizabeth, 1918–1945.   2. World War, 1939–1945—
War work—Red Cross.   3. World War, 1939–1945—
Women—United States—Biography.   4. American
Red Cross—Biography.   5. Women—United States—
Biography. I. Title.
D807.U6M24 2007
940.54'771092—dc22
[B]
2007014985

1 2 3 4 5 12 11 10 09 08 07

DEDICATED TO THE MEMORY OF
CATHERINE M. MADISON, HOME-FRONT NURSE,
AND
WILLIAM A. MADISON, COMBAT INFANTRYMAN,
ENGLAND, FRANCE, GERMANY, CZECHOSLOVAKIA

Contents

Preface

Growing up in the 1950s, my heroes were the men of World War II. I read about ordinary GIs in Ernie Pyle's stories and about decorated heroes such as Audie Murphy. Some war heroes I knew personally, including my friend Gary's father, whose burn scars resulted from a Nazi shell that hit his Sherman tank. All kids in my small hometown knew that our friend Paul had no father. He died in the war. My own father survived combat but seldom talked about it. At the back door of our house hung his old army jacket, a spark to my boyhood fantasies.

These heroes shaped my world. They still do. But as a history professor reading and teaching about the war, I've expanded my list to include men such as Kurt Vonnegut, who told his war story in *Slaughterhouse Five*; Dietrich Bonhoeffer, the German Lutheran pastor who defied the Nazis; and Edward R. Murrow, who reported the news from London. Other heroes have joined my list over the years, but nothing has changed my connection to this war more profoundly than my accidental discovery of Elizabeth Richardson.

That discovery began on a spring day not long ago when I visited the American Cemetery in Normandy. I walked slowly among the 9,387 grave markers that stand above Omaha Beach. As I'd done before in such troubling places, I tried to find the dead from Indiana, my home state, as a way to make the overwhelming numbers more real and believable. It was easy to find Indiana men and to imagine the heroes among them. But then on this sunny day I read, etched in marble:

Elizabeth A. Richardson
American Red Cross
Indiana July 25 1945

Who was Elizabeth Richardson? Why was this woman buried among men who died fighting the Nazis? What did she do to deserve a place in this sacred soil? This book is the answer to my questions, offered in my words and, more importantly, in Elizabeth Richardson's own words.

When I returned home I wrote the librarians in Elizabeth Richardson's hometown of Mishawaka, Indiana. They sent me copies of a page from her high school yearbook and her obituary from the local newspaper. Those two pieces of paper might have satisfied my curiosity, except that I stumbled onto her brother Charles Richardson, Jr. (known in the family as "Butch"), who I learned had boxes of letters, a diary, photographs, and paintings. Charley's treasure boxes of first-hand source material pulled me deep into his sister's story.

So much of what I learned about Liz Richardson seemed ordinary. She grew up in a middle-class family in northern Indiana, near South Bend; attended Milwaukee Downer, a Midwestern liberal arts college; worked in advertising for Schuster's Department Store in Milwaukee; and then, in 1944, joined the American Red Cross. Even her wartime work in England and France might seem prosaic. From a converted London bus known as a Clubmobile, she served coffee and doughnuts to men going into or coming back from combat. Compared to the usual war stories I read as a kid, hers might seem slightly frivolous, just another example of women's work of the sort often judged inconsequential.

I eventually learned that the women slinging doughnuts and pouring coffee from Red Cross Clubmobiles were hardly typical and their work anything but ordinary. I've interviewed several Red Cross women, now elderly, who served in World War II, and I've read the letters and memoirs of many more. While the word "hero" is readily attached to men who fought in the war, this book suggests that among the Red Cross Clubmobile women there are candidates for similar accolades.

Without firing a weapon Liz Richardson came to know war—far better than most Americans at home and even better than many men overseas. The heart of her work was listening to and talking with GIs. In a windswept tent camp or on a nighttime dock near a troopship, she offered doughnuts and coffee to American boys as she smiled and wisecracked, laughed at their jokes, listened to their gripes, and, more quietly, sympathized with their frustration, loneliness, and hurt. Many GIs remembered her long after they first met, and she remembered them. In France, on April 2, 1945, she wrote her parents:

we were cruising past some resting troops, when I heard them shouting "Hey, Liz! Hey, Milwaukee!" It was a whole unit that we had known in England and we had a wonderful reunion right there on the road. And yesterday I met one of the cooks who had helped us brew our coffee during that week of the invasion of Holland. It's funny how they remember you and stranger yet how we can remember them after seeing thousand and thousands of faces.[1]

Like most Clubmobile volunteers, Liz developed strong feelings for these soldiers. They told her stories not reported in newspapers, stories of combat and brutality, of choices grimly made, of fears and deep regrets—stories that a GI might not write home to a wife or girlfriend, not tell children or grandchildren in the years to come, and sometimes not even confide to a best buddy. There is evidence, indeed, that Liz Richardson knew war. "I'm used to the men going over every minute on the line," she wrote her parents on May 28, 1945. In another letter home she lamented, "If you only knew what combat does to these boys—not in the physical sense, although that's bad enough—but mentally." She came to understand, as one historian has written, that war forced men "to do things which did not come naturally" and to know too that "it would have been a tragedy for their societies if it had been otherwise."[2]

Knowing war, certainly this war, meant seeing the best and worst of humanity. Liz lost her innocence in her first months overseas. Her letters and diary reflect a growing weariness shared by all who had seen too much. In a Mother's Day letter on April 8, 1945, she recalled the previous holiday: "a lot has happened since then, making me a wiser and sadder creature (the latter in itself a sign of wisdom)."

Americans in the decades after 1945 created a powerful "good war" myth that centered on heroic deeds, generous sacrifice, and proud victory. Few then or since would doubt that World War II was a necessary war, a just war, a war the Allied nations absolutely had to win. Liz Richardson believed passionately in the cause, but her experience suggests that the appellation "good war" is far too simplistic for the complexities, ambiguities, and heartaches she experienced.[3]

Red Cross Clubmobile women learned about war's hardships not only by listening to the GIs but also by experiencing it themselves. These women suffered cold and rain, days without baths, bone-jarring jeep rides, and shortages of food. Incongruities abounded. There was often plenty of liquor but, during Liz's first eight months overseas, no fresh milk and little fruit. Sometimes the food was abundant, embarrassingly so compared to British and French civilian diets, and sometimes it was only K rations. Food was a special hardship for those like Liz who had a large appetite and loved good food—excepting the Red Cross doughnuts she served every day ("repulsive, greasy things"). Sometimes the mail from family and friends came through; often it did not. Camaraderie only partly disguised the loneliness and homesickness that seeped into the core of these young women overseas. "Home seems far away," Liz wrote her brother John, two days after Christmas, 1944. Holidays were especially difficult times. Thanksgiving that year produced this laconic diary entry: "I ate my Thanksgiving dinner in the enlisted men's mess out of my mess kit. No one was very thankful."[4]

Like many curious Americans, Liz Richardson often delighted in the excitement of living and working overseas, but English and French cultural differences and routine inconveniences at times overwhelmed the spirit. Clubmobile women generally suppressed their own problems as they went about their daily work of lifting soldiers' morale. As Liz wondered in a letter to a friend, however, "Who takes care of the Red Cross's morale?"[5]

The Clubmobile women faced too the challenges of living as a sprinkling of females in a sea of men. Liz wrote soon after arriving in England, "You feel sort of like a museum piece—'Hey, look, fellows! A real, live American girl!'" In a letter to a Milwaukee friend she explained:

If you have a club foot, buck teeth, crossed eyes, and a cleft pallette [*sic*], you can still be Miss Popularity. The main thing is that you're female and speak English. It's certain that all of us will have more than a work-able knowledge of the ways of men. "Men, men, men," one of my co-workers was heard to exclaim the other night, "I hope I never see an-other"—a rather vain hope, as she no doubt knew.[6]

Matters of gender and sex were never far from the lives of Clubmo-bile women.[7] Unlike some of her colleagues, Liz was determined not to marry as long as the war confused and distorted personal relationships. Liz liked men and enjoyed being feminine. She wore perfume and lip-stick on duty and off; she went to dozens of dances and parties; she spent lots of time with men beyond serving them doughnuts and coffee; she fell in love with two lieutenants, the second passionately so. But she re-mained resolute when it came to marriage, even when her refusal to rush to the altar meant a falling out with the man she loved. Nor did she suc-cumb to temptations to feign girlish immaturity or flightiness, traits she disliked in other women. She was tall, athletic, physically strong, and not beautiful in the Hollywood way, so that playing the role of little girl was practically difficult as well as personally repugnant. More important, she knew that many of these men were still boys and that behaving like a silly girl was not what they most needed.

Much of Liz's ability to cope with war came from within—her intel-ligence, education, and personal character. She described herself in one letter as an eternal optimist. When writing home, she focused on good news and moved quickly through or around the bad. She wrote of home-sickness and hardship, but she seldom whined. Her keen observation of people and places helped her cope. Well educated and well read, she was quick to make comparisons and references that ranged from Gilbert and Sullivan operettas to Siegfried Sasson, John Keats, and Hollywood films. Her interest in art sparked attention to the natural world and prompted comparisons to a Bruegel landscape or a Cézanne or Van Gogh palette. On a rare day away from doughnuts and coffee, she went off with her sketch pad or watercolors. Liz saw too the ugliness of war's devastation of people and places. In a single letter or diary entry, she could capture the contrasts in her daily life—of war and tranquility, of ugliness and beauty, of brutality and generosity.

Liz liked to write. She found pleasure in trying to convey in words what she saw and learned. She wrote well, especially in describing people and places. Her art training helped. So did her reading, a part of an earnest effort at continuing self-education. Rather than seeing letter-writing as just an obligatory chore, she took it seriously and wrote engaging and informative letters—despite the military censor looking over her shoulder. She was witty and adept at word play, referring, for example, to captured German soldiers as "pouting gentlemen of the Wehrmacht-that-was."[8]

Liz's writing can be enjoyed on the surface. More interesting, however, is to read between the lines and to imagine what she was thinking. Her letters home were not always candid. Like most GIs, she usually obeyed the censorship rules and also willingly spared her family most of the worst news. She did not want them to worry. Yet, her letters differed somewhat depending on the intended recipient. In those to her parents she was a loving and respectful daughter. As she wrote her mother on April 8, 1945, "you and Daddy remain as always a very firm anchor from which I can't drift too far." Yet, her parents, Charles and Henrietta Richardson, sometimes frustrated her, especially her mother. Letters to her brother John, a marine, were more frank about family and military matters. And those to college friends were more revealing, particularly in matters of romance. Her diary entries, of course, suggested more than her parents knew.

Liz's correspondence is marked by modesty. There are glimpses nonetheless of her excellent skills in administration, human relations, and leadership. The Red Cross recognized these abilities in promotions and added responsibilities. Her colleagues respected and admired her. She was only twenty-five when she entered the service but mature and self-aware. She knew who she was and what she wanted.

Elizabeth Richardson died on July 25, 1945, in a military plane crash in France. She was twenty-seven. She never regretted her choice to serve in World War II. Referring to herself as "Auntie," she wrote to her best friend on September 4, 1944, "Damn glad I have a [college] degree—it helps so much in making doughnuts. However, I wouldn't trade this for anything else and it has more satisfaction in the doing than anything Auntie has ever done."[9]

abeth Richardson in England and France, 1944–1945. *Courtesy ISS Graphic Services, Indiana Uni-*
ty.

Chronology of
Elizabeth Richardson's Life

June 8, 1918	Birth
1936	Mishawaka High School, Indiana, graduate
1936–1940	Milwaukee-Downer College, Wisconsin
December 8, 1941	[United States enters World War II]
1940–1942	Mishawaka, back home with parents on Dragoon Trail
1942–1944	Milwaukee, Schuster's Department Store
May 15–July 7, 1944	Washington, D.C., American Red Cross training program
June 6, 1944	[D-Day, Allied invasion of France]
July 7–July 14, 1944	New York City
July 14–20, 1944	*Queen Elizabeth*, Atlantic crossing
July 21–August 1, 1944	London, Red Cross orientation
August 1–November 17, 1944	Leicester, England
September 1944	[Operation Market Garden, Holland]
November 17–November 28, 1944	Biddulph, England
November 28, 1944–February 2, 1945	Barrow-in-Furness, England
December 1944–January 1945	[Battle of the Bulge]
February 2–19, 1945	Warrington and Cornwall, England
February 19–25, 1945	London
February 25–March 1, 1945	Paris
March 1–July 25, 1945	Le Havre, France
May 8, 1945	[V-E Day, Germany surrenders]

(handwritten annotation: 1944 Join Red Cross)

CHRONOLOGY

July 25, 1945	Death
July 29, 1945	American Military Cemetery, St. Andre, France, interment
July 1948	Normandy American Cemetery, France, re-interment
June 6, 2007	Normandy American Cemetery, France, new visitor center, honoring Elizabeth Richardson, dedicated

Slinging Doughnuts for the Boys

[1]

Growing Up, Leaving Home, and Preparing for War

Some of Elizabeth A. Richardson's strength in war came from her secure and happy childhood. She was born June 8, 1918, in Akron, Ohio, where her father, Charles M. Richardson, Sr., was an executive with the Goodrich Rubber Company. The oldest of three children, she soon had a brother, John, born in 1922. When Liz was eleven her father took a position with Hood Rubber, near Boston, where her second brother, Charles, Jr., was born. In 1931 the family returned to the Midwest, to Mishawaka, an industrial town in northern Indiana where her father worked for Ball Band, a unit of the United States Rubber Company.[1]

Liz was close to her father, who she always called "Daddy." A farm boy from West Virginia, he became a successful business executive. He was a quiet, distinguished-looking man and "all business," one of Liz's high school friends, Anne Bodle, recalled, yet he remained down to earth. Liz's mother, Henrietta Mehlbach Richardson, was more vocal and more sophisticated in background and style. She had grown up in New York City and had studied music in Berlin for three years before marrying in 1917. Anne remembered that Henrietta was a "very correct New Yorker" and proud to be from the East. She clearly loved her three children, but Liz and her friends had to play quietly in the house and she seldom joined in their games. Both parents were Episcopalians and staunch Republicans, with no affection for Franklin D. Roosevelt and his New Deal. Even during the Great Depression the family had a maid who did the cooking.[2]

Liz and Anne Bodle met in the eighth grade and were inseparable through Mishawaka High School. After graduation they stayed in close touch. Like everyone else who remembers Liz, Anne spoke decades later of a very energetic girlfriend who "saw the funny side of everything" and was "always good for a laugh." At the same time, Anne wrote in 1982, "if there had been a women's movement in her day, she'd have been at the fore of it." Henrietta Richardson wanted the teenaged Liz to be more ladylike, to dress more stylishly, to let her hair grow longer and get a wavy permanent, but Liz stubbornly refused. Conscious of her large size as a teenager (and all her life—she grew to be 5'10" tall), Liz preferred a more active and simpler life. She and Anne went to parties, but there was not much real dating in high school, and there were no serious boyfriends. They walked to school, but depended on Liz's father for transportation farther away. Liz did not learn to drive until she was in Europe. Liz and Anne were both excellent students. Interested in current events, they worked together on the Mishawaka High School yearbook and the school newspaper, with Liz serving as managing editor of the latter. She already had a strong interest in painting and drawing cartoons and was president of the art club. Never shy, Liz performed in the class play and joined other school organizations. At home she was understanding of her kid brother, Charles, Jr., "Butch," a self-described "pain in the ass" who adored his big sister even as he tormented her.[3]

By the time Liz graduated from high school in 1936 she was the sort of accomplished, small-town Midwestern girl eager to move on. She found her place in Milwaukee at Downer College. Liz loved Downer, set on a beautiful campus, high above Lake Michigan, where the sounds of fog horns cut through the nights. Inside buildings of red brick with slate roofs she eagerly embraced the social and academic life of this small women's college. Downer was blessed with good professors, nearly all single women who lived on campus and were dedicated to a traditional liberal arts education. Liz majored in English and art. She studied hard and earned good grades in an academically demanding curriculum. Her painting became so accomplished that in her senior year she won the prize for the best student work at the Annual Wisconsin Art Salon in Madison. While she joked lightheartedly about professors and classes,

Downer College girls at play, with Liz Richardson in the center, laughing. *Courtesy Lawrence University Archives.*

she developed a lifelong curiosity that kept her engaged with art, music, literature, and international affairs in the years after graduation.[4]

There were many women's colleges in America in the early and mid-twentieth century. Most, like Downer, expected more than academic achievement. President Lucia Briggs wanted her students to be not only well-grounded in the liberal arts but also, as one recalled, "ladylike" in dress and behavior. Liz generally cooperated, as did the other students. They were not permitted to wear slacks to class. They wore hat and gloves to go to downtown Milwaukee for shopping, concerts, or a movie. They had to be in their dorms by 10:00 PM weekdays and no later than 12:30 AM on weekends. They ate all meals in the college dining hall, where a faculty member sat at each table to keep manners sharp and conversations on a high level.[5]

Downer students were not prissy hot-house flowers, however. Most had fun, and few more so than Liz. Everyone on the small campus knew her, and all knew her quick wit, her sense of humor, and the big smile she

Liz's cartoons of "Beulah" offered a wry commentary on Downer student life. This one, titled "Term Paper," shows Beulah in the uniform of college women of the late 1930s—saddle shoes, ankle socks, and a baggy sweater. *Courtesy Lawrence University Archives.*

usually wore. Strong and athletic, she was an active member on the rowing and field hockey teams. But she was probably best known for her drawing talent, which produced a popular campus cartoon about a fictional Downer student named "Beulah." Wearing saddle shoes, ankle socks, and a baggy sweater—the uniform of college women in the late 1930s—Liz's Beulah offered a clever and wry commentary on Downer life. Beulah appeared in all sorts of campus publications and flyers. Liz showed only close friends one of her more irreverent cartoons: Beulah sitting with students and faculty in the college dining room; everyone wearing a pair of shoes but nothing else (the students in their ubiquitous saddle shoes); a naked President Briggs saying to the naked dean, "Your shoes are untied." The girls thought it hilarious.[6]

They all played practical jokes, and Liz was a master. On several occasions she typed a letter to her roommate on official college stationery and signed President Briggs's name. Sometimes she got in trouble, even though as an upper-class student she served on the student board that heard cases of rules violations. Her college friend Betty Twining recalled that few students were as smart and quick as Liz in sneaking out a dorm window and then back in after hours. There were parties with boys and alcohol, although Liz never had a serious boyfriend during these joyous college years.[7]

There were less happy moments, too. One of the few who saw that Liz was "discouraged sometimes" was Ann Bumby, her roommate their junior and senior years. Ann recalled that "she could easily see thru the pretense, sham and bureaucracy in the world." Some of this was doubtless related to her prickly relationship with her mother, who believed that rules and social formalities were to be obeyed and who expected a great deal of her daughter. Liz complained to close friends about "St. Henrietta," a woman of strong opinions who did not indulge in frivolities. And she joked also about her aunt Lily Kimbel, a sort of New York jet-set type far removed from Liz's world.[8]

In some of the stories and essays Liz wrote for the Downer College magazine and especially in her personal diary it is apparent that she was anything but a simple-minded or frivolous girl. She thought for herself and gradually drifted from her parents' conservative politics to embrace Franklin Roosevelt and especially Eleanor, who seemed more like the kind of active, intelligent woman she and her friends wanted to be. By her senior year the joys of college rituals and pranks were waning, the sadness of parting from good friends wearing, the prospect of finding a job disconcerting. What upset her above all was the European crisis, which she followed closely in newspapers and on radio.[9]

Liz's attention to international affairs was heightened by Dean Amy M. Gilbert, a widely traveled historian, who was deeply interested in European affairs. In November 1939, just after Germany invaded Poland, Liz wrote her parents about an eight-part series of "excellent lectures" Dean Gilbert gave on international politics and diplomacy. Like many of her generation, Liz believed that America should remain isolated from Europe's tangled quarrels. The Great War of 1914–1918 had taught that lesson. The beginning of another European war found Liz and her friends in agreement that "the U.S. will be suckers if they enter it." In February 1940, Downer students heard a strong case for American intervention in a lecture by Clifton M. Utley, a foreign policy expert who strongly condemned the Axis aggression. As she read about the Nazi march across Europe in the last months of her senior year and as she listened to CBS radio reporter Edward R. Murrow describe the Blitz of London, Liz remained opposed to American involvement. She thought of her brother: "nothing could be more wasteful than a boy like John going to war, especially a modern war of efficiency the aim of which is to kill." Like nearly all Americans, Liz could not imagine what this war would become.[10]

Liz's happy undergraduate days ended with a whimper in June 1940. Not only did the terrible news of the Nazi conquest of France dampen spirits but Liz's trip to Chicago in search of an advertising job failed. By late June she was back home in Indiana. Her family had just moved to a house on Dragoon Trail outside of Mishawaka, which she called "The Patch." The property had a barn and large acreage so that her father could indulge his dream of becoming a gentleman farmer. Later, when writing from the other side of the Atlantic Ocean, Liz referred fondly to The Patch and the vegetables and melons her father grew. But living on Dragoon Trail in 1940 and 1941 with her mother, father, and kid brother, Butch, caused her life to take on a "discontented blur." A desperation job clerking at a Sears, Roebuck store in nearby South Bend only added to her unhappiness. "Someone give Eliz. a good kick," she lamented in her diary late that summer. She continued her unsuccessful search for an advertising job in Chicago and Milwaukee. After visiting with best friend Betty Twining in March 1941, she lamented that "my career is still at a standstill" and suggested that the two friends "go into business digging bomb shelters—that seems to be the coming thing."[11]

The war overseas helped end the Depression and create a welcome prosperity and jobs for Americans, including Liz. In early 1942 she received an offer to join the advertising department at Schuster's, a large Milwaukee department store chain. She eagerly left The Patch and jumped into a job she soon loved and excelled at, quickly earning more responsibility and promotion. As she joked to her aunt Lily, "I write signs— you know—Glamorize your legs with Slinky-Slank hosiery—79¢."[12]

Milwaukee roommates at 1718 N. Prospect apartment, ca. 1943. Liz is on the far right, with Betty Twining next to her. Others are not identified. *Courtesy Charles Richardson, Jr.*

Liz enjoyed the single social life in Milwaukee, too. The city was booming with war production, so much so that housing was in short supply. She shared a small, one-bedroom, second-floor apartment at 1718 North Prospect Street, overlooking Lake Michigan. Although temporary roommates came and went, the core were Liz and two friends from Downer: Chris Hanson, who also worked in advertising for Schuster's and who Liz sometimes called "Little Clarey"; and Betty Twining, known as "Twine," and sometimes "B-bub," who worked for the *Milwaukee Sentinel* newspaper. Life for the 1718 North Prospect gang was often "a big party," Chris recalled, with movies, concerts, dances, and lots of fun. Six decades later Chris and Twine would still remember Liz with a deep joy that conveyed an enduring friendship. (Each woman would name a daughter for their Milwaukee roommate.) Liz tended to be the organizer at 1718 North Prospect, the "responsible one," Chris Hanson recalled, as they shared chores and rotated beds (since one had to sleep on the couch). They made little pretense of traditional home decorating, not bothering to put up curtains in their one bedroom, for example. None much cared for cooking either. For Thanksgiving dinner, 1942, they bought a pre-cooked turkey "so we don't have to be too domestic about this business," Liz wrote her brother John. Liz was far more interested in art. She painted a wonderful watercolor, which she titled "The New Hat," depicting one of her roommates in front of their dresser mirror. She entered the painting in the Milwaukee Art Institute annual exhibition in spring 1944.[13]

Twine introduced Liz to her first real boyfriend, Ernst Kuenstner, who had immigrated to the United States from Germany in 1928. In her teasing voice Liz described Ernst to her brother John as "very nice, but ugly." In fact, he was rather handsome. She told her parents, more seriously, that he "was very bitter about the Nazis." The couple dated regularly, and Twine thought they were "lightly" in love. In late 1942, Ernst was drafted and soon left for basic training. He was thirty-four and had a brother in the German army. Ernst came back to visit Liz on military leave, but separation cooled the romance, at least on her side. They continued to correspond when Liz worked in England and France and Ernst was a GI in Italy. She dated other men in Milwaukee, including one named Andy Anderson, whom she would resume seeing in Washington, D.C.[14]

The war dominated the news by the time Ernst became a GI. Victory gardens, bond drives, and rationing of food, shoes, and gasoline convinced home-front civilians to do their part. Women entered war factories and other jobs in large numbers, sometimes taking jobs recently considered appropriate only for men. Far from home Americans died in combat. Milwaukee's youthful mayor, Carl Zeidler, volunteered for service and was lost to a German U-Boat attack in the Atlantic in late 1942.[15]

From 1718 North Prospect Liz closely followed the war news in Milwaukee papers, the *New York Times*, and on radio. She joined a discussion group on world problems and "the peace to come." Pearl Harbor had convinced her, like most of her generation, that this was a necessary war, yet she regretted the necessity. "Like a toothache, I hope it ends quickly," she wrote Aunt Lily three weeks after Pearl Harbor. She worried about male friends in uniform, including John Richardson, who left college to join the marines in summer 1943, Ernst Kuenstner, and a Milwaukee friend stationed on Guam who no one had heard from since Japanese troops overran the island. As Ernst prepared to leave for duty, she wrote home: "We all have weltschmerzlich [pain and sadness with the world] tonight—the war is rather overpowering, and it seems tough that we are the people who's [sic] friends are off fighting with such an indefinite future and so much horror to live through." In another letter to her parents she lamented, "This business is so upsetting—I wish I could be calm mentally about war and its various nasty manifestations." As much as she loved her job, "advertising," she confessed, "seems so awfully trite when I'm away from it." A cover illustration for the *Saturday Evening Post* in September 1942 doubtless captured her feelings. It showed a young woman in American Red Cross uniform as she walked by a store window displaying the height of civilian women's fashion; her look of disdain suggests the triteness Liz also felt.[16]

Elizabeth Richardson's eventual response to the pain of war was to volunteer at the Milwaukee USO, the club for visiting servicemen. On duty there, she explained to her parents, "I feed coffee, frankfurters, coke, and cheer to the armed forces once a week." She also volunteered to sketch portraits of GIs to send home. Off duty she painted a watercolor of the men in uniform and the women serving them. Working as a USO hostess was an introduction to war work and to GIs but not a sufficient remedy for her need to do something.[17]

In early 1944, Liz, her roommate Chris Hanson, and another Downer graduate, Margaret Flood, decided to join the American Red Cross. "We just had to go," Chris recalled. Liz's parents approved of her decision. She was so enthusiastic; they never imagined harm would come to her. It was her brother John, now a marine, they worried about.[18]

Liz's choice was logical, although there were female military units she might have joined instead of the Red Cross. She briefly considered the navy, but she wanted to go overseas, closer to the war. And the WAVES (Women Accepted for Volunteer Emergency Service), WACs (Women's Army Corps), and other women's units did mostly clerical and other support work at home. As Red Cross volunteer Katy Kirkpatrick recalled, "I wanted to be more of service than sitting in an office taking shorthand

and typing." There were gender issues as well. Many Americans questioned whether the military was a proper place for a woman. Men went to war, not women. Women needed protection; they might be hurt; they might become "mannish"; they might become sexually promiscuous. Less so than an army or navy uniform, a Red Cross uniform did not so directly challenge 1940s definitions of femininity and masculinity. Red Cross service seemed less troubling in mixing categories of "soldier" and "woman" (or more often in the 1940s, "girl"). It's unlikely Liz had such concerns, though her parents might have had.[19]

The American Red Cross was also more socially respectable than the military. Red Cross leaders were businessmen, often from the upper classes, who during the First World War had built a reputation for responsible and effective service to the troops. Some people thought its leaders a bit snobbish, yet the Red Cross was also a fixture of main-street America. The organization rose to unprecedented popularity with the beginning of another world war. Even before Pearl Harbor, for example, women in local chapters sewed flannel nightgowns for English children whose homes had been bombed by the Germans. American entry into the war brought an intense and sustained response from Washington headquarters. The number of employees increased from 935 in 1940 to 24,300 by 1945. Annual Red Cross war fund drives created enormous radio, newspaper, and movie newsreel publicity. The 1945 campaign distributed 1.3 million posters to be hung in libraries, offices, and train stations. Americans at home read magazine stories of Red Cross workers around the world comforting their sons, brothers, and husbands, doing, as Eleanor Roosevelt said in 1943, "the things which we would want to do ourselves, if we could be with our boys." Millions of dollars flowed in to support the organization's quest to "Keep the Red Cross at His Side." Home-front civilians volunteered to serve food in canteens, roll bandages, greet GIs at train stations, and donate blood. And some volunteered to serve in the European and Pacific theaters of war. Even though by the time of World War II the organization no longer had many nurses in its ranks, it offered a better chance to do more substantive service abroad because the War Department had decreed that the Red Cross would be the only civilian service agency permitted to work with overseas military personnel.[20]

The Red Cross created a sophisticated campaign to recruit women like Liz Richardson. As one Wisconsin volunteer, Margaret Kelk, remembered years later, "the American Red Cross had the reputation of only taking the cream of the crop. . . . If you could get in the Red Cross, that was way above the [military] services. . . . You have to be special to get in the Red Cross." Applicants had to be college graduates and at least twenty-five years of age. The rigorous selection process accepted only one in six applicants. Recruiting teams traveled the country interviewing candidates. Reference letters and physical examinations were essential, but the personal interview was the clincher and, as one official wrote, "often centered around the intangibles of personality."[21]

Earlier, in World War I, Red Cross posters and other recruiting methods focused on the sweetness and angelic qualities that young female volunteers could bring to support men in uniform. With World War II the organization focused more on attracting bright, educated career women and promised them real, roll up your sleeves work. In early 1944, for example, *Life* magazine published an amply illustrated article about American Red Cross women working in England. *Life*'s headline proclaimed, "Their job on the fighting front is romantic, but their days start at dawn and their work is never done." The women "are hand-picked for looks, education, personality, and experience in recreational fields. They are hardy physically and have a sociable, friendly manner. The majority are in their late 20's." When film actress Madeline Carroll, known as "America's favorite blond," abandoned Hollywood to volunteer for Red Cross overseas service, news stories focused on her sincerity and dedication and downplayed her movie-star glamour. The Red Cross benefited too from Eleanor Roosevelt's endorsements in speeches and writings. The President's wife visited the Red Cross training program in Washington in late 1943 and proudly wore the organization's uniform when she traveled to visit troops in the Pacific Theater. The American Red Cross and Elizabeth Richardson seemed a perfect fit.[22]

Twenty-five-year-old Liz passed her medical exam in Milwaukee on March 8, 1944, and whizzed through the all-important personal interview. The second week in May she returned to Mishawaka for a last visit to The Patch and her parents, brother Butch, and Freckles, the family dog, before heading off for training in Washington, D.C. A photograph

American Red Cross posters recruited volunteers and contributions on the home front. The organization's publicity often featured the phrase "at his side," connecting home front to battlefront. *Courtesy Hazel Braugh Records Center and Archives, American Red Cross.*

Butch took on May 13 as she prepared to leave for the railroad station shows her parents dressed in their best outfits, her mother, Henrietta, wearing white gloves and hat, Liz smiling.[23]

An overnight train, the Baltimore and Ohio's *Capitol Limited*, took an excited new war recruit eastward. Liz climbed down from her upper Pullman berth in time to see picturesque Harpers Ferry, "like some toy village

Charley (Butch) snapped this photo of his sister with their parents, Charles and Henrietta Richardson, as Liz prepared to leave the Dragoon Trail farm for Washington, D.C., May 13, 1944. All dressed up for the important day. *Courtesy Charles Richardson, Jr.*

against the hillside," and to enjoy a "super B&O omlet" for breakfast before arriving in the nation's capital at 8:45 AM. Washington's beautiful Beaux Arts–style Union Station teemed with people in uniform, eating, sleeping, reading, and waiting for their trains. Exiting Union Station in search of a taxi, Liz had her first glimpse of "fairy land Washington, complete with picture-card capitol against unbelievable blue and green."[24]

As her cab drove across the city, she saw everywhere the signs of war (though nothing compared to what she would soon see in London). Antiaircraft guns on rooftops guarded the Washington Monument, the Capitol, and the White House; hundreds of temporary office buildings lined the Mall; victory gardens dotted every piece of open land. The city was bursting with people. Liz was one among thousands of young women flooding into the wartime capital, some in uniform, others taking jobs as civilian typists and clerks—the "government girls" who did much of the clerical and administrative work essential to the immense war effort. The influx of people overwhelmed the city's buses, restaurants, hotels, and shops. Although 1944 offered one of the city's most beautiful springs, with trees and flowers in colorful glory, the weather was already warm and marching toward the relentless heat and humidity typical of a Washington summer. There was little in the way of air conditioning, certainly not the room the Red Cross assigned to Liz in the Emery Hotel on G Street, two blocks from the White House. Like many other newcomers, Liz in nearly every letter home to The Patch commented on the heat: "Weather is hotter than hades, and if not hotter than hades, it's damper than Africa's jungles. What a place!" And "a curse on our country's fathers when they picked this ex-marsh for the nation's capital."[25]

Liz's training began May 15. Among the first tasks were fittings for summer and winter Red Cross uniforms. The summer suit was light blue; most women thought it very good looking and wore it proudly so that, as one reporter noted, "you could spot them all over Washington." The winter uniform was less attractive, dark gray, of 100 percent wool. It included a winter overcoat that Liz's college friend Margaret Flood said was "designed by a cunning blacksmith in a mad moment." And there was the first of several trips across the Potomac River to get immunization shots at the newly completed Pentagon ("the most amazing thing you've ever seen," Liz wrote, "with an interior like the World's Fair").[26]

The American Red Cross operated its training program on the wooded campus of American University, located in the northwest corner of the District of Columbia. Military and government agencies had leased nearly all campus space from the university, most of whose regular male students were away in uniform. A Navy Bomb Disposal School, WAVES barracks, and several hundred Red Cross trainees dominated the campus by 1944, leaving only a few classrooms and the library for the civilian female college students still trying to get a degree. Red Cross classes filled Hurst Hall, an attractive college building in the center of campus.[27]

Increased demand for more women overseas led the Red Cross to compress its basic training course from six weeks to two weeks. A new class entered every Monday and another graduated every Saturday. Twenty Red Cross staffers provided instruction. Training began with basic orientation on history, procedures, and policies of both the Red Cross and the American military. There were lectures on military security with severe warnings that anyone leaking information would be sent home. As with all military training, there was also considerable attention to dress. The Red Cross uniform manual was ten single-spaced pages. It stipulated that women were to wear the uniform at all times, "except in the privacy of their living quarters.""Collars must always be pinned at the neck line since V-necks are not permitted." There were to be no earrings, hair ornaments, "brilliant nail polish," or "excessive use of cosmetics." Women in uniform were always to wear a "foundation garment." The instructor in charge of uniforms regularly snapped girdles to check that all were appropriately dressed. Instructors explained too that men overseas would be eagerly seeking courtship and even proposing marriage, and that if a woman married she would be transferred back to the States or to a different overseas post. One area in which some veterans later felt that they had received insufficient preparation was the emotional and cultural challenge of overseas work.[28]

At the end of the first week of basic training, the 58 women in Liz's class endured a mid-course evaluation that included a series of personal interviews. The interviewers attempted especially to ascertain whether candidates could engage in small talk, tell stories and jokes, laugh at silly comments, and be comfortable around lonely GIs far from home.[29]

Liz seldom boasted, but she could not hide her pride in the outcome of her interview and evaluation. She excitedly reported to her parents on May 19:

We finished section one of our training and I had my first interview, or rather interviews, and the upshot was that I have been offered a better job than Staff Assistant—and shall have the super deluxe 5 week training program. Only two in our class of 58 were offered advancement and I was one. He he he. Salary: $175 plus maintenance. However, it means that I will be sent to a very isolated spot and will be in a camp rather than a club. The job is almost purely recreational (and now boys, let's have a jolly spot of volleyball).[30]

The Basic Recreation Training Course was four weeks of intense mental and physical activity, with classes in Hurst Hall and in the gym that extended from morning into the evening. The women learned about crafts, music, dancing, games, program planning, group dynamics, and discussion techniques.

We work like mad, not only in listening to lectures on leadership and group management, but classes in table games (today we learned how to play Casino, Michigan, and Fantan), classes in crafts (learn how to block print in 55 minutes at the American University!) classes in recreational dramatics, dancing and last but not least, leadership skills as applied to volleyball, baseball, badminton etc. etc. etc. Naturally, I'm not the same sporty girl I was back in my hey-day circa 1937, but I daresay I shall soon develop that Physical Education stalk.[31]

A week later Liz wrote that the work "ordinarily would be fun, but the pressure is so great and there's so much to learn." Yet, "I'm learning—it's a wonderful adventure." Her twenty-sixth birthday, June 8, was an ordinary day of classes, more shots at the Pentagon, and uniform alterations at Hecht's Department Store. By this time, despite the fact that she was "eating like mad," her aching body was seven pounds lighter.[32]

Liz completed the recreation training course June 18 and resumed the basic orientation training, "which consists of sitting in a chair and sticking to same while we listen to lecture after interminable lecture. Frankly, I think I've reached a saturation point—the lovely words beat at the air vainly." Graduation came on June 24, preceded by a bit of slapdash training in close-order drill before the ceremony, in which they wore class A uniforms, including white gloves and girdles. Afterwards, "a few of us went to the Statler [Hotel] for a soothing lunch with much string ensemble in the background. I felt like a 'New Yorker' cartoon." She was now a trained Red Cross Staff Assistant. Her temporary assignment, while waiting posting overseas, kept her on the American University campus to organize recreation activities for "200 SPARS [U.S. Coast Guard Women's Reserve] who are badly in need of recreation—but I have an odd feeling that the R.C. is not going to offer the kind of recreation they are necessarily craving." In fact Liz spent most of the time swimming, playing tennis, and growing more impatient to be off.[33]

New recruits in Red Cross training, Hurst Hall, American University, Washington, D.C. *Courtesy American University.*

Despite the demands of training, Liz enjoyed an active social life in Washington, making new friends and visiting old family friends and relatives there and in New York, including Aunt Lily and John. A boyfriend she had dated in Milwaukee, she learned, was stationed nearby. She and Private Andy Anderson explored the city, mostly on foot, from the Tidal Basin and Jefferson Memorial (dedicated the year before by President Roosevelt), to picnics in Rock Creek Park, to the newly opened National Gallery of Art, which enthralled Liz even though many of its masterpieces had been removed to North Carolina for safekeeping. Her interest in painting pulled her back to the National Gallery several times. On one visit she focused entirely on nineteenth-century French painting. In the bustling, crowded, and hot city, she and Andy sought swimming pools, parks, and air-conditioned movie theaters. As Liz waited for her final orders, with no idea where she would be sent, she had a last date with Andy. They had become close, and it was a stressful parting, one of many to come and one common to wartime romances. The next day, July 1, Liz confessed that "today I feel as if I'd been through an emotion ringer—the natural suspense of the R.C. situation, plus 4 shots (2 in either arm), plus l'affaire d'Anderson has left me a limp rag. We did have wonderful times together." On July 5, at last, the Red Cross ordered Liz and 22 other women to the New York Port of Embarkation for transport to London.[34]

Liz wrote her last letter from Washington on July 6 to send details about her income tax and a new life insurance policy and to ask her mother to ship her black lace dinner dress and evening shoes. Wartime censorship prevented her from saying directly that she was leaving or where she was going, but she cautioned, "Don't worry if you don't hear from me for a short while—we are busy as little beavers." And then she made a sly family reference they would know meant she was on her way to England, though she cautioned them not to let the secret out to anyone else "except Freckles and then, only in the privacy of his kennel."[35]

On a hot July day the Red Cross women in winter uniforms marched in double line through Union Station to board a train that arrived that night at Pennsylvania Station in New York City. They climbed into buses to cross the river to Brooklyn and rooms at the massive St. George Hotel, which bustled with uniformed Americans. The military issued them helmets, canteens, and web belts. They had training in poison gas attack and more lectures, including stern warnings about censorship and security. They were not to make phone calls or write letters. There was time to take the subway into Manhattan to see plays, movies, and the sights. Much of the time they spent playing cards and wandering from hot room to hot room in their slips, talking and waiting. They got to know each other better. One, Rosemary Norwalk, from San Francisco, wrote in her diary: "The biggest surprise has been the girls—almost without exception they're outstanding, a cut above, and for some reason I hadn't expected that. There's not a dull one in the bunch. They're educated and interesting and motivated and, of course, because that's what the Red Cross seeks, generally outgoing and gregarious."[36]

On July 14, the women—"only slightly encumbered by life belts and steel helmets"—joined a massive stream of GIs walking up the gangplank and onto the *Queen Elizabeth*. Designed as a luxury ship to carry 2,000 passengers in grand style, the "Queen" became instead a cattle boat that transported 15,000 Americans to war. Liz and seven other Red Cross women shared an inside cabin, all with last names beginning with "R," since alphabetization was the standard form of organization. The eight were "wedged like sardines on a quadruple bunk." It was so crowded, one of the "Rs," Eloise Reilly, later recalled that "we had to undress one at a time to go to bed, . . . but through it all we laughed, thanks mostly to Liz." The "Rs" ate their two meals a day together in the officers' mess, where Liz and Second Lieutenant Bob Walker became good friends. They all had their first experiences of being a handful of women among thousands of young men, of being obligated to make small talk, learn names, and laugh. The Red Cross women spent much of their time on one of the sundecks, known to some as the "Bird Cage," which they shared with officers over the rank of captain. In the officers' lounge at night there were card games and songs, ranging from "God Bless America" to increasingly bawdy versions of "Roll Me over in the Clover." Liz had time to read Somerset Maugham's popular short story, *Rain*, a character study of a doctor, missionary, and prostitute set in the South Pacific.[37]

The Nazi U-boat menace was still real, so the *Queen Elizabeth* ran her customary zigzag course designed to outrun the enemy. Daily lifeboat drills reminded everyone of the danger, although thoughtful participants could see that there were far more passengers than lifeboat seats. Nonetheless one of the "Rs, Ruth Read, packed her prized possessions into her musette bag every night in case of attack." This trip across the calm, summer Atlantic was uneventful. On July 20 Liz saw the green hills of Ireland and then Scotland and the River Clyde, where they anchored near Greenock. The next day a British officer welcomed the Yanks and added as an afterthought, "Oh, you'll find the buzz bombs a bit of a nuisance!" After a breakfast of kippers, they boarded a cold, blacked-out troop train and ate mostly K rations as they traveled through the night toward London and their new jobs.[38]

[2]

The Yanks in England

A calm Atlantic crossing placed Elizabeth Richardson in a country that had been ravaged by nearly five years of Nazi bombs, food shortages, and the horrors of total war. The English were bearing up in their particular way, sacrificing, fighting hard, and carrying on, but England was a dark and tired place by 1944.

The London Liz entered on July 21 was a disheveled city, radically different from the Midwestern heartland or the bright, untouched American capital she had recently left. Londoners had staggered under the big blitz of 1940 and more bombing by the Luftwaffe in 1941. As she traveled across the city Liz could see gray buildings with boarded-up windows and piles of bricks stacked beside dusty bomb sites. St. Paul's Cathedral still stood, majestically, now more visible than ever because so many buildings around it had been destroyed. In the National Gallery on Trafalgar Square empty walls signaled paintings removed for safe keeping. People on the streets looked battered too. Their clothing was mismatched and shabby, their shoes long worn out. Meals in homes and restaurants were monotonous at best. Years of food rationing meant that vegetables grew in St. James Square and around the Tower of London. The blackout continued and presented a special challenge for foreigners attempting to negotiate dark, winding streets on foot. And it wasn't over, even though the D-Day invasion of France that June brought greater expectations. As British air defense strengthened and as the Allied offensive moved toward Germany the Luftwaffe's bombing raids on London had diminished, but then on June 13, 1944, Hitler's scientists launched a new weapon of revenge.[1]

The new V-1 rocket forced many Londoners to flee the city just as Liz reported to Red Cross headquarters near the American Embassy in Grosvenor Square. Hitler's vengeance weapon was an unmanned bomb, fast and difficult to stop. Londoners called them "buzz bombs" or "doodle-bugs," but they were anything but cute. They hit buildings and people at random, including several dozen of the 148 buildings the American Red Cross occupied in London. Those on the ground heard the engine's sputtering noise and then in the last seconds the silence as the engine cut off before the terrifying explosion. The nauseating sequence of engine, deadly silence, and explosion happened dozens of times a day in London that summer. Before it was over the V-1s caused 5,375 deaths.[2]

Red Cross Clubmobile worker Charlotte Colburn was among those eager to leave the city and its V-1s for her assignment in France. She thought she would be safer closer to the front: "nothing that you may read," she wrote her family on August 4, "can exaggerate or describe the horror and damage that they cause." Another Red Cross colleague estimated that "it takes about three days of concentrated work to get over the 'buzzie' jitters." The Red Cross's "Tips for Troops in South England" advised GIs, "Don't be ashamed to duck—Joe Louis isn't. And, remember, the old soldier always takes cover. That's why he's an old soldier." With more experience perhaps the Americans would learn to behave like the stoic English described by Mollie Panter-Downes, whose reports from the city appeared in the *New Yorker*: "Londoners make jokes about what they call the doodlebugs," she wrote on July 9, 1944; "after an assault, they get up from the pavement, dust their knees, straighten their hats, and move off with the slightly embarrassed smile of someone who has been caught leaping for dear life from a mad bull."[3]

If there was to be an end to the V-1 attacks and victory over the Nazis the British needed the Americans at their side. The wartime alliance of the two nations turned out to be one of the greatest in history. Yet despite a common cause and despite the so-called special relationship between the two English-speaking peoples, each struggled to move beyond simple stereotypes and real differences.

The Americans caused the English no end of frustration and despair.

Everyone said that the only problem with the Yanks was that they are "overpaid, oversexed, and over here." The Americans certainly arrived without direct experience of the horror of war, without much real sacrifice on their own home-front, and yet with a cockiness that their superior ways would bail out the British.[4] The arrogance and provincialism of so many Americans overseas embarrassed their more thoughtful countrymen, including Liz Richardson, who, although she had her own frustrations with English ways, grew increasingly fond of these mostly patient and kind people. By mid-December 1944, she would write that "the more I live in this strange isle, the more I like it and understand the British and their foibles. We Americans are loud and gauche and have much to learn from them."[5]

There would have been fewer problems if only a handful of Americans had crossed the Atlantic, but over three million of them spent time on the tiny island during the war. In July 1944, when Liz arrived, there were nearly a million Yanks scattered across the land. They overwhelmed the city of London and the tiny villages. Their jeeps and 2½-ton trucks were everywhere, along with their chewing gum, slang, music, and eagerness to date English women. There were so many Americans and so much heavy equipment that wits said that the purpose of the barrage balloons attached to cables was less to distract German bombers than to hold up the island under the weight of the occupation forces. And there was Ernie Pyle's story about the GI who complained that "these English are beginning to act as if this country belonged to them."[6]

The British government tried to explain the foreigners' strange ways. A 1943 government pamphlet, titled *Meet the U.S. Army*, described American differences, from uniforms to Jeeps to food. Language was a problem, for example, not only with different vocabulary words but with American slang, which "is richer and more colorful than our own," the pamphlet writer confessed. The British had best concede that the Americans pioneered in popular music and dance and "tend to regard some of our imitations as amateurish or 'corny' (old-fashioned) or merely dull." They should accept the likelihood that Americans who danced with English women "tend to be disappointed by dancing standards of their partners." So too was British food a disappointment: "we should admit that even in peacetime English meals, on the average, were not particularly good." As for the GI, "do not be misled by his easy line of talk, his wise-cracks, his love of jazz or—often—his schoolboyish smile, into thinking that he has any illusions about what he is here for. He regards your island as a halfway house to the Front and he knows what that front will be like."[7]

From the other side of the cultural divide, the American government tried to prepare its citizens for life in Britain. A film titled "Welcome to Britain" and a seven-page pamphlet, *Over There*, were among several ways authorities introduced the English. The foundation message was that Britain and the United States were allies against Hitler, followed by examples of the ties that bound together the two peoples, including "our common law and our ideals of religious freedom." And then there were the differences, such as vocabulary (the word "bloody," for example, which "is one of their worst swear words") and accents: "Don't make fun of British speech or accents. You sound just as funny to them but they will be too polite to show it." The newcomers learned that the British liked their money in pounds, shilling, and pence, "and all your arguments that the American decimal system is better won't convince them. They won't be pleased to hear you call it 'funny money,' either." There were tips about warm beer and pubs. There was information meant to be reassuring about the English weather: "Most people get used to the English climate eventually." And there were several cautions about arrogance: "remember that crossing the ocean doesn't automatically make you a hero. There are housewives in aprons and youngsters in knee pants in Britain who have lived through more high explosives in air raids than many soldiers saw in first class barrages in the last war."[8]

By late 1944 American Red Cross workers had seen so much of this cross-cultural-sensitivity propaganda that their newsletter ran a parody that pretended to prepare overseas Americans for the cultural shock of coming back to the States. "A Short Guide for Your Return to the U.S.A." offered such tongue-in-cheek advice about American life as: "If your drinks are served ice cold, or even with ice, you must not criticize; they like them that way."[9]

The Yanks had their own problems. Most important, they were far from home, most of them for the first time. They were homesick for family and friends, for the comforts of familiar food, music, and fun. Most were very young. The majority had not graduated from high school. Many really didn't much like England. They weren't interested in Gothic cathedrals, art museums, tea, or the rural countryside. Even the pubs were often unappealing, with weak, warm beer and early closing hours. Few Americans ever visited an English home or really got to know a native. They stayed close to their bases and their fellow Americans. They were bored, the food was monotonous, the women too few. And hanging over them was the uncertainty of knowing when they would go into combat and when they would go home. There were, of course, other sorts of Americans, those few who fell in love with England and the English. About 40,000 married English women who then joined them in the States after the war, many with babies. Some Americans learned to enjoy the pub culture, to explore the countryside on a bike, to visit its cathedrals and museums, to meet and really begin to know the individual English person. Liz Richardson was one such American.[10]

Liz and the other Red Cross women were not in England to sightsee, however. Military leaders had always known that building and maintaining troop morale was a necessary part of victory. No less an authority than General Dwight D. Eisenhower wrote that "morale, given rough equality in other things, is supreme on the battlefield." Leaders such as Eisenhower knew too that morale was especially difficult to maintain when bored young men lived among a foreign population. One necessity was an escape off base to sample civilian pleasures. The challenge, of course, was how to keep men on leave from overwhelming local facilities and from running wild. This large responsibility the War Department assigned to the American Red Cross. By designating this one organization as the sole provider of welfare services to military personnel, the government expected that efficiency would increase and duplication and rivalry diminish.[11]

The Red Cross created for American servicemen on leave a massive network of hotels and recreation clubs. Here the soldier found, as the director of London's Hans Crescent Club wrote, "not only a home away from home, but the fraternity house, the Elks Club, the corner drug store and Mom's front parlor all wrapped into one." London had eight clubs because it was by far the GIs' first choice as leave destination. The most famous was Rainbow Corner, near Piccadilly Circus, where GIs and airmen flocked for a few days of rest and recreation in a blacked-out and dreary city. At Rainbow Corner they found American food (and consumed 30,000 doughnuts a day), music, dances, movies, and Red Cross women they could talk to. There were tours of London and tickets to West End shows as well as French language lessons. They all received a London map marked with locations of other Red Cross clubs, places to see, and routes for buses and the underground. At the clubs too they could find discreetly placed prophylactic stations to minimize venereal diseases. The military had requested space in the clubs for this service because men claimed to be unable after sexual intercourse to locate the regular stations in the London blackout. Red Cross officials eagerly publicized the clubs, but not the prophylactic stations, one of many ways in which the home front was kept ignorant of the sexual side of the war.[12]

By 1944 Americans were stationed all over the British Isles, most in places ten miles or more from London or other cities with clubs. One GI complained that the "Red Cross in London is doing a marvelous job, but we ain't all in London seven days a week." The Red Cross response to such massive troop dispersion was the Clubmobile, created in fall 1942. The Red Cross Commissioner in Britain, Harvey D. Gibson, put the basic club facilities on wheels so they could be taken to remote bases. Most Clubmobiles were single-decker buses acquired from the Green Line, a defunct English company. Fitted with coffee and doughnut-making equipment, the Clubmobiles also carried chewing gum, cigarettes, magazines, newspapers, a phonograph, and records. A lounge in the back provided a place to sit and talk. A British driver piloted the large vehicle as it rattled through village streets and down narrow muddy lanes. But the most important contents of each Clubmobile, more so than coffee and doughnuts, were the three Red Cross women inside, always called "girls." They were the stars of the traveling show. As one Clubmobiler later wrote, "Doughnuts and coffee were our props."[13]

The role of the Clubmobile and its contents was captured in a postcard prepared by the Red Cross and given to GIs to mail home. The card showed a Green Line Clubmobile and troops gathered around it. The label read "American Red Cross Clubmobile 'Somewhere' in Great Britain," and, in reference to the doughnuts, "Sighted Sinkers—Sank Same." Printed on the reverse side was an explanatory line: "Red Cross

The American Red Cross prepared this postcard to give to GIs to mail home. Yanks training for combat on the Continent gather around a Clubmobile "somewhere in Great Britain." *Author's collection.*

Clubmobiles staffed by American Girls bring free hot coffee and dough-nuts, cigarettes, gum, candy, etc. from the folks back home to U.S. Forces at their camps in foreign lands." One GI mailed home one of these post-cards and wrote on the back:

> Hello Mom,
>
> This is a picture of the Red Cross clubmobile that visits our camp about every week. They serve us doughnuts & coffee. Also at times books, candy, gum, and cigarettes. It is operated by our own American girls. They certainly are a swell bunch.
>
> Leo[14]

Homesick young men like Leo hungered for the sight of a friendly female face, "our own American girls." Nothing so distracted them from the frustrations and fears of military life. Nothing so reminded them of home or assured them that they might someday go home to an American woman. Of course, there were English women (and very few English men as competitors). Many GIs made connections with local women as

Liz's watercolor, made in London, February 1945, shows the common sight of an English woman and an American soldier, in this case a paratrooper. *Courtesy Charles Richardson, Jr.*

smiling dance partners, eager prostitutes, real girlfriends, and marriage partners. Liz painted a watercolor of a Yank with an English girl on his arm, a common sight all over the island. The guys also tacked up their pinups of Betty Grable, Rita Hayworth, and the girl next door. Real American women in Britain were few, however—about 1 of every 100 Americans in mid-1944.[15]

The Red Cross women were among those few. Short supply made them precious. One Clubmobiler, B. J. Olewiler, wrote home that the GIs "[are] so glad to see an American girl and hear American English spoken they just stand and look at you." When Hattie Brazier returned to the spot where she had talked with a lonely GI a few hours earlier she found "a monument of white stones piled one on top of the other and . . . a sign on it that says, 'A girl from the good old USA stood here'."[16]

It wasn't just their small numbers that made Clubmobilers special; they had been carefully and deliberately selected by the Red Cross. They knew the right slang, had the right look, knew how to take and make a wisecrack, and knew how to talk about Chicago, Brooklyn, or San Francisco, about baseball, Glenn Miller, and apple pie. They encouraged banter. Eleanor Stevenson explained how they'd yell out to a truckload of GIs, " 'Hi, soldier. What's cooking?' and the guys would yell back, 'Chicken! Wanta neck?' " Standing beside their Clubmobile at an isolated, windswept military camp in England, Red Cross women knew how to look at pictures of girlfriends and wives and how to listen to stories, including the sad news from home that ended a romance or told of the death of a loved one. They could join an impromptu jitterbug dance next to the Clubmobile or sing along as their well-worn phonograph record played the same few songs from home.[17]

Aged twenty-five and older, the Clubmobilers could see that often the men in uniform were really boys. Military historian Max Hastings has observed that the "people who fight wars are customarily referred to as 'men.' " "Yet in truth," Hastings asserts, "irrespective of their ages, most of those engaged in combat behaved, thought and talked as boys—exuberant and emotional, careless and naive."[18] The Red Cross women had grown up with American boys. They had dated them in college. They knew a lot about them and quickly learned much more on the job. In many small ways these women knowingly played the role of the American girl, the touch of home and the symbol of what the GIs were fighting for.

Red Cross and military leaders made the most of these symbolic connections to home. As one Red Cross official told a *Los Angeles Times* reporter in August 1944, the girls "represent everything the boys admire in American womanhood—vivacity, grace, charm, virtue, beauty, enthusiasm, intelligence and that wholesome friendliness and interest that reminds them of sister and wife, girl friend and mother." To a *Washington Star* reporter the Red Cross girl was "the sweetheart of World War II." An

Avon cosmetics wartime advertising campaign featured an attractive woman in Red Cross uniform under the title "Miss America 1944."[19]

Gender and sex mixed with war and loneliness to create challenges for all. Men waiting to go into combat lived in exaggerated masculine environments, deliberately segregated from women and from civilians. Their lives seemed filled with officers they often thought arrogant, training routines that seemed senseless, and petty military rules that they called "chickenshit." Many sought relief from boredom, loneliness, and military discipline in alcohol and sex, the latter, of necessity, often with prostitutes.[20]

Red Cross women were not sexy, at least not in the provocative sense. Their uniforms had a military styling, enhanced often by muddy combat boots and odd bits and pieces of clothing. *Life* magazine glowingly described a Clubmobile arriving at a camp in England "with a smartly uniformed crew of three girls," but more often the soiled pants and jackets the women wore in the field to keep warm and dry left them looking bedraggled or, at best, "somewhere between dowdy and glamorous," as Clubmobiler Mary Metcalfe recalled. Sometimes they hadn't had a bath for several days, often they smelled of doughnut grease, always their hands were red and raw, their hair flattened by the uniform cap they were supposed to wear. Yet they avoided the "mannish" or "Amazon woman" stereotypes that invited disdain from 1940s Americans. They usually took time to put on lipstick, nail polish, and perfume. These smart women quickly came to see that such small feminine connections to the girls back home meant worlds to the boys in the field. Clubmobile women could sing slightly bawdy songs, respond to off-color jokes, deflect a sexual advance with what Liz called "evasive tactics," and remain respectable women the guys loved to be near. Often they heard wolf whistles, especially when GIs first saw them. They learned, as one wrote in a 1944 issue of *Ladies Home Journal*, "to get over the embarrassment of walking through lines of men all thoughtfully extending their complimentary whistle. Now, instead of getting red-faced and awkward, we throw back our shoulders, wave and whistle back."[21]

Men tried hard to behave when Red Cross women were around. Red Cross women seldom heard "the f word," likely the most oft-used word in the salty GI vocabulary. A GI out of line in language or conduct was usually told where to get off by his fellow soldiers. The GIs knew that the Clubmobile women were volunteers. They had willingly signed up to work overseas. They were as far from home as the guys and perhaps as homesick too. They knew all about GI mess food and K rations, cold and rain, military bureaucracy, and many of the other hardships of war. Though never "one of the guys," the Clubmobilers quickly won the respect of the men they met. The Red Cross uniform brought status and courtesy. The woman wearing it, even if a bit bedraggled, was a living antidote to the loneliness, violence, and barbarism of war.[22]

To everyone they were "girls," from the top Red Cross administrators and field officers, who were all male, to other Red Cross women, to the lonely GI. One Red Cross administrator wrote an evaluation of a new recruit after he interviewed her in Washington, D.C.: "27 years of age. Very attractive girl, has open face and wonderful smile and dimples. She impresses me as being the wholesome type of American girl that will fit into the work overseas splendidly."[23]

Sometimes called "doughnut girls," they were not warriors and usually stayed distant from the front lines. They did not consider themselves feminists and did not willfully seek change in traditional gender roles. They could be dependent and allow men to protect them when necessary or convenient. Men often felt obliged to help them, even if it only meant carrying heavy coffee urns. The jobs Clubmobile volunteers did might appear as traditional women's work: cook, clean, and serve men. Yet, these women did essential war work that included demanding physical labor and stressful emotional costs. Their jobs required sophisticated organization skills and superb interpersonal relations. And they carried out their duties in a foreign culture far from home with limited resources and scant administrative support. Their experience, maturity, and education gave them a self-awareness and understanding of the job they were doing. They saw the contradictions between their ordinary daily chores and their college educations and also between their image as "girls" and their work as women. "Who ever thought that my M.A. degree would prepare me for this!" wrote Gretchen Schuyler from England in 1943, and later to her father, a veteran of World War I, "I may be a mere *girl* but we girls sure do get around these days."[24]

From the thousands of hours they spent with GIs, they came to know far more about the boys and their war than all but the small percentage of men who actually saw combat. From her Clubmobile base in England in October 1944, Margaret Gearhart wrote her parents: "Believe me, Mom and Dad, we Red Cross have seen more of this war than anyone—and what we've seen and heard could make an excellent book. We feel the sprit and soul of the war."[25]

Despite the long days, they seldom whined. In fact, they worked hard to make what they did look so simple: the Clubmobile pulled up at a tent camp and soon there was a hot cup of coffee, a fresh American doughnut, a smile, a flash of lipstick, and a cheery "hello, soldier, where you from?"[26]

[3]

V-1 Rockets, the *Kansas City,*
and the 82nd Airborne

The German V-1 rockets falling on London introduced Elizabeth Richardson to war, a first step in her education about its horrors and in her developing impatience with those ignorant of war's meaning. In her first letter from the other side of the Atlantic she only briefly mentioned the buzz bombs, doubtless not wanting to alarm her family. She filled her six-page letter instead with enthusiasm for where she was and joy in the likely assignment to a Clubmobile, for many women the most sought-after posting.

This was the first of many letters home that would downplay her hardest experiences by eliminating details and softening horrors. Already, there was a tinge of homesickness, a disease rampant among the other million young Americans in Great Britain that summer of 1944, all waiting to do their part to defeat Hitler and then go home.

July 24, 1944
[London]

Dear mother, daddy, Butch, Freckles,

By now, you must know that I am safe and sound in Great Britain—that the impossible has happened and that I won't be using those rubber boats paddling through the jungles. Instead, I'm juggling shillings and half crowns and crouching on the floor in an artistic attitude of prayer when I hear the wailing ups and downs of the siren.

How long I'll be here, I don't know, but much as I love London, I'd just as soon be out in the country where the wind blows free. We were told at our port of embarkation that the buzz bombs were "a bit of a nuisance" but my words for them are much fruitier and stronger.

There's so <u>much</u> to tell you, but you know that most of it will have to wait until we meet again. Be sure to ask me about it then, because it's all so wonderful that I have a hard time containing myself. We had our first inkling that we were coming in this direction back in Washington and then began the process of our clearance in the course of which we acquired some of the trappings of war—anyway—by the time we mounted the gangplank, we were the better for steel helmets, gas masks, canteens, first aid kits, not counting our musette bags. Our voyage over was ideal—not very rough seas and good weather. It would have been interesting though, if we had had rough weather—I'd probably come up with somebody else's head. Our best companions were our life belts and our helmets, which made us look like droopy pigeons (very big). Our first sight of the United Kingdom was something I'll never forget—in fact—I'll never forget all of this. Of course, you both know this country and can share some of my enthusiasm and in spite of this constant atmosphere of fourth of July, I love it all.

So far, it looks as if I'm getting Clubmobile, which pleases me no end, although I won't be an able-bodied Recreational Worker as originally planned, but I'm asking for it in preference to the lonely grass shack or equally lonely igloo. Well, Paw, London hasn't changed much since you were here. Americans still get ice water at the Savoy [Hotel] and the 2-deckers still go lumbering down the Strand. God knows how they do it, but they do. We were quite touched at the port with the enthusiasm with which we were received—it was like something out of Quentin Reynolds or something equally dramatic. Being female and sentimental, we all were busy blinking and blowing our noses.

The R. C. here is a magnificent thing—clubs all over the place, efficiently staffed by Americans and British—in old homes that are still going strong. The group with which I came over, is grand—our leader was a girl who had returned from the South Pacific—perhaps you read about her in the Reader's Digest a couple of months ago. As for Chris [Hanson], the last I saw of her was in Washington after we were alerted, trudging down the street with my laundry bag. We really finished our time in Washington in a bang-up fashion with 2 boys from Ft. Meade and a gay jaunt to Baltimore, so at least Chris and I celebrated our epoch together in true 1718 N. Prospect style.[1]

Although I don't know when and where I'll see them, I'd like John Bodle's and Laurence Rolston's A.P.O.'s.[2] And if you feel like sending packages, soap, Kotex and wool socks are in order. When you mail it, show this to the postmaster and he'll O. K. it. Daddy, you'll be glad to hear that I was not deprived of my hot bath going over, even though the water was salt. But that fresh water certainly felt good!

The English countryside made me just a little homesick for the Patch—I can see it now and I can also see Butch cleaning out the chicken house and cutting the grass (joke). By the way, tell John to write—how is he getting on? This is not my permanent address; we're awaiting assignments and I'll send on the real thing as soon as possible. But my mail will be forwarded from this address.

Meanwhile, I think of you all a lot, so eat the beans and peas and lettuce, and, Daddy, have a cold bottle of beer for your

Elizabeth

Military and Red Cross leaders very much wanted Liz and the other fifty-two new arrivals to move into the field as soon as possible. In the weeks following D-Day the Red Cross had transferred some 400 women from England to France, leaving only 130 in Britain and forcing the closing of some operations even as large numbers of troops continued to arrive. New Clubmobile recruits from the United States landed in England later that summer and fall and by October there were about 200 women slinging doughnuts at 60 locations. Nonetheless, military requests for Clubmobile service continued to exceed available women and vehicles.[3]

Liz's days in London were filled with more orientation and training and included getting British ration cards and instructions in air raid drills and first aid. She and the other volunteers had lessons necessary to obtain a British driving license and instructions for making doughnuts and coffee in enormous quantities. Often the sound of a buzz bomb punctuated a meeting. They went to Wigmore Street to pick up their "battledress," a trouser uniform more suited to the work ahead than the skirts of their Red Cross uniforms.[4] One of Liz's colleagues, Rosemary Langheldt, wrote, "We all love the outfits—Eisenhower type battle jackets (short and belted at waist with deep pockets on the front of the jacket) with slacks in the same shade of RAF blue and a jaunty billed cap." Liz would eventually tire of the battledress and refer to it as "the monkey suit" and "Clubmobile Clown suits," along with "those awfully Kraut-style hats."[5]

Liz's second letter from London showed that even in a war-torn city under frightening V-1 bombing there were tourist sites to see, from the Tower of London to Buckingham Palace. There were nice dinners and dances too, with lots of music, the American swing and dance music that swept England and then Europe along with the Yanks. Here Liz expressed her first reservation about pushy fellow Americans.

July 28, 1944
[London]

Dear mother and daddy,

Here sits your foot sore daughter, making up for lost time in the writing department. We have had a good week in which to see London—all the high spots and some of the low—and my ground grippers are not reacting as they should. So far, no mail has come through from home, but I keep on hoping!

We are being assigned alphabetically (as usual) and I'm seriously considering sending a memo to Washington, recommending that hereafter, a list should begin with the Z's or else I'm going to change my name to Abigail Abbey (or Aaron). Slowly but surely, we will eventually be issued our additional equipment and we will be taught how to manufacture a mean doughnut and a neat cup of coffee. The funniest thing of all is my new British Driving License—"You, too, can drive a ten-ton truck." Anyway, we've had lots of time, even time to see the changing of the guard at Buckingham Palace. Of course, the color of days of yore is missing, but it's still a grand sight. Today, we started out for the Tower, but ended in the Old Temple, a sad sight since the blitz of '41. This destruction is most tragic and it's just as well that you are not here.

We are now living in a Red Cross dormitory, once a very lovely town house, but now occupied by lots of wooden bunks, and I do mean wooden. Before, I was comfortable enough so that I had time to worry about the buzz bombs—now—I don't think about the things. Too busy feeling sorry for myself. Our headquarters is a grand hotel for Clubmobile personnel run by a charming Englishwoman—we have most of our meals there, or else we eat at one of the Officer's messes where the food is American and good.[6]

I won't bother you with a list of the places I've seen—you know—the customary things. There are Americans everywhere, some are wonderful, but others make me ashamed to be one, but you know the American habit of walking in and taking over. However, on our walk today, we were taken over by all sorts of people who are still eager to show you around—Bobbies, little fellows just proud of their city, even a retired Army Officer who once had an "American sweetheart woman I used to meet right here under the Marble Arch." But she stymied him when she came over the second time with her husband. So you see how it goes.

Last night, we had dinner at one of the hotels, dinner music provided by a tuxedoed dance band—and did we hear English tunes? No, indeed—they were the same songs they're whistling back in the States. Even a spontaneous community singing circle in Hyde Park featured that lovely thing, "Mairsie doots and doesy doots. . . ." Or how do you spell it. But this weather is certainly a benediction after Washington—like a perfect day in October. I'm anxious, though, to get out in the countryside and see what it's really like. Also, it will be fun to be settled in one place for a week or so.

Have my checks come through from Washington? You should have received a few by now. And I hope the luggage arrived, so that Butch can pack up for his interlude in New York.

Forgot to tell you that we saw the Ballet the other night—it begins early and between acts, everybody has tea at their seats. This startled me, but I'm beginning to find out that tea comes first and after that, anything else.

You know, I can see now how the Londoners have managed to maintain the even pace of their lives. At first you think, "Good God, I can't live like this, shaking hands with eternity." But after a while, you adjust your life to that strange new element, accept it and continue as before. It's a form of fatalism, but it just shows how flexible the human mind is.

It's almost dinner-time (we dine at the fashionable hour), so I had better give this up.

Please write—letters do mean a lot. And I'll do the same.

Love,
Elizabeth

Liz also wrote her aunt Lillian Kimbel in New Canaan, Connecticut, using the V-Mail service. V-Mail was designed to save cargo space on shipments overseas. The correspondent used special stationery, which was microfilmed and then enlarged after reaching the overseas destination. Liz complained about the difficulty reading V-Mail and used it only occasionally.[7]

July 28, 1944
[London]

Dear Aunt Lily,

You see, the best thing of all happened and so I'm here and not chopping a path through the jungles! We're awaiting assignment and meanwhile, seeing London and learning how to run a doughnut machine (believe it or not). Wish I could tell you about our subsequent adventures before landing in the United Kingdom—it's been a wonderful experience. London has changed, I imagine, since you last saw it. There are hoards of Americans and sometimes you can almost imagine yourself in Manhattan. But the British continue to go their way and they are the stabilizing influence. It's just as well that you can't see some of this—it makes me a little sick and very angry. Give my love to Aunt Josie—and to you,

Elizabeth

The news in Liz's mostly upbeat letters from London was confirmed by the diary that she began keeping only in January 1945. The diary also included details the censor would not have allowed in a letter home and occasional comments she doubtless didn't wish to share with her family. In this first diary entry, more than five months later, she recalled V-1 rockets falling on London.

Diary, January 10, 1945

At 5 o'clock, we pulled into London. An alert was on and we saw our first buzz bomb over the dim bulks of the railroad yard. We marched through the station (a cold and bleak place so early in the morning) into waiting trucks. London seemed a haunted city. For two hours, we stood in line outside the Princes' Garden Club [an American Red Cross club] in Kensington and I don't remember even going to bed. None of us heard alerts that day. Late that afternoon, be-showered and refreshed, we took a walk through Kensington Park and stared politely at the Albert Memorial—garish, Victorian thing that it is. The next morning, we reported at the Hans Crescent [Red Cross] Club for clearance. When an alert sounded, a small bell inside the club rung by the roof watchers announced the arrival of the buzz bomb in the neighborhood. They always seemed to be right, too, for presently from our crouching positions on the floor, we'd hear the now familiar chug-chug of the infernal machine and then the pause as the motor switched off—and then the explosion. During those seconds, one had time to think about one's whole life or in my case, "This is a hell of a way to die." Lindsay Rand and I walked over to Hyde Park where one had fallen during the afternoon (turning at least three of my hairs white in so doing). For blocks, shop windows were shattered and trees were down for at least 300 yards. There were no signs of casualties.

Our group began to break up, but the Clubmobilers were the last to leave, for we had to learn to make doughnuts. This was accomplished in a dank garage one morning. We were transferred from Princes' Garden to Gloucester St. in Marylebone. The beds were of solid wood, including mattresses. Every night, Mary Read and I climbed to the top floor and watched the bombs coming in. Sometimes the ack-ack would get them as they were caught in the search lights, but mostly, they didn't.

When they appeared to be headed in our direction, we'd scamper down the five flights and warn the lower regions. Then we'd crouch on the basement floor with pillows over our heads and wait. In the daytime, between alerts, we saw all the sights—Westminster, Buckingham Palace, the changing of the guard (no bright uniforms this time), St. Paul's rising majestically above the ruins, Fleet St. and so on. One afternoon, a Canadian lady took us through the Inner Temple, horribly bombed. After 10 days of London, I received my assignment—Leicester, in the midlands.

Liz departed London on August 1, the day before more than a hundred V-1 bombs hit the city, the largest number of the war.[8] Now part of a newly formed Clubmobile unit, Liz and two other Red Cross workers settled at their new base, the city of Leicester, in the midlands north of London.

Leicester's population of a quarter million people knew the privations of war. The Germans had bombed the city several times, most heavily the night of November 19–20, 1940, a raid that killed 108 people. By 1944 the city was far safer than London, a comfort Liz appreciated. In fact, British authorities evacuated approximately 10,000 women and children from London to Leicester that summer. Locals suffered from severe shortages of food and fuel through the war years and into the 1950s. With occasional access to GI food supplies and their British ration cards Liz and her two colleagues ate reasonably well, but they also came to know first-hand some of the wartime shortages.[9]

August 4, 1944
[Leicester]

Dear mother and daddy,

Still haven't had any mail from you, or anyone else, for that matter, but I'm hoping that it will come through in big gobs. Anyway, here I'm sitting on the floor at Mrs. Tipper's house with the telephone in front of me—and at five minute intervals, I dial the station master to see if our doughnuts have arrived for tomorrow's work—but the English are worse than the Southerners when it comes to taking their time. This is supposed to be our day off, but we have spent it gazing at our doughnut machine and dangling our new G.I. Shoes.

My assignment came through on Tuesday morning and on Tuesday afternoon [August 1], little Elizabeth was on her way. We were hoping that three of us might be together, but no luck. However, I'm with 2 very swell girls and an English driver (as yet unseen) somewhere in the midlands. We live in the lap of luxury after London—a real home, with a bathtub of our own, hot water and a garden! And our landlady is a dear—she has just brought us coffee on a silver tray. Ah! Civilization.

Naturally, I was most happy to be leaving London—can't say that I enjoy living dangerously. But, in spite of everything, we had fun and more important, we ate well and food has assumed gigantic proportions, and is second only in proportion to the buzz-bombs.

I wish you could see me in my new battle dress—a sadder sight you wouldn't see this side of the St. Joseph Valā [Valley]—

[At this place in her letter, Liz drew a sketch of herself serving doughnuts and coffee.]

This is British issue, except the coffee & doughnuts. We make the latter in our little clubmobile and consequently are constantly saturated with a new perfume, Eau de Doughnut.

As for the English countryside—it's unbelievably beautiful—the flowers are so numerous and the hedges so clipped. I can't wait until I get a bicycle so that I can go out and see it on my own.

One of my or our crew members is an ex-singer from Henry Busse's and Bob Crosby's orchestra—she's at the piano now, lulling a visiting major to oblivion, so you'll pardon my jerky composition.

Well, fond parents, I hope I'll hear from you soon. Did Butch take any pictures of John & Sue [Stevens] & you? Please send <u>lots</u>—and special request, would you send a subscription to Time of the overseas edition of Time and Life, please. No magazines here, except "Yank" & "Stars & Stripes."[10] And you probably know more what's going on than we do. And write <u>soon</u>.

Love
Elizabeth

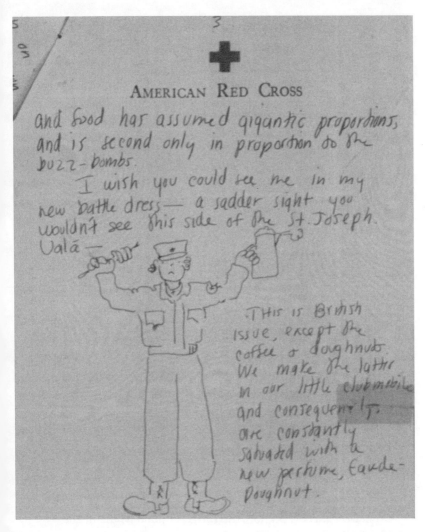

AMERICAN RED CROSS

and food has assumed gigantic proportions, and is second only in proportion to the buzz-bombs.

I wish you could see me in my new battle dress— a sadder sight you wouldn't see this side of the St. Joseph. Vala —

.THis is British issue, except the coffee & doughnuts. We make the latter in our little clubmobile and consequently. are constantly saturated with a new perfume, Eaude-Doughnut.

On this page of her first letter from Leicester, England, written August 4, 1944, Liz sketched herself in Red Cross battledress, holding a coffee pot in one hand and a doughnut prong with three sinkers in the other. *Courtesy Charles Richardson, Jr.*

In her diary, Liz provided more detail about Leicester, the *Kansas City*—the converted Green Line bus that was their Clubmobile—and her fellow crew members Margaret Morrison from Watertown, New York, and Aileen Anderson from Kansas City, Kansas, who would be with her for some time in England and then again in France. Liz thought Aileen a bit naïve and flighty. Margaret became an especially close friend, who shared Liz's sense of humor, spunk, and appetite. And she introduced their landlady, Mrs. Tipper, and "the boys" they were serving, the famed 82nd Airborne.[11]

The 82nd Airborne quickly won a special place in Liz's heart. They were the army's elite. On their chests they wore silver parachute badges; on their feet distinctive jump boots. These veterans had seen hard combat in Africa and Italy. In February 1944, they arrived in Leicestershire to rest and train for the invasion of France. Most of the 82nd jumped into Normandy on June 6, in advance of the D-Day beach landings. During the 33 days they fought the Germans in France they suffered large casualities: 47 percent of the 11,770 men who went into Normandy were dead, missing, or wounded. They were pulled back again to their Leicestershire bases for rest and for the incorporation of replacements. It was at this point that the *Kansas City* joined the 82nd, working with them until they were off for their fourth combat jump, into Holland, on September 17, 1944. The men lived in tents outside the city. It was not the most comfortable accommodations in damp England, but after the foxholes of Italy and France "a tent city," one recalled, "seemed like the Waldorf to us." The 82nd overwhelmed Leicester and the county of Leicestershire. They came to know well the pubs, fish and chips shops, dance halls, and many of the women.[12]

Diary, January 10, 1945

From St. Pancreas Station, the LMS [London Midland and Scottish Railway] took me through softly rolling country to Leicester. My first night there was spent at "The Stag and Pheasant Hotel" in a rather strained atmosphere, as my co-traveler (I can't remember her name now) got mixed up with two glider pilots on the train, and naturally, a bottle, so the Stag and Pheasant weren't exactly cordial. The next night, I met a new captain, Margaret Morrison and my co-crew member, Aileen Anderson. Aileen had come over on the boat with me, but owing to the alphabet system, my circle of acquaintances had been limited to the M to Z group. Our clubmobile was the "Kansas City" and it smelled of doughnuts. We were billeted in a nice middle class house on a nice middle-class street. Our landlady was an Irishwoman, a recent widow, who looked and acted like Billy Burke. As for Leicester, it was our home for three wonderful months and we grew to appreciate its somewhat doubtful charms. It had had its own blitz in 1941, at the same time that Coventry had gotten it. We were attached to the 82nd Airborne Division who had recently returned from Normandy. They were a wonderful bunch of boys who had seen and done too much.

The best fun in Leicester was the regimental dances and gradually, the blob of faces became individuals. Our favorite regiment was the 504 who had been pulled out of Anzio too late for Normandy. They were a crack outfit, with perfect cooperation between officers and men.

I bought a bicycle for £8 something. I'd ride down to the clubmobile in the morning and home at night. Our route covered the hunting district pretty well—Husband's Bosworth, Melton, Nottingham, Market Harborough. We got used to the doughnut routine and I did some painting.

Liz described a day in the life of the *Kansas City* crew in a report she sent to London after the first three weeks in Leicester. *The Sinker*, the Red Cross Clubmobile newsletter, published a portion of her report in its issue of September 15, 1944. Her good humor masked some of the dreary and frustrating details of Clubmobile work. The work was physically demanding, with long and irregular hours of heaving heavy coffee urns, mixing dough, moving supplies, washing coffee cups, and scrubbing out the greasy doughnut machine as well as the Clubmobile. Another Clubmobiler wrote that "this is without doubt the simplest work I've ever done, yet the most demanding physically. And the most satisfying."[13]

The Sinker included with Liz's article a simple sketch she drew depicting her serving doughnuts to a sea of GIs. By October 1944, when the Clubmobile program had celebrated its second anniversary in England, approximately 600 women had been trained as "doughnut queens."[14]

Everything's Up to Date in "Kansas City" or
We've Gone about as Fur as We Can Go
Elizabeth Richardson

The good Clubmobile <u>Kansas City</u> is, by some strange coincidence, a long, squat, converted Green Liner. It has all the characteristics common to others of its species, including the ability to get lost in a blackout. And it has taken three weeks for its crew to get sufficiently acclimated so that there were energy and time to spare for the joys of diary keeping.

The <u>Kansas City</u> lives in the backyard of the Red Cross Club at Base 21. Small boys are especially intrigued with it and people in bus queues on the street beyond have been known to miss their bus because they were captivated by the activities centered in Doughnut Alley. They also like the smell, which gives them a vicarious sort of pleasure.

Every day (except Sunday and days when the Division chooses to go on extensive and mysterious manoeuvres rather than eat doughnuts) the K.C. produces enough doughnuts to fill its trays— oh, heck, we might as well admit it: some come in boxes from a doughnut kitchen—and then sets out on the day's schedule. Our particular Division is a very special and wonderful one. It's Airborne and has seen combat ever since Africa, and although we are very new and green, we already feel as though we belonged to them. Take Wednesday for instance. It's August, but blindfold us and take away our sense of time and we'd say it was early December in the near vicinity of Hudson Bay. And there's a fine, misty rain that's supposed to be so good for the complexion. The K.C. is supposed to be at a camp by 9 a.m. because . . . well, because. So, singing paeans of thanksgiving for the Doughnut Production Center, we load up at the station (having whipped through our thirty pounds of home-made mix) and proceed to the camp, only getting lost once en route. Local yeomen and stray jeeps finally land us in a sea of mud that we perceive to be our destination. On time too! The captain bustles off to investigate the coffee water situation, while the rest of the crew (one befogged creature—the Ranger Crew has the other) artistically arranges chocolates and cigarettes and GIs. The captain returns and reports mission a failure. They want the doughnuts on the chow line, not enough water, etc., etc., etc. The mud rises, the phonograph blares, the doughnut supply dwindles. The latest flash from H.Q. comes thru the mist just as we are ready to perform via chow line. Could we serve tonight at the field rather than today? Of course we can! We'll go right back to the Base and make some more Unmentionables (doughnuts, to the uninitiated) and we'll be at the camp at six and a jeep will lead us to the field. We wave good-bye, the gears of the K.C. grind, the wheels writhe, and we are on our way. No sooner are we installed over a cup of pre-doughnut tea when a telephone call comes through. Everything is off, and would we serve this afternoon instead?

We gather up our woolies and once more go through Routine No. 1 (i.e. getting lost) which inevitably lands us at the camp and this time there's water for the coffee, a bright sun and renewed zeal for doughnuts. It is five o'clock when the last coffee urn is washed, and we are richer by a magnificent cake, bedecked with pink frosting and strawberry jam rosettes!

Doughnuts dominated the lives of Clubmobilers. Next to the women themselves, doughnuts and the coffee that accompanied them were among the GIs' most beloved symbols of home. They were also the trademark of the wartime Red Cross. Red Cross doughnuts had a special appearance, less wrinkled and readily distinguished from those made in the army messes, which reinforced the sense that the Red Cross "sinkers," as they were lovingly called, came from civilians and from home. The Red Cross went to great effort to get its doughnuts to the boys. The organization entered into a contract with the Doughnut Corporation of America, which loaned at no cost for the war's duration 468 doughnut machines, each with a capacity of 48 dozen an hour. In return (and much to the regret of the Pillsbury Flour Company) the New York City company enjoyed exclusive rights to sell to the Red Cross all the doughnut flour it needed.[15]

Shipped across the Atlantic in barrels, the special doughnut mix contained flour, sugar, egg powder, skim milk powder, and salt. To this mix the women added water. They were instructed to measure the water accurately by weighing it, the source of the sardonic line on the masthead of their Clubmobile newsletter: "We Weigh the Water." In fact, they seldom did, learning by experience how to adjust to changing weather and other conditions to get the doughnut mix to the right consistency. In a scrapbook she made after the war, Patricia Maddox wrote next to a copy of *The Sinker's* slogan: "We weighed the water when the boss was looking." That seldom happened since Clubmobiles were so far from direct supervision.[16]

From the large mixing bowl the Clubmobiler transferred the dough into the machine. Most of the doughnut-making machines were "Lincoln" models, which worked well in America's main street doughnut shops but proved cantankerous in a Clubmobile parked in an English field. The machine's intricate moving parts shaped the dough, cooked it in hot fat, and flipped it over. GIs liked watching the moving parts and the doughnuts coming down the chute at the end. But the machine operator, as Mary Hall reported, could "get dizzy and feel weird as we watch the donuts turn round and round in the hot fat until they flip out the opening." Clubmobile women were never to touch a doughnut with their fingers. They used a prong to remove each cooked doughnut from the machine, which was why an instructor at orientation in London offered only one piece of advice that Clubmobiler Barbara Pathe remembered: "Do not get the prong caught in the flipper." More than a few tired women made this mistake while "pronging" doughnuts, as did some GIs who tried to help. The machines required an electrical connection, which often presented difficulties in wartime England. They had a hand brake that had to be set properly before moving the Clubmobile. And the process required obtaining, storing, and moving large barrels of doughnut mix and lard. Clubmobile crews would sometimes turn out several thousand sinkers a day when all pieces of the process were working. But that was not often.[17]

Clubmobiler Harriett Engelhardt wrote a friend in July 1944, that "the doughnut machine is the instrument of the Devil." It "has never been known to work properly." The many challenges caused the Red Cross to conclude finally in early 1944 "that it is not practical to install a doughnut machine aboard a mobile unit." Even if the "delicate parts" were working well, "the machines cannot turn out doughnuts as fast as the boys eat them; therefore, the only value of making doughnuts on the spot is the entertainment value of watching the ingenious machine in action." The Red Cross moved to set up central bakeries to supply Clubmobiles each morning. The crew could then concentrate mostly on serving and on talking with the guys, sometimes making a few batches with the dough-nut machine for the entertainment value it added.[18]

Liz would benefit from access to central supply bakeries, especially later in France, but she would spend much more time fussing with the cantankerous doughnut machine as well as performing the other chores necessary to hand out a fresh-made sinker and cup of coffee to a GI in the field. She and her colleagues grew very, very tired of smelling and even seeing doughnuts, but they could often joke about them. "I smell so much like one," Gretchen Schuyler wrote home, "that I'm afraid a solider will grab a cup of coffee in one hand and me in the other!" Clubmobiler Margee Main described herself to her family as "the gal behind the donut behind the man behind the gun."[19] And there was a Clubmobile song with the verse:

> Oh, you'll never get to heaven
> With a doughnut in yo' hand
> 'Cos they can't abear the smell
> In the promised land.[20]

Among the Milwaukee friends Liz wrote from blacked-out Leicester was Winifred Wood, who had worked with her in advertising at Schus-ter's Department Store. Here, with wit and intelligence, Liz explained her work and her uniform, the aggressiveness of English women, and some of the things she most missed.

Commenting to W.W. on the novelty and excitement of her experi-ences, Liz made a reference to John Keats's "On First Looking into Chap-man's Homer." In this 1816 sonnet Keats expresses his wonder and de-light at reading George Chapman's 1611 translation of Homer: "Then felt I like some watcher of the skies, When a new planet swims into his ken."[21] Liz's memory of this poem and her reference to it reveal more so-phisticated and intellectual qualities of mind than she usually showed in letters to her family or, doubtless, in her banter with most GIs. Just as Keats read Chapman's Homer, Liz was a thoughtful and passionate discoverer of a new planet as she "read" England, the war, and the men fighting it.

Aug. 8, 1944
[Leicester]

Dear W.W.

This is just a note—thought you might be interested in the enclosed. Poor old Liz is working like a beaver 12, 14, or even 16 hours a day and half the time is spent bending over an old doughnut machine! We have a grand clubmobile that takes us over the lovely English countryside, but remind me to never mention the word doughnut again.

I was darn glad to leave London, needless to say! This is the end of my first week here in the midlands and we are looking for our second wind! Our captain has been over 7 weeks and myself and partner are so green it hurts, so we all feel like kening a new star or whatever the man did on looking in Chapman's Homer. Our route covers about 8 or 9 camps in one week, most of them Air Borne and veterans of everything from Africa on. They are wonderful fellows, but it's been awfully hard for them—as for the camps, we will now delve into the kitchens. We have cultivated every mess sarg. in our radius and what with the doug—whoops, almost said it! What with our stock in trade, we are waxing very well indeed. We live on the outskirts of what is called in a Hugh Walpole novel, "a provincial town," and our landlady, an evacuee of the London blitz of '41 is a gem—crams tarts and tea down us and owns a bathtub with <u>hot</u> water.

The crowds do <u>not</u> cheer when the yanks go by around here—it's more mutual toleration. The British girls, however, are in there pitching, and I don't mean hay. Far as I can see, our native land is going to be flooded with a lot of new faces, come the peace, or else somebody's giving the ladies an awfully good line! 5 years of war has also done something for their inhibitions. I doubt very much if that something called English reserve still exists.

I miss milk, ice cream, Milwaukee beer (it's called "mild" or bitter" here and served at the temperature of tired dishwater), readable newspapers (although the stars and stripes does a swell job), the New

Yorker, windows open to the night with light coming out of them, and a few other things—but all in all our life is quite civilized, though our wardrobe is not. The Red Cross has presented us with British-issue battle dress of R.A.F. blue, complete with hat a la Helen Hokinson.[22] This, added to our summer issue, winter issue, and various hats—all of different weights, colors, and materials makes the Red Cross the most ununiformed bunch in captivity. Except the Free French. I attempted to carry on a dashing conversation with one last night (he knew one word in English—"Good day") who sported a pinstripe shirt, a dotted tie, and a threadbare uniform dimly reminiscent of the motorman on the North Ave. streetcar. A slight language barrier kept us apart.

Didn't mean to become so involved with this—it's late and my roommate is snoring.

Liz

The mail from home finally caught up with Liz the second week in Leicester. The *Kansas City* was now fully rolling, carrying doughnuts, coffee, and, most important, Liz, Aileen, and Margaret to the GIs spread around the area. There were long days and hard work and all the time smiling while on stage.

At night there were dances, often with the 82nd Airborne Orchestra, sometimes in Montfort Hall, sometimes, for the enlisted men, in the Palais de Dance, or for officers in the Grand Hotel. The Red Cross women were nearly obligated to attend the dances and to dance. Since they were all over 25 and sometimes too old to have learned the new jitterbug steps that the younger GIs knew, they simply had to learn. As one of them, B. J. Olewiler recalled, "To uphold the honor of my country, I had to learn to jitterbug." Couples danced to slow numbers too, while the orchestra played the romantic and smooth sounds captured in tunes like Glenn Miller's "Moonlight Serenade." For many lonely GIs a dance with a Red Cross girl was a special opportunity to be physically close to an American female. Wartime lyrics such as "We'll Meet Again," "Don't Sit Under the Apple Tree with Anyone Else but Me," and "Paper Doll" only highlighted the separation from home.[23]

English women came to the dances too. They watched the way the

Americans jitterbugged and soon joined the vigorous action on the floor. With their Hollywood style and their easy money, the Yanks were irresistible to many English women. Some men took off wedding rings to pass as single and catch a "bird." They benefited not only from smooth talk but also from an abundance of cigarettes, candy, food, and pub money, essentials that distinguished them from English men and made them both liked and disliked. Clubmobiler Rosemary Langheldt wrote in her diary in early 1945 of the English women that "they seem overly aggressive in their search for a date." A Leicester woman later recalled that "the girls went mad about them." Another remembered of the GIs, "They'd all got money, they had everything; all the beautiful young girls wanted somebody then, and they got them."[24]

One Leicester resident, Jean B. Sleath, recalled mixed feelings about the Americans, including compassion for young men so far from home:

> The Yanks were both welcomed and disliked. They were generous, cheeky and had "candy," "tinned fruit," and food we had not seen for years. They were very good to the children, who followed them everywhere as they whizzed about in their jeeps. They were often at a loss as what to do during their off-duty hours and wandered the town mainly trying to pick-up a "dame." . . . It must have been boring, dead, depressing for the Yanks to come to a shabby, war-torn rationed town with its dullness accentuated by the blackout, to which we were accustomed and they were not. "Put that bloody light out!" vied with "Goddammed Limeys!" and Tom, Dick and Harry turned into Bud and Joe. You could make an easy 'buck' out of our American friends by selling at inflated prices all kinds of rubbish which they found "Cute," though this was not overdone unless our overseas guests became exceptionally boastful, brash, and boring.[25]

Liz continued her avid interest in current events, more so than most GIs. Throughout her service she regretted the scant supply of reading material and made several requests home for magazine subscriptions. GIs read too, though most did not share Liz's more sophisticated preferences. Everyone wanted to read *Life* magazine, with its carefully presented photographs and upbeat stories. A survey of the reading tastes of over 2,000 soldiers in Great Britain in 1943 ranked *Life* as one of their top favorites. Liz included in this letter home a request for the *New Yorker*, a more text-oriented and serious periodical. Only a handful of GIs surveyed included it on their reading list.[26]

This letter is one Liz typed rather than handwrote. She had the day off and planned to go swimming.

August 9, 1944
[Leicester]

Dear mother and daddy,

At last, the mail is beginning to come through, and very well, at that. I received your letter, daddy, written on the 4th today and day before yesterday, I got one addressed to Washington. So according to those communiques, the Patch must be deserted while C. M. and Henrietta frolic and Butch makes enemies on the east coast. Hope that Freckles is being well fed and that somebody is around to keep an eye on the melons.

This is our day off. After a week of it, I have never appreciated a whole empty day as I am doing right now. We have been working 12 and 14 hours and I almost whoops when I hear the word doughnut. The payoff came when our supervisor dropped in and presented us with a new record to play on our recording outfit. It's called "Dunkin' in the ETO" and in theory is supposed to be the theme song of all the clubmobiles. Ugh and ugh again. All joking aside, we mix a mean doughnut and the coffee is certainly better than the G. I. variety. Our clubmobile is a converted Greenline bus, fixed up with a lounge, sink, and doughnut machine and serving facilities. Also a British driver and us. We start out about six in the morning, either make our doughnuts parked outside the local Red Cross Service Club [on Granby Street near the city center], or else we make them at camp with ten million G. I.'s and an occasional Colonel watching the operation. Then we turn on our recording machine and serve, all the time smiling like mad and dividing our time between the doughnuts, the mess sgt., the coffee and the sea of faces. You can see why we especially pay attention to the mess sgt., he feds (feeds, get it) us and we are partial to Army food. Mrs. Tipper, our

51

landlady, does very well by us and between the two, we are waxing fat. This is a provincial town in every sense of the word and many are the lace curtains that are parted as we wend our merry way down the street. The Yanks are no novelty around here, although American women are, but there is not too much love lost between the two. But the British girls are having a wonderful fling and are for the most part looking forward to a happy wedded life in the States. Our little guys take awfully good care of us and we are sort of community property—they get us our weekly rations, fix us up with boots, see that we see the dentist and all that. This afternoon, we are going swimming. I shiver at the prospect, but the British say that this is a nice warm day. So—we are going swimming. We also go to battalion and regimental dances and officer dances. And then the cold bleak dawn and the doughnut machine.

I am very near John Bodle and expect to see him soon, that is as soon as I can get hold of him. We have a little difficulty with transportation and as the trams stop running almost as soon as they start we have to depend on miscellaneous jeeps, weapons carriers and our own two feet. So I am going to buy a bike. They are about £8 and I can sell it if I have to. I love the countryside and can't get enough of it. That's the beauty of being in a Clubmobile—we do get around.

Ernst [Kuenstner] is now a Staff Sgt., so at this rate, he should be a general by 1955. By the way, if you are wondering what I want for Christmas, it's a bright red scarf,[27] ditto socks (wool), good dog tag chain or identification bracelet with name and serial number, subscription to Life, Time or New Yorker, camera. I could go on at great length, but won't. If you think I'm a bit previous, it's just because we hear that Christmas packages must be mailed before the end of September. Do tell me if the checks are coming through from Washington. They certainly aren't from this side. In fact, they told me at the London paymaster's office that I wasn't here! This is an interesting new angle—perhaps it is all a dream.

Please write as often as possible—mail is a lovely thing to get. Airmail is by far the most satisfactory in this theatre. And anyway, V mail hurts my eyes.

Love to you all,
Elizabeth

→helped GIs & their families

Clubmobilers sent special pre-printed postcards to the families of some of the men they served. The card had a photo of a Clubmobile and crew at work and the greeting:

> We have just served your [e.g., son Bill] with coffee and doughnuts from the American Red Cross Clubmobile. He is looking well. With sincere best wishes from the Clubmobile Crew.

The crew signed their names. The *Kansas City* sometimes received replies to the postcards, such as this one:

> Many thanks for the card telling me about my son, Cyril. This is the first news that we have had of him in over seven weeks . . . Yours is very fine work, and may God bless you in it.[28]

The work days became even longer as the *Kansas City* now made occasional night runs to serve the 82nd as it trained for night jumps. In the blackout Liz had to read direction signs by flashlight and then talk and laugh with paratroopers who faced, as one recalled, "the prospect of stepping out of a comfortable plane into black oblivion . . . like voluntarily deciding to step through a black portal into a coffin."[29] The social life intensified too, with dance after dance for the American women in such short supply—dances, like military life generally, divided between officers and enlisted men.

The Red Cross struggled with the necessity of maintaining a line between officers and enlisted men. That line was often wobbly, and particularly so when it came to females. The Red Cross was obliged to follow military policy that its officers date only other officers, not enlisted men. Since the Clubmobile women had officer status this meant they were to date only lieutenants and higher. This policy often matched the self-interest of most Red Cross women. Officers tended to be more attractive as social and romantic partners because they were generally better educated, older, and more mature, and they had access to better creature comforts, particularly food and alcohol. Moreover, to do their jobs Red Cross workers needed cooperation from the commanders. There was a downside, however. Women sometimes felt compelled to attend officers' parties and dances, fearing reprisals if they did not. They resented some officers' notions that they were on call for command performances. And

Liz could only date to higher officer [?]

doubtless there were occasions when an officer moved into areas of sexual harassment with a Red Cross woman. On the other side of the divide were the enlisted men, who naturally resented a policy that restricted their company with the women. They put pressure on Clubmobile crews to dance, to go for a drink, to date. GIs, particularly those who had little or no direct contact with the Red Cross, sometimes charged that the Red Cross women were "brass happy, out every night shacking up with officers." Some griped that they were "snooty dames" and "officers' whores." Caught between enlisted men and officers, the women were often torn and uncertain about what was best for their work and for their personal lives. Some were so partial to enlisted men that they refused to date officers because of adverse GI reactions. Most spent not only work time but social time with enlisted men and some dated them. As Clubmobiler Rosemary Langheldt wrote in late 1944, "Despite our instructions during Washington training that we date only officers it's a rule often ignored." Only an irresponsible Clubmobile woman would have snubbed a soldier because of enlisted rank.[30]

Liz tried to walk both sides of the divide. She likely spent more personal free time with officers than enlisted men (and would fall in love with two lieutenants), but she came to know and to respect dozens and dozens of ordinary GIs. They were among the male friends she spent time with off duty in restaurants, pubs, dances, and concerts. She would join one GI, Private Bernie Levine, on a weekend trip to Edinburgh.

Her landlady, Mrs. Tipper, was very alert to the officer/enlisted status differences, doubtless because of the resemblance to Britain's class differences. But Americans noticed too. Class and gender came together in the enlisted men's common gripes about officers.

Dating was perfectly ok, but premarital sex for American women had to be kept quiet even though there was lots of it overseas as well as at home. Several unmarried Red Cross women became pregnant and had to be sent home. And there were a few unplanned babies the organization had to find ways to have adopted.[31]

Already Liz's conversations with hundreds of men in the 82nd had given her a fuller sense of war's costs. In this letter she combined comments on the frivolity of social life with a vague reference to the hard combat the paratroopers had already seen and her anger that Americans at home were not sufficiently aware of the cost of war. This letter arrived at the post office in Mishawaka, Indiana, on September 8.

August 18, 1944
[Leicester]

Dear mother and daddy,

At last, the mail is coming through like the Pony Express and I am so glad to have news of all of you—did you have a wonderful vacation? Of course, Mother stayed at Whitehaven a little longer, I hope. How do Aunt G. and Uncle J. [Gertrude and John Richardson] feel?

We have been having wonderful weather, but I still refuse to call it hot. Today is the sort of a semi-day off, so I'm going to buy my bicycle and paint the clubmobile. We are thinking of decorating it with murals, although where the time is coming from is a different matter. Tonight, we have a night run—not bad at all. In fact, we had one last Monday and after we were through with tossing doughnuts at the sea of upturned faces, we were loaded into a jeep and taken to a dance, during the process of which I dimly remember jitter-bugging. This must have been quite a feat, shod as we were in heavy G.I. boots.

Our social life is a little too active for my taste. The work is purely physical and at the end of the day, we don't feel too much like exuding even more personality. But we do. This is Friday and so far we've been to three dances and the G.I. ones are rough! The real fun ones are the Officers' Dances which are quite civilized—flowers, good music and wonderful dancing with a miscellaneous assortment of very nice partners. We are called for and taken home in anything from a Jeep to a Weapons Carrier, both of which I recommend highly. And you know how I love to dance! Our division is the best one in the Army, but they have gone through so much—I wish I could tell you. If only we could, people back home would be more aware of what's going on and there wouldn't be this chasm between the men over here and the home team.

If only you could see these charming hamlets and villages! We stopped in one the other day—myself, Margaret (our Captain) and Eddie, a little G.I. While we were buying flowers—large red carnations—a woman came in the shop and welcomed us to her town. We were the first American women to shop there, she said. She was an American herself who had married a British diplomat during the last war and she invited us to her home for a drink, which we had to refuse because our Clubmobile was full to the gunwales with G.I.'s that we had acquired en route. I also had tea with one of the native families of this town—the kind who drop their aitches and speak in such a dialect that I can't quite catch all that they say. This continual drinking of tea amuses me muchly and of course, I am only too willing to cooperate. A G.I. took me there—sometimes you feel sort of like a museum piece— "Hey, look, fellows! A real, live American girl!"

The news from France is quite good, but don't be too optimistic.[32] Our men have a most healthy respect for the Germans as fighters and they don't seem to think that they'll fold up like a tired balloon. But you never know—even if it did happen, there will be much to be done and I imagine it will be a long time before we see the Old Lady with the Torch.

It's strange and beautiful to ride through the blacked out night in our merry Clubmobile. Everything is so very dark and yet filled with a feeling of alertness and a thousand muffled sounds. The stars seem closer and there are more of them. I feel like Columbus himself as I swing out of the door to investigate the sign posts with a flashlight. Of course, the very names of the cities and towns are still magic to me and a signpost in a blackout adds to the spell.

In my last letter, I optimistically made out a Christmas list. Amendment: Cancel dog tag chain—I have a brand new G.I. one—add red wool mittens to match red scarf (very long) and durable notebook, sort of like a Journal. Hate to have all this happen and no place to put it down!

It's good to hear that John liked Parris Island. He'll make a good officer and if not that, a good Marine. There's nothing else that I need or want, except mail and magazines.

Mrs. Tipper, our landlady, "from the right part of Ireland," is calling us for lunch (we just finished breakfast a half hour ago), so I must leave you temporarily. Mrs. T. is most class conscious and does not approve of enlisted men. She says the neighbors talk, so you see what sort of reputation the Yanks have in this neck of the woods. Robin Hood must be whirling in his grave.

Love,
Elizabeth

Late in the English "summer," Liz wrote by a coal fire. She had finally found a bicycle, a goal from near the beginning. Doughnut making and dancing continued, but by now she had come to know the American GIs sufficiently well to see them as "wonderful kids," yet "oddly old," and herself as a "big sister."

Aug. 22, 1944
[Leicester]

Dear mother and daddy,

Each day, our packet from London brings me mail ante-dating the last received and it's an interesting sensation to read letters backwards. By this time, you are all back at the Patch, watching the melons ripen—ah-ah-h! And I am sitting by an open coal fire this August day, for at last the famed English weather has caught up with me with everything in the books and it is with great difficulty that I recall those sweltering days in Washington. This morning, I had to go down to the Clubmobile to whip up the doughnuts for the day and a sadder figure you can't picture as E. Richardson, clad in sweater, heavy shirt, battle dress, WAC raincoat and a light drizzle, plodded through the morning mist to the tram, her breath trailing behind her in graceful clouds. Frankly, I expect snow tomorrow.

The best thing I have is my new bicycle—a lovely black thing with hand brakes and attached tire pump—and I am the Clubmobile's messenger de luxe. I carry laundry on the handlebars, investigate the doughnut situation at the station and anything else, thus partially overdoing the evil done by Uncle Sam's good food and our retinue of favorite friends, the mess sergeants—also, our doting Mrs. Tipper who does noble with British rations, plus our donations from the M.S. (mess sergeants). I feel very British, pedaling away with the rest of the population, until some urchin interrupts me with a "Have any gum, chum?" So my disguise isn't so good, as that's the way every American is greeted.

I wondered, Mother, if you were listening to the radio at about 1:00 P. M. today. It was 6 o'clock here and we heard a program destined for home with a round table discussion on the buzz-bombs. I could picture you reclining in the "library," relaxing (I hope) while outside the nice <u>warm</u> Indiana sun bathed the green and not <u>too</u> civilized landscape.

People here are quite thrilled by the news from France, although nobody thinks of the end as an actuality. This seems so queer to me. The Americans, of course, think of the end as going home—they have been away so long and our particular charges have seen so much—but the British! God knows what they think. I think they've forgotten what it's like to live without fear or small privations. It makes my hackles rise to hear some of these kids tell of their experiences and to see their faces which are oddly old—do you know what I mean? And some of them are much younger than Johnny. They place such small value on human life—I wonder what will happen to them when they come back to that Utopia they firmly believe exists.

Last night, after serving until the final crumb vanished, we went to a G.I. post dance—Margaret with the mess sergeant of the moment (he threatened not to give us some eggs if we didn't go) and me with a boy from Milwaukee and afterwards, we sat on a brick wall and sang, or rather, they entertained us—especially with that most charming and pathetic of songs "Lili Marlene" both in German and English. All of them are such wonderful kids—already we feel like big sisters to them.

This is a request, which you may give to the postman. Understand that the pkg. can't weigh more than 5 lbs., so could you send the following?

1 pkg. currents
1 Sweat Shirt (size 40)
2 White gym Socks (size 11)
3 bars good soap (preferably Yardlys—or Cashmere Bouquet
Small combs

When you send these bothersome things, please use the money coming from Washington.

Keep writing and send some snapshots!

Love to you all,
Elizabeth

A weekend free of doughnuts allowed time for painting and a long bike ride in the country with an American lieutenant.

Aug. 28, 1944
[Leicester]

Dear mother and daddy,

Mother's letter written from Whitehall arrived this morning and it sounds as if you all have been having a gay time—awfully glad that Mother stayed on another week. As for Butch, I received a Travelogue of a letter from him, a paen of appreciation to the Stevens family and Westchester County. No news from Pvt. Richardson but that would be expecting too much.

I'm sitting at the breakfast table, while Mrs. Tipper prepares breakfast. Outside, there is a very blue sky and very green leaves and I'm anxious to be up and off on my trusty bicycle. This is our long weekend and I was intending to meet one of my Washington colleagues, but sitting on a train, especially a crowded one, is not my idea of a holiday, so I'm contenting myself with the local variety. Yesterday, therefore, I did a watercolor of some jumbled houses, quite the usual thing here, but all the chimney pots intrigue me. Then a Lieut. named Hank and I pedaled out in the country for tea under large, vari-colored umbrellas, the only trouble being that we didn't drink tea. Hank brought beer along in his musette bag, which we drank as a passable substitution. And then more rural roads, narrow, lined with hedges and twisting gently up and down hill and dale.

Mrs. Tipper's house is so much like home that our little friends enjoy sitting in the living room and basking in front of the fire. As I've said before, Mrs. Tipper is Irish and anybody with the name of O'Malley or equivalent is O.K. by her—so we have assembled a retinue of Kelly's, Murphy's and Kennedy's and if they happen to be blessed with an occasional Schmidt or Jones, we invent grandmothers named MacNamara. On her birthday, one of the mess sargts. gave us a magnificent cake, covered with curlicues of pink icing and the fellows produced Scotch, so that we really had a gala party.

The news from France continues to be wonderful—I'm looking at a headline now that says "As one week of Disasters Ends for Hitler, Another Opens." Doesn't that sound British? Very little said and in the longest way! We can't help but wonder what will happen to us if the war in this theatre is over and we are hoping that whatever happens, we'll stick to our division wherever they go.

In my pedalings about the countryside, I've found some wonderful old churches and ditto churchyards—one, especially, has parts that are 14th century. However, the British can't understand our feverish delvings in search of ancient architecture. To them, on old building is an old building and they are much more proud of a Victorian atrocity of a tower to which their fathers each subscribed a sixpence back in 1906.

At this moment, I can hear the radio giving forth with much German and a krauty version of Yankee Doodle. How we are supposed to absorb the propaganda when the only words we understand are "Amerika und Deutchland" I do not know. The boys probably believe, in their supreme conceit, that <u>every</u> body speaks German.

Please have a dozen ears of corn for me and 5 big melons each.

Your fat and sassy daught,
Elizabeth

In an unusually short letter, Liz expressed some frustrations but also her good fortune to be doing her part in the war, as she looked forward to homecoming and dawn-to-dusk storytelling beyond the censor's eye.

September 1, 1944

[Leicester]

Dear mother and daddy,

The last mail from you had you on a terrace overlooking Lake Michigan, with Daddy, and the Chicago Richardsons returning to cruel civilization and leaving poor Henrietta all alone. And meanwhile, Elizabeth is sitting in front of the fire, surrounded by the babblings of four miscellaneous females, plus the BBC, so you realize under what handicaps I'm working. Anyway, this is going to be a very brief note—and I'm having a hard time getting this off. Mrs. Tipper is like Mother—she grunts and groans during the current radio program to signify appreciation. Oh Gawd . . . I can't write, but anyway, you know that I'm thinking of you. We had peculiar day No. 6330 today—our supervisor plus Mr. Red Cross in Great Britain were to pay us a visit and in eager anticipation, we polished and scrubbed, and I drew many cartoons to decorate our walls, until we had a model Clubmobile, indeed. Then, of course, they did not turn up, which has left us with a feeling of frustration and a clean clubmobile.

I just asked Margaret what else to ask for Christmas. She looked up, animal-like from her occupation of the moment and grunted "Food." Margaret is our Captain, my eating partner who almost rivals me in appetite. By this time, you must be sick and tired of requests, requests and more requests. But if you only knew how barren the stores are of even the necessities (and then it takes coupons) and (Thank God) I am far away from the Officers' Q.M. Depot in London . . . that's my only excuse.

Someday, I'll be able to tell you about this, without the base censor leaning over my shoulder and when that comes, we'll have a dawn to dusk session, preferably in the melon season, with plenty of ice cold beer on hand. At least, I consider myself fortunate to be in Clubmobile—can't conceive of anything else. It's a rugged and irregular and weird life, but it's wonderful. That is, as wonderful as anything can be under the circumstances.

Love to all of you

Elizabeth

[handwritten annotation: →Not getting a full picture]

Liz wrote her Milwaukee roommate, Betty Twining (now married to Robert Gleisner), who she often addressed as B-bub or Twine. This letter contained the usual gossip about mutual friends, the love of wit Twine and Liz shared, a few serious observations, and a bit more candor than letters to her family.

September 4, 1944
[Leicester]

Dear B-Bub,

I don't know what got into me, because I wrote a letter to one of the Prospect Avenue gang last week, but the occasion was so magnificent when at long last I received a letter from the Gleisner that I rushed to out [sic] landlady's typewriter and found myself doing this . . . This is our day off, because we have just returned from a little session in the field, the details of which I can't bear to go into—too much like a chapter from the Rover Boys in the Wilds. And now that I have washed the accumulated dirt of three days from my bodee, I can face the world again.

Your letter was loaded with news and as far as I can see, everybody is either reproducing like mad or playing Rosalind Russell[. . . .]

To hell with this typewriter, pardon me while I change horses. Our clubmobile is an ex-London green bus, not particularly adapted to rural country lanes. The front of the thing has a serving counter, many doughnut racks, a doughnut machine and lots of loose odds and ends that fall on your head when we take a corner at any speed over 10 mi. per. The back has a lounge with a PA system, extinct records, magazines dating back to Pearl Harbor and usually a horizontal member of the crew. We also have an English driver named Jimmy [Saunders]. He is good at oiling my bicycle and mooching from mess sergeants. The work is in spurts and gasps and then we have one or two days in which to gather our forces. Damn glad I have a degree—it helps so much in making doughnuts. However, I wouldn't trade this for anything else and it has more satisfaction in the doing than anything Auntie has ever done. Our captain is a girl from upstate New York, with a swell sense of humor, while the other is of the type who calls everybody "dearie" and is

over qualified but happy nonetheless

simple and sincere as a frisky peasant girl. She used to be a vocalist with Bob Crosby and God knows how such an experience could leave her so completely naïve. She loves 'em all and we no longer run a clubmobile—it's a kissmobile from now on in.

If you could only see me jitterbugging. I just grit my teeth and let gravity do its bit. You'd have enjoyed London in spite of the buzz bombs. It's a magnificent city with a sort of sad and bedraggled dignity. One day while we were standing by a bus stop on Fleet street, a passing woman (who turned out to be of the press) attached us and took us through the Temple Gardens, a beautiful spot, even now. And a Czech movie producer took us to Soho for tea at his club. The atmosphere is very Bohemian, far more so than Greenwich village. I could go on for sometime, but I'll save it for our reunion in your F.H.A. [Federal Home Administration] home in 1966[. . . .]

Love, Liz

[4]

War Comes Closer

The Red Cross women continued their daily routine of driving out from Leicester to the surrounding camps and making and serving coffee and doughnuts in huge volume. A new experience came when the Kansas City crew spent three cold, wet days in the field working with the 82nd Airborne as they prepared for a jump into Belgium, set for September 3. At the last minute, as Liz later noted in her diary, the mission was cancelled. Two weeks later she would see the beginning of the real thing.

As she often did, Liz imagined her family back home in Indiana, symbolized by ripe melons. Such an imagined scene was all the more comforting after the long weekend in the field.

September 6, 1944
[Leicester]

Dear mother and daddy,

Mother's letter from her solitary beach chair in Michigan has arrived and I find it hard to bring the two pictures together—because although it's still September 6, I picture you according to the latest communiqué from Mother. In reality, Butch must be getting ready for school and the rest of you must be eating melons . . . ah, yes.

We have just come from three days in the field and I do mean rugged. Now I know what it's like to hear the wind and rain sweeping down on a Nissen hut and how it feels to be huddled under 5 army blankets and <u>still</u> be cold. We didn't change our clothes at all and neither did the weather. It's also quite an experience to wake up in the cold, grey dawn, share a pail of cold water with a colonel and then stand in chow line out under the threatening sky with your mess kit dangling artistically from one purple hand. Another interesting fact is that the Army evidently labors under the illusion that ladies don't use a biffey.[1] This added suspense to our little outing. Of course, our good Clubmobile got bogged down in the mud and so we took a jeep; after the first 50 miles, I was ready for anything—even a trip by rocket to the moon. We filled the rear with doughnuts and coffee urns, the front with an M.P. (military police) driver, ourselves and phonograph. I carried the records cradled in my arms and naturally half of me floated in the breeze. Before long, I expect to have one of those peasantry English complexions—<u>not</u> the kind lauded by Yardley's. However, it was a wonderful experience and some day I'll tell you all about it. Believe me, Mrs. Tipper's glowing fire and tea and tarts looked awfully good to us, not counting the luxury of the bathtub.

Mother, you asked how we function. If I haven't told you, it's like this. Every day we have a schedule of camps and we either manufacture our delicious doughnuts hooked up behind the local Red Cross Club— or else we hook up at the camp-for-the-day. (This happens rarely, as we seem to have a tendency to blow all the fuses.) The camps always (well, most of the time) have coffee water ready for us and we usually are ready to serve within 1/2 an hour after reaching our destination. The doughnuts are a cinch—there's a machine in each clubmobile, sort of like the ones in F. W. Woolworth Stores and all we have to do is mix the dough with water in the approved fashion and adjust the pressure and this gadget and that gadget, turn on the machine, and voilá! They start coming. We make good coffee, too, even though it's on a rather large scale. Yes, Maw, it's real, honest to goodness coffee, as good as any you can get at home. To supplement the doughnuts we make, we receive a daily shipment from a Red Cross doughnut center, so that takes care of that.

Did I tell you that Chris [Hanson] is in the Azores? I certainly didn't learn this from the lady herself—her letter was so veiled that she could have been any place from Ascension to Siam, but Twine wrote me that it came out in the Milwaukee Journal. By the way, the other Clubmobile crew based here tells me that there's a pkg. for me at their roost—I imagine that it's the dress which you so kindly had repaired and dispatched. We're going to a regimental dance tomorrow, so maybe I'll be able to wear it. Don't worry about my other mounting requests— just send them when and if you feel like it. Bath powder is always nice, too. I am not as grasping as I appear.

And now I must give this up, in favor of my favorite place—bed. It really is a lovely thing, especially in contrast to our little rest in the field. Butch, give us more about your journey into the world and how about some snapshots?

Love to you all, even Freckles—
Elizabeth

In her diary Liz provided more detail about the 82nd as the men prepared to take off on September 3. It was another jump into combat that these experienced veterans were not eager to make and were happy to have cancelled.

Diary, January 10, 1945

About the first part of September, we began to hear rumors of a new jump. And one beautiful September day, we followed the 82nd in to Lincolnshire and hoped that something would happen to cause it to be called off. For two days, in mud and rain, we served doughnuts and one night, sitting in a glider 2 hours before the takeoff, we heard the boys cheering in the hangar and we knew it had been called off. Patton's army had moved fast and the 82nd was not needed—not for a while— anyway.

Still unable to divulge her location to her family, Liz did make clear she was near airfields. And that it was cold. The black lace dress she asked her mother to send in July finally arrived, a welcome change from her daily uniform.

September 10, 1944
[Leicester]

Dear Family,

At this moment, I'm sitting in "the garden," (we'd call it a back yard) where there is late afternoon sun, a crabapple tree laden with red and uneatable crabapples and convenient stone steps. It could very well be some spot at home, except that there is a sort of permanent chill in the air and the almost continual roar of aircraft. Today is our day of rest, which I have observed by eating and taking a spin on my bicycle. I regret to say that I discovered nothing of particular interest with the latter activity—all the lanes I turned into, although charming and picturesque, ended abruptly for no reason at all and after mediating over the view for a few moments, I was forced to turn back to the main highway and its row of uninspired suburban houses. The English need some architects with just a small spark of imagination.

Which reminds me—yesterday took us to a base that was most interesting—an estate that was indeed one of the stately homes of England.[2] The stables are now occupied with motorized steeds, the mansion by the Army, but otherwise, it was unchanged. The front of the main house overlooked a terraced formal garden with all the ingredients—rococo fountain, rose bushes, and an erstwhile velvet lawn that neglect could not spoil. And all this sloped down to a vista of undulating hills and woodland. Nearby, so that you could see its spire through the trees, was a 13th century church—swell Norman exterior and the interior I will investigate the next time if I can slide out from my duties. One of the G.I.'s told me that the stained glass windows were from all periods, 14th century up. This is in the heart of the hunting country—no, Daddy, not with Freckles, but the red-coated Tally-Ho sort—and things like this are just one of the sad traces of its past glory.

We have acquired a dog, very young and of doubtful antecedents. His name is Jerry and he is going to be awfully big if one can judge by the size of his paws. But he looks dimly like a police dog and he is in the midst of being house-broken. Poor Mrs. Tipper is frantic, especially when he appeared with a stuffed toy cat that for no apparent reason has decorated the foot of the stairs. He is now out for a walk with Patsy, Mrs. Tipper's sedate and convent-bred daughter.

The dress arrived safely and thank you so much! There will be plenty of opportunity to wear it, although I rather wish it were electrically heated. There is a wonderful future in this country for some central heating magnate. Butch, thanks for the V-Mail letter, and I'm glad to hear that you saw so many plays. What happened to "Oklahoma!"? I have a long weekend next week and plan to make an expedition a-field if all goes well, to Cambridge and surrounding countryside.

Love to you all—
Elizabeth

A letter to Winifred Wood, her Milwaukee co-worker, included a report on Glenn Miller's concert for the 82nd Airborne at Leicester's De Montfort Hall on September 11. Miller's big band orchestra was the most famous in the world of popular music at the time. They played numerous concerts for American servicemen in England in the summer and fall of 1944. The 82nd's officers, enlisted men, and a few Red Cross women packed De Montfort Hall that evening. Because of the paratroopers impending combat jump, however, there was no publicity or photographs of the Leicester concert.[3]

Sept. 12, '44
[Leicester]

Dear W.W.,

Your nice letter of August 23 was received and read and re-read—ah! the blast of hot air from Garfield and the man selling the "Watchtower" at 3rd and North; it all came back across the miles. And today, the crew of the other clubmobile told me that I had a package at their hotel. So, breathlessly, I mounted my good bicycle and pedaled up to welcome what I knew would be mounds of goodies; but no, it proved to be an expertly layed out ad, extolling the virtues of the Army Show at 12th and Vliet Street in Polish, to make it better. I could see Helen and Mr. Cornehls slapping their thighs in childish glee and I did likewise, although it's a bit difficult on a bicycle. Thank the dear kiddies for me.

→ constantly busy

It's now next morning—as any fool can plainly see, I was interrupted. Anyway, I was leading up to the fact that all these things combined were drawing me to a letter writing effort. The other two members of the crew have left to indulge in a doughnut-making orgy and this is my turn to play Mrs. Astor.

What do you think of our little Clarey in the Azores? My idea of the geography of the islands is so dim that I picture her enthroned on an ocean-bound rock, waving occasionally to passing ATC planes. And little Clarey does nothing to change my ideas.

This is a beautiful month, rather like October at home, but with a perpetual chill in the air (and the English have as yet to be converted to central heating.) How flowers bloom and trees remain green is quite beyond me. And I've never known such penetrating rain—our rain-coats are as much a part of us as our skin. But when the day is fine, it's the finest you've ever seen, which makes me a firm believer in compensation. Pooh, I wish you could see one of our bases—an ex-stately home of England, complete with rococo fountains, a horse graveyard (an especially big tablet to the horse who won the grand national) and velvet lawns, terraced to perfection and opening up to a view of rolling misty hills and woodland. I feel like some gross intruder, but the army must be hardened to it all by now. This particular estate is in the heart of the hunting country and as I'm now reading Sigried Sassoon's, "Memoirs of a Fox Hunting Man,"[4] it's all like stepping in the pages of a book and the motorized steeds now occupying the beautifully appointed stables seem awfully out of place. I have a long weekend coming up (one a month) and I'm planning to go to Cambridge—in fact, there are so many places that I'd like to go, but it's astounding how distances double on this small isle and whoever planned the railroads must have been a genius at mazes. By the way, I have met a Dutch Commando, very natty in a green beret and with a story that would put Raphael Sabatini to shame.[5] He was a native of Rotterdam and didn't leave until 1941, so you can figure it out for yourself. When you talk to people like that, you realize what a burning thing hate can be—it is a totally different emotion than what our G.I.'s feel, even those who fought through Italy and Normandy. Well, I find the whole business damnably tragic, and I hope people realize what a terrific readjustment must take place when and if this is over.

Glenn Miller played for our Division the other night and I was quite impressed with them—the Division, I mean. It was the first time I saw them en mass and it's quite a different thing than seeing them through the hole of a doughnut. As for Glenn, strictly in the groove, Jackson, strictly in the gro-ove. Our Division is the best in the army, better than the Rangers and if you read that article in The Sinker about meeting them at the station, you'll get some idea of what they are, because we inherited that same bunch when the other girls were sent to France. There is so much to write about—I could go on for some time at great risk of completely boring you and wasting paper—but the clock says that the hour has come for me to climb into my monkey suit and keep my rendezvous with a doughnut.

Please keep on writing those nice letters—mail from home is most welcomed, even more than when we used to ride the trolley home at noon for want of it. Give my regards to your mother and go down to the fountain this afternoon and have a hot fudge sundae for me. Wash it down with two cokes.

The dances continued, mixed with a serious note of a military decoration to Ed Kennedy, a hero in their "favorite regiment," the 504th.

September 15, 1944
[Leicester]

Dear mother and daddy,

It's 24 hours, Greenwich mean time, the female radio announcer just told us—what that is, I couldn't tell you. Just another way to make things more difficult. This has been a rotten week so far as the mail situation goes, although V-mails from Miss Julia and Aunt Lilly came through. When I come home blind, you may say that your daughter got that way trying to decipher V-mails.

Mother, you asked about the checks from Washington. The great white mother is quite correct. I was paid in Washington up to the 15th of July and my salary didn't start going home until at that time (As you can see, I'm having fountain pen trouble). Then you asked what sort of troops we were attached to, but I can't tell you that. Golly, it's wonderful to be mysterious. And here, Agnes let out a fiendish laugh.

We are recovering from a gala night—Aileen's (one of my co-workers) brother, a lieut. in the air force, paid her a visit and we celebrated with champagne from France, Bourbon from the U.S. and Scotch from the U.K., along with some other little friends. There was a Division dance mixed up with it somewhere and a gay time was had by all. Did I tell you about the Dutch Commando we have met? He escaped from Rotterdam in '41 and a more fascinating story I have never heard—I was frankly open-mouthed. Then, I was terrifically impressed with having come face to face with a real, honest to goodness Commando. I was dancing with him last night during a particularly jitter-buggy number and we were accomplishing nothing at all, so I asked him if he waltzed. Oh yes, he did, and in spite of the opposing rhythm of the band, we waltzed, much to the amusement of the spectators. The whole evening was great fun, even excluding the champagne.

And day before yesterday, we saw the general present the Silver Star to one of our friends for gallantry in action in Italy. It was a wonderful experience to be standing by a hedge beside an English lane and see stretched out before us, our favorite regiment, complete with regimental band, and then to see Ken march forward across the meadow to receive his citation. By the way, this particular boy reminds me so much of John—he looks like him and although he's more mature (which he owes to Sicily, Italy and Normandy) he has the same ideals and outlook that Johnny has. His men adore him—the perfect officer, believe it or not.

This should be our long week-end, but we're working instead. I'm still going to Cambridge sometime. It doesn't pay to make plans in this racket. I'm having such difficulty with this pen that I'm afraid I'll have to sign off for tonight. Please don't take those little men on the radio too seriously and never think that this business is all over but the shouting. If that were only true . . .

XXX to you both,
Elizabeth

~personality!

Liz experienced a week of roughing it in the field as the 82nd prepared for a jump into Holland, a bold drop behind German lines as part of Operation Market Garden. Saturday, September 16, was especially busy as officers and men checked maps and equipment, attended final briefings, walked to the latrines, wrote letters home, and visited with the Red Cross women. Few slept well that night. The next day, Sunday morning, September 17, the anxious troopers boarded the C-47s, some for their fourth combat jump. These men knew what antiaircraft flak did to planes and the people inside them and what jumping with the enemy below entailed. More than one was a fatalist who believed his luck had run out. Soon the skies above Leicestershire were filled with planes, circling and forming up to move across the English Channel toward Nazi-occupied Holland.[6]

Although she wrote home of some of her own hardship during the week of preparation, Liz included mostly upbeat news and left out the details the censor would not approve. Clubmobile women had to deal not only with the censor but with their conviction that folks at home could not understand their work. "The type of work we do," Gretchen Schuyler wrote from England, "is hard to explain. . . . How I wish I could write details of things seen and done." A year later Schuyler lamented, "I can't imagine anyone at home really being able to understand our feelings and attitudes about this bloody business."[7]

Between the lines the reader can detect Liz's frustration at being unable to explain the realities of being so close to the men as they prepared to jump into combat. More evident is her disappointment over the impatience at home. A Gallup poll that September reported that 67 percent of Americans thought the war would be over before Christmas.[8] Liz knew it was not over. And because she had now spent lots of time with combat veterans she knew the costs of this brutal war far better than did Americans at home.

September 23, 1944
[Leicester]

Dear mother and daddy,

Please notice my new APO—until further notice it's 413—so spread the tidings far and wide. However, I'm still at the same base, so it doesn't mean anything particularly.

We returned today after a week in the field to find a fine stack of mail which needless to say, was greedily devoured. It's been a hard, strenuous week, both emotionally and physically and we are just the people who waved goodbye.[9] Last Saturday night, we didn't go to bed at all and the next night, what sleep we had was in our clothes. We finally found a resting place among the WAAFs [British Women's Auxiliary Air Force] who sleep on strange 3-sectioned mattresses (a courtesy title)—which are apt to part during the course of the night. They must be hardy souls, we thought, as we'd tramp the miles to the "ablutions" of a cold, misty morning. The British have a curious habit of separating such inseparable things as biffey and wash basin. Don't ask me why. This has been a most terrific experience and we are very proud of our guys—you have no doubt been reading about them. Anyway, we worked long past union hours, all the way around the clock. Please don't say that the war in this theatre is almost over, because as long as lives are being lost, it isn't. Remember how disturbed I was about Ernst's letter last Christmas. Now, I can see what he meant, only it is not the fault of the people at home, but of the radio, the press and the movies.

So much for that—we ate good Air Force food—the best in the army, believe me. Our one recreation was a movie last night—"Thank Your Lucky Stars"[10]—in a mess hall, along with all the G.I.'s it could hold. And how we enjoyed it! I wish you could hear the reaction and if I could only convey to you the atmosphere of a place like that. We were escorted by the cooks, who afterwards took us to the Red Cross Club as if they were taking us to the Empire Room! Now, it is wonderful to be home, bathed, in clean clothes, in front of a roaring fire—and I only wish our men were in a similar position.

As for the local situation, the most momentous thing that has happened is to the blackout—we now have a partial one and the first night, the poor souls were out as if the millennium itself was about to occur. All oogling at the lights, even babes in arms. Now, we have 4 days accumulated leave coming up and this time, I'm really going to Cambridge, although I lean slightly towards Cardiff. By the way, I'm sending a few things home under separate cover and please keep them in a safe place. The picture is of the group with which I came over, and the "Sinker," our Clubmobile newspaper contains something about our

Clubmobile written, of course, by that talented and darling doughnut pusher, E. Richardson.[11] And the Stars & Stripes I want to keep for special reasons.

There were some bright spots to light our rough time. One night we were traveling from one place to another under M.P. escort and I was riding with the M.P. in a jeep. We were whizzing o'er the rain spattered roads in the gathering dusk as only a jeep can whizz, and in our love of speed, lost the Clubmobile and ended up with a flat tire and no spare in a damp ditch. A passing civilian took the M.P. to a pub to call for a tire, leaving Aileen and myself to care for the jeep. We soon hailed an RAF pilot on his way to the same pub for a gay evening with his crew. Soon, crew appeared—all 7 of them—and we had a gay time talking with them until we were rescued. All this was in the pitch black and is typical of the spirit of the thing.

Mother, your letters are wonderful, and Daddy—a gold star for you—yours, too. Haven't received "Time" yet, but I'm certainly looking forward to it. We gobble up April and May editions of magazines as if they were hot off the press.

So much for tonight, parents. If only I could tell you all about this . . . I'll have to talk for a week straight when I get home in 1966.

Love to you all—

Butch
Freckles
Chickens
And you,
Elizabeth

Later, in her diary, away from the censor, Liz provided more details of the 82nd's departure for Holland. She wrote in a sparse, matter-of-fact style so different from the upbeat letters home.

Diary, January 10, 1945

The morning after the dance, we were told to pack up—the Division was moving out again and we were to go with it as far as we were able. This time it was the real thing. The jump was to be in the Netherlands—we knew that by Friday afternoon, the 16th of September.[12] We worked all Saturday afternoon, Saturday night and I remember the dark hangars, the men wide awake, the night which was cold and dark. The clubmobile had a 2 1/2 ton truck following it, loaded with our supplies. At 4 o'clock in the morning, we drove with MP escort from one field to another, through the silent Lincolnshire villages—I rode in the truck with Ralph, the Pfc. driver. He talked about his wife and I fell asleep sitting upright. By 9 o'clock we were on the perimeter. The planes were warming up, the men were grotesque lumps of equipment. The sun was brightly shining and there was a cold wind. The boys still laughed and joked, but their faces streamed perspiration. We said our goodbyes to all of them— George, Bill,—all of them. Then we moved to the center of the field with the rest of the stay-behinds and watched C-47 after C-47 taxi off, wheel around the field and strike off for the channel. Then came the C-47's with gliders. Two of the gliders' tow lines broke and they were quickly moved off the runaway and the steady stream went on until the sky was almost dark with thousands of rendezvousing planes. → fear and guilt/regret

Liz and the "stay-behinds" waited for news of the 82nd and especially worried about reports that the 504th had high causalities at Nijmegen, where they led the assault under heavy fire.

Liz finally took her long-planned trip to Cambridge, a joyous immersion in a far "different world" from Leicester and the Clubmobile. The Cambridge architecture entranced her, as it has other tourists for centuries. A highlight was Kings College Chapel, finished in 1547 and one of the architectural gems of the world. On the opposite side of beauty, she got her first glimpse of German POWs. And she remembered Milwaukee boyfriend Ernst Kuenstner. She recommended a film, *A Canterbury Tale*, a wonderful 1944 British mystery that celebrated the English countryside, the decency of the people, and their kindness to an American soldier traveling to Canterbury Cathedral. It was the England she was coming to know and to love.[13]

September 27, 1944
[Leicester]

Dear mother and daddy,

The mail brought a letter from Johnny Bodle today and from it, I gathered that he will be home soon—he was very near here, but Uncle Sam's mailing system being what it is and leaves and passes being what they are, we didn't get together. What a happy day at 406 Niles Avenue when he arrives! Also got a letter or rather a card from Dean Groton [Mishawaka clergyman] from Cape Cod—very nice of him to think of me and if you will give me his address and initials, I'll write him a note.

I came back from my 2 day stay in Cambridge last night, replete with a surfeit of antiquity—I can't begin to tell you how much I enjoyed myself and my surroundings. I arrived in Cambridge Sunday night in the most black black-out that exists and (of course) it was raining—a sort of soupy mixture of rain as we know it and a peculiar opaque mist peculiar to this isle. If it hadn't been for one of the ever-present G.I.'s who escorted me from station to the Red Cross Club, I'd still be wondering about. But even in the blackness, I could see the Gothic silhouettes of innumerable spires against the sky. The Red Cross got me rooms a few blocks away, which I found by sheer instinct. The room was on the top floor of a house filled with stiff pictures of past cricket teams, crews, stern young men in blazers and in every corner, inscribed oars and cricket bats. And of course, no plumbing, but a bed comfortable enough to make up for these lacks. I woke up in the morning to a blue sky over those fairyland spires and the landlady with a steaming cup of tea. She served me breakfast in a pre-Raphaelite parlor overlooking that interesting thoroughfare, Tennis Court road. Even an egg, mind you, served like this. After brushing my teeth at the Red Cross Club (located in an ex-hotel and practically in King's College grounds), I set off on Richardson's own Tour of Cambridge. It was like being in a different world—the green lawns, the narrow and placid Cam, the well-worn stone bridges and King's College Chapel—well—I'm not equipped to describe its soaring Gothic beauty. Surely, if ever god was reached, it was in a place like that. Between the buttresses were smaller chapels, each one perfect in itself, and the lovely lines lead up to heaven itself. Tudor roses and lattice work abounded and I left very humbled and inspired, if you can feel two such different emotions at once. From King's, I wandered into Trinity and from Trinity, into St. Johns. Trinity's refractory (dining room) was a wonderful thing in dark worn paneling and good and bad portraits of various alumnus. In the afternoon, a little man showed me about the new library—Rockefeller Foundation sponsored—and Thank God, no pseudo Gothic, but very nice functional modern, discretely removed from those that it can't compete with on quite the same grounds. I also wandered in Trinity's own library, unoccupied except for one preoccupied and gowned gentleman in a far corner. I also walked about Peterborough, the oldest college, and its neighboring church, St. Mary's the Less. The evening I spent about my landlady's fire, along with a fat spaniel, a molting parrot, a lady who liked American cigarettes, a youth who was about to "go up" to Pembrooke and who actually flaunted an old school tie and the landlady's father, the retired cook at Pembrooke—(on which Tennis Course Road borders) who whiled away the evening with tales of past cricket matches and crew races—he even showed me how to pitch a cricket ball, even though he was shaped like a nine-pin or a daschhound—I couldn't decide which.

The next morning after a pleasant breakfast with the under-graduate-to-be and an art collector (with an accent who wants to show me about London), I met Marion Travis of White Plains—we visited a lovely round Norman Church and Magdeline College (pronounced Maudlin) which is the most charming of them all—small and compact—or perhaps it was the Handel Mass that someone was playing as we looked in the small but perfect chapel. We finished up with tea in the Officers Club in front of a warm fire and then Marion's own Command Car and driver (advantages of being in an Aero club) took me to the station.

By the way, I have had my first glimpse of the master race en masse—dirty, bearded but darn healthy and not too old or too young. And quite self-contained . . .

Mother, will you buy a nice fruit cake and some heavy wool socks (size 11) for Ernst and send them to him, with Christmas Greetings from me, by proxy? It's next to impossible to get things like that here and the prices are hideous[. . . .]

By the way, if you can see "A Canterbury Tale," a British movie which I think is showing in the states, be sure to treat yourself. It catches the England as we know it very well.

There is a chance that we might be moved to another base—I hate to leave our comfortable home with Mrs. Tipper and her tarts—but we have been lucky and I guess it can't go on forever. And now, pore Eliz's hands are so chilly that they can hardly wield the pen, so I'll say goodnight with lots of love to you all,

Elizabeth

Liz wrote her brother John, a marine, about the Cambridge trip and other details, including his pending marriage to Sue Stevens.

October 1, 1944
[Leicester]

Dear Johnny,

Your letter, penned on the 9th of August, arrived day before yesterday and it was the first letter I have had in a week and everybody is suffering the same plight. However, that's part of the racket—mail comes in gasps and spurts—but it's certainly hard on our morale. By this time, you are no doubt away from the joys of Parris Island and naturally, I'm most anxious to hear when and how. A gyrene is a rare and lovely sight in the ETO, although there are a few in London. Of course, it's stupid to even think of it, but it would be wonderful if, when the day comes that you are shipped (which I hope will be never) it should be in this direction . . . You said that you thought it would soon be over and I'm glad that you think so, because we certainly don't think. I found out long ago that it's a bad habit. It's good to hear that you like the life, because whether you know it or not, it's not

For a day

not for a week

and I hope not for always.

Are you still considering matrimony? The family is wildly enthusiastic about Sue and if even Butch approves, you may picture me as cheering you on in the background.

This is a beautiful country, as I think that I've said before. But it's cold and it's damp and the sun is an elusive thing. This last week has been a sort of leave for us, so I took off for Cambridge for a few days and Johnny, I wish you could have seen the place, including my rooms overlooking a picture-card scene of gothic turrets and spires. . . . You'd love the trains—just like an Alfred Hitchcock movie, but you wouldn't love their slow, leisurely progress over hill and dale. I also went up to London, which is now figuratively shaking itself and has less the aspect of the deserted city. We had lunch at one of the hotels and if I half closed my eyes, it could have almost been any dining place in a big city back home.

By the way, Johnny Bodle was stationed very near our base, but Evangeline like, we missed each other. He wrote me a nice letter and has evidently completed his tour of duty and will be home shortly. That's the nice part about the Air Corps., outside of their food, which is wonderful. We had a week or so with them (Air Corps—not Johnny B.) and when we weren't working, we were eating but frantically. We always work on the mess sgts. sympathy by saying in a tearful voice, that we live on British rations, which is half way true, anyway, and the good little guys immediately bombard us with enough vitamins for 3 months. In fact, that's why I invested in a bicycle—to work off, shall I call it, accumulated energy? I pedal energetically to and from Clubmobile, threading recklessly through trams, more cyclists cursing drivers and horses.

There is much that I'd like to tell you, but you know what they told us earlier in the [illegible]. "When you write a letter, reread it in 2 hours, and if it's so dull that it bores you to pieces—then it's O.K." This masterpiece, I believe, fulfills all requirements.

So please keep on writing and tell me all about it. Sue must be back at Wells by now. Does she miss you?

Your secret admirer
X-pma

Again Liz mentioned listening to the BBC, the voice of calm reassurance throughout Britain and beyond. With the 82nd gone, life in the provincial town of Leicester was beginning to wear, exacerbated by lost ration cards and a broken-down Clubmobile. But Liz could find contentment in a long bicycle ride in the countryside and in her chances to sketch its beauty. And she kept a close eye on the news from Holland where the men to whom she recently served doughnuts and coffee had been stopped by the German counteroffensive, taking heavy losses.

→ content on a long bike ride alone

October 6?, 1944
[Leicester]

Dear mother and daddy,

despite pressures of navy, finds time for herself

Please pardon the star-spangled stationery and the pencil, but it's all we have available at the present and my pen hasn't acclimated itself to British ink. Therefore, the equipment at hand. I'm sitting as close to the fire as humanly possible, listening to the calm creature from the BBC who gives us the latest in the world of news. This has been a gloriously beautiful day, marred not at all by the requisite number of showers and I have spent it on a 34-mi. bicycle ride from which I am now recovering. I started out with my sketch book, 4 tomatoe sandwiches and a bottle of beer and I had a lovely, solitary day, eating and drinking in the shadow of a very neat, house-shaped haystack and pedaling leisurely over hill and dale and through villages unspoiled by my beloved countrymen. We are recovering from the <u>dull</u> week, to boot. Margaret got an infected tonsil from our episode in the rough and Aileen (the other crew member) and I were doing our duty right heartily on a night run last Monday, when our engine caught fire. Our driver, Jimmy, a London Cockney, aged 21, heroically put out the blaze and we rode back to our base in state in a passing lorry. Since then, the Clubmobile is being repaired with typical British dispatch and we are <u>hoping</u> to get to work tomorrow. I wouldn't wish my best enemy to be stuck in a provincial midlands town with nothing to do. We have seen every movie in town (gay things of 1940 vintage) and I have bicycled myself muscle-bound.

On top of everything else, we haven't had any mail for 3 weeks and that means we haven't any morale left. Pardon me, I did get a letter from Johnny dated August 9th—it must have come over by raft.

Mrs. Tipper is calling—dinner is served—and even that is sad as

London has neglected to send up our ration cards and we are living on bread fixed in various artistic ways. However, that's all that is wrong and one can't be unhappy with such beautiful countryside about one. We have heard from Holland and things are as well as can be expected.

So all my love to you—
Elizabeth

Mrs. Tipper continued to serve her tarts as the wind and rain blew outside and mail from home remained scant. There were memories of a weekend trip to the "picture-postcard place" of Stratford-on-Avon.

Liz struggled with dereliction of duty by their Clubmobile driver, Jimmy Saunders, not the last time he would go on a drinking binge. Jimmy was something of a character (he refused to eat vegetables, for example), but the Kansas City crew accepted his shortcomings in return for generally good work. Moreover, everyone knew that the converted Green Line buses were difficult to maintain and drive and that good drivers were in very short supply.[14]

October 11, 1944
[Leicester]

Dear mother and daddy,

Having borrowed a pen (that scratches), perhaps I'll be able to express myself a little better and at more length . . . maybe. Big event the other day! A letter from Mother dated July 16th came through, giving me all the details of the shipping off of the formal, which I appreciate muchly. Other than that, no mail, except for some V-Mails, including one from Anne Bodle Schuknecht. Right now, I have my feet in the fireplace and the wind is howling about our provincial home—also rain (naturally) and we are awaiting Mrs. Tipper and coffee and tarts.

Had 48 hours last weekend and managed to get to Stratford-on-Avon, a picture-postcard place—I felt as if I were in a toy town—especially since 15th century Englishmen obviously were much smaller and erected their doors accordingly. I met an Army nurse and a Red Cross girl on leave from Iceland and we actually went punting on the

81

Avon. At first, the boat seemed to prefer to go in circles, but we finally got the nack of it and managed to go in a fairly straight line. The weather was mild (no sun, but what do we want? Egg in our beer?) and the leaves were beautiful and the landscape idyllically calm. The Avon was lined with Sunday fishermen and we stole some apples en route. The Red Cross has a wonderful Officers Club there, which provided us with bed and breakfast.

Margaret (our Captain) is off on leave, so Aileen and I are carrying on alone, only slightly handicapped by the activities of Jimmy, our driver, who has taken to the bottle and yesterday got blind, staggering drunk—leaving us with the intricacies of a diesel engine and our temperamental doughnut machine.

I am sure that everything is alright on Dragoon Trail—Daddy must be getting some good hunting in. This would be good country for Freckles and his children, all of whom possess a good nose for a pheasant. Hope that the mail will be coming through <u>soon</u>. Do you have any new snapshots? I'm enclosing some pictures of Stratford for Butch.

Lots of Love,
Elizabeth

Again it was the mail, or lack of mail, that frustrated Liz, as only those far from loved ones can appreciate. She continued to think of home and the details of savings account, insurance, and voting in the upcoming presidential election.

October 15, 1944
[Leicester]

Dear mother and daddy,

The mail situation is still very bad and I am beginning to be a bit worried about your activities, although I know that you are all alright. But I haven't heard from Dragoon Trail for more than a month except for that letter from Mother dated July 16th, which I keep to read over to remind me that I still have home and family.

Autumn is really here and everything is basking in a lovely yellow light. Fall is not the violent and speedy thing that it is at home, but it's beautifully gradual and the weather appears to be milder—or maybe I'm getting acclimated. Just as I get used to seeing my breath while sitting in the bathtub, they'll send me to the CBI, which is Army jargon for the China-Burma-India theatre. Don't worry. Just joking.

We have been working hard, thank God, and I hope it keeps up. Margaret returned from her leave in Scotland yesterday and has given us such a glowing report of the scenery and local yokels that we are most anxious to see it for ourselves. My first real leave is due in about another months time and by then, I'll have to hire a dog sled to get anywhere. Yes, I know it doesn't get that cold, but this weather must be indicative of something and it couldn't be of the flowers that bloom in the spring, tra la.

By now, Washington must have sent you enough money to have paid off my national debt of $200 and something. I'll leave the kind of savings account you're putting the rest in up to you, but don't forget to buy an occasional bond for me, say one a month, payable to various members of the family. Hope that somebody is wearing my raincoat— it's a good one and somebody (namely, Daddy or Butch) should be getting some wear out of it. Thanks for taking care of the insurance— glad that's out of the way.

I hopefully sent in my ballot application to Wisconsin on the forms provided by the Red Cross—this was about two months ago, and I haven't heard even an electrical peep from them since, so I guess I don't get to cast my ineffectual vote. It's just as well, as for all we hear, there might not be an election going on AND I DON'T LIKE IT A Bit. Wait until I see Franklin D. face to face, and then I'll tell him! Meanwhile, there's nothing to be done but grin and bear it.

About Christmas, I am sending a money order to you Mother in a week or two and you can either give it out in cash or get things with it. It really is silly to get things over here and then the mail situation is so stinky, I'll be fortunate if the money order gets there by next Easter! And now, I must hop on my bicycle and investigate the golden afternoon (it's Sunday and our day off). Please keep writing, even though I'm not receiving. Incidentally, mail coming from home is not censored, so don't be so mysterious and ambiguous[. . . .]

83

Have been doing some painting—an English lady got me some beautiful water color paper which I'm not particularly worthy of.

XX and love,
Elizabeth

Mail finally arrived, with report of a new family dog named Topsy. A visit from a paratrooper just returned from Holland with news of the disaster of Market Garden reinforced the hard side of war. In her diary Liz identified the visitor as Maggie Megellas.[15] And Margaret and Liz battled the unwanted advances of drunken GIs.

October 20, 1944
[Leicester]

Dear mother and daddy,

At last, the mail is beginning to come through, but there's still a lapse of a month or so and I imagine it will catch up to me some day soon in a big clump (known as wishful thinking), but right now nothing would be more welcomed than a big clump, specially of mail. I'd love to see Topsy and I hope that the new tall and handsome Butch will take some snapshots and dispatch them to me soon. And it's also good to hear that Mother's cow reproduced successfully!

We have just returned from work via jeep—our clubmobile blew out a front tire (spelled tyre) on the main drag of a largish hamlet and after calling our maintenance man, the Ministry of Works (who won't fix a tire unless they have an order signed by the King) and finally our headquarters in London (all of which completely exhausted our supply of sixpences, shillings and thru' penny bits) we hailed a passing jeep and left our driver to entertain the curious. You see how it goes—if it isn't a tire, it's the engine and if it isn't the engine, it's the driver, dead drunk in "The Rainbow and Dove." So we have a long weekend to do something in—I'd like to go to London and have a very rich and handsome Colonel take me to Claridge's for dinner and to the Dorchester for dancing. Regret to say that this wish can't be carried out because of complete lack of very rich and handsome Colonel. Something will no doubt come up, spake the eternal optimist.

The rains have come, not that they haven't been coming all the time, but they are coming with a sullen and awful persistence that doesn't go well with my bicycle rides. I did have a long ride last Sunday after writing to you, past droves of families airing themselves, dogs and babies in prams, out to an incredibly golden countryside. The bicycle traffic, however, was like Sunday traffic on route 20, but it was great fun and I stared at them and they stared at me. I suppose they think that I am a weird creature in my old saddle shoes, slacks and G. I. jacket—and I in turn, am transported back to the golden 20's when a gentleman in trim plus fours whizzes past me or I pass a gray-haired grandmother with a fur piece twined about her neck pedaling away for dear life.

Well, I'm still with Mrs. Tipper and will be, I imagine, for at least a month. We still have the stay-behinds to take care of and replacements, which gives us plenty to do. The other night, we had a wonderful thrill when one of our friends from Holland walked in on us—he looked like a different boy, minus about 20 pounds, with a shaggy dog mustache— but arrived with a bottle of Champagne from Brussels which was pure heaven to drink. It was hard to believe that 24 hours before, he had been in the front lines with what are left of our fellows. I suppose I will never get used to the matter-of-fact way in which life and death are accepted, but I suppose under the circumstances, it's the only way to face things— sort of stopping up the emotional valves. *women in war w/o emotion*

Talking about emotion, Margaret and I cleaned our doughnut machine the other night until 11 o'clock and Margaret flagged a jeep to take us home. The jeep driver and friends turned out to be most amorous in a beery sort of way and at the most convenient place, Margaret and I got out and waved goodbye from some good citizen's gate, not wishing to continue the slightly hazardous journey. The jeep riders suspected AII and spent the next 15 minutes cruising the street, which meant that I'd run for one gate, get in somebody's yard and lie flat until they went by. Then we'd emerge and run like crazy until they came again and so on until we reached our own abode. I feel that I know a little bit about hedgerow fighting now.

I met a G.I. from South Bend. He comes up to my chin and wants to take me dancing. People appear to lose their sense of proportion when they hit the ETO. Now me, I can't see us as the ideal couple, even though we both hail from Northern Indiana.

No, I haven't received "Time," but I considered myself lucky to be able to buy a September 11 issue in the PX this afternoon.

Must combat the elements in the bathtub now. I'm getting to be quite a Spartan—only 1,000,000 goose bumps instead of the 5,000,613 I had in August.

Love to all of you,
Yr fat daught.
Elizabeth

[p.s.] Daddy, the enclosed is from the Champagne bottle. Hope I make you jealous.

A V-Mail letter to her brother John reflected Liz's love for him and the misery of war separation.

October 22, 1944
[Leicester]

Dearest Johnny,

You've probably left Parris Island months ago, but since I haven't heard from you since the "a" or ditch-digging period of your life, I do wonder what and where you are. Mail has been lousy the last month and I am looking forward to hearing from you—it seems centuries since I saw you—was it only last spring? This is a dull Sunday in the United Kingdom and when a Sunday is dull here, it out does itself. Even [illegible] cooperates. You and I make a hell of a brother-sister team—the years seem to be sending us in completely opposite directions and I hate to think of it happening like that, old goat, especially as I intend to spend WEEKS with you and Sue in your little FHA home after the war, taking care of little John Jr., Beulah and Gwen. God forbid. I've had a nice weekend in Stratford-on-Avon, punting right merrily down the Avon and humming an old Shakespearean sonnet. You'd love this country, in spite of the atmosphere of perpetual dampness. Work hard, Sweetie-Pie (remember?) Lots of Love to you—

Elizabeth

A promotion to captain came for the hard-working and talented Liz. The Red Cross stipulated that a Clubmobile captain was "responsible for the running condition and the producing ability of the Clubmobile. She should check oil, petrol, water and tyre pressure before leaving on a trip and on return." And there was paperwork for the evenings. The captain was to "keep an accurate weekly log of where her machine has been each day, how many doughnuts it has served, how many cups of coffee it has served, how many packets of cigarettes it has given away, how many cartons of gum it has give away, and how many miles it has been driven." Red Cross administrators compiled these weekly logs into monthly reports and produced large charts to show the organization's output and productivity, just like an automobile or steel company. A report for the month of December 1944, for example, proudly showed that 205 Red Cross women in Great Britain served 4,659,728 doughnuts. Liz proved to be an excellent leader and manager, but she would tire of some of the bureaucratic tendencies of her employer. With her new promotion also came "people problems," starting with responsibility for supervising a newly hired doughnut cook and a row between Aileen and Mrs. Tipper.[16]

October 29, 1944
[Leicester]

Dear mother and daddy,

This is one of those lovely opportunities—a glowing fire in the grate, Aileen in the bathtub, Margaret in bed and Mrs. Tipper frying tomatoes (she does not approve of them in their natural state)—that leaves me with myself and my thoughts. I received a letter from Mother dated September 11th, so I guess the back mail will begin to saunter in, taking its own sweet time, of course.

The clubmobile department is celebrating its second birthday in Britain this week, and we are dispensing Coke instead of the usual coffee—British Coke, that is—and that ain't nice. And we have inherited all the runs of the other Clubmobile, plus our own, so we are really slinging it. Our latest innovation is a London evacuee, a sweet little lady with horn-rim glasses, who cooks doughnuts for us from 6 o'clock until 11 in theory, but so far, one of us has had to stand by and tell her how and finish up, which usually leaves me, because I have a bicycle. Which in turn leaves me cycling down the main drag at 2 A.M., hoping that one of those mad yanks doesn't knock me off with his 2 ton truck. Margaret is leaving to be Captain of a new crew and I am now Captain Richardson, a title which will not bear fruit in the form of $$$ for 3 months or so.[17] I get a new crew member Monday and Aileen is staying here, along with ten million headaches, such as how to keep the rats out of the doughnut floor and how to figure the wages of the sweet old thing from London. When we cook at night, we really have it, it being a constant stream of hungry visitors, varying in character according to the hour. From 6 to 10, we get civilians (hungry) and children (hungry) with a sprinkling of G.I.'s (also hungry). From 10 to 10:30, we get G.I.'s (drunk and hungry), because that's when the pubs close. From 10:30 on, we get G.I.'s sobering up and British Army and R.A.F.—too poor to be drunk, but still hungry.

We have also had Domestic trouble. Aileen (who calls <u>every</u> body "honey") had a scene with Mrs. Tipper. As I wasn't here, I can't tell you what the scene was about, but Aileen screamed and kicked and Mrs. T. and Aileen have not been speaking. It's all very dramatic and exciting. And it's also one of the problems I am inheriting. Otherwise, our life is chilly, but normal. The leaves are falling, but they're taking their own sweet time about it, a characteristic they no doubt inherit from the human population. The air is very cold, but the flowers persist in blooming, in spite of rain, fog and not enough sunshine. We had our first real fog the other night, when we came back from camp in a jeep, crawling at about 5 miles per., with the driver extending half of himself outside to try to see through the fuzz.

Well, now that the melon season is over, I can relax for a while and stop dreaming. Anyway, I managed to get quite a few in Washington before I left. So there. Hope that Topsy is relaxing also, and being good—same applies to Freckles and Butch.

Love to you both,
Elizabeth

P.S. Telegram just came—Margaret is not leaving for a while, pending new arrangements, so I can really relax. Goodnight!

Margaret Morrison did leave for London, and soon wrote a piece for *The Sinker* on her regrets at the parting and starting over with a new crew: "One short week ago, I was happy and contented. We were only working night and day, but there was such a pleasant click-click about it all, known only by crews that have worked and haggled things out together."[18]

Captain Richardson was now in charge of the *Kansas City* and responsible for a broken-down doughnut machine. Along with such daily frustrations there were small pleasures, especially in Mrs. Tipper's sitting room, where they listened to American entertainer Bob Hope and even the Nazi propagandist Lord Haw Haw, who played popular American music. The prospect of prep school for her kid brother raised Liz's antipathy to snobbery. She explained more about why they were in the field earlier, helping the 82nd make ready for the jump into Holland. Those days had already moved to a special place in her memory.

November 1, 1944
[Leicester]

Dear mother and daddy,

This afternoon's mail brought a big pile of back mail, which I gobbled up with much gusto. So I have devoted the evening to the art of letter-writing and rereading that nice stack. And do I love it! Mrs. Tipper has some new coal.[19] Her last batch burned with a smoldering sullenness as if reluctant to give up any heat—this new stuff has made my usual seat by the fireplace a burning inferno. But, as the G.I.'s say, what do I want, egg in my beer? [...]

As for Butch going to Prep School—well—it would be nice, but I don't think too necessary. He'll be able to drive the Model A next year and then he won't lack a social life. I'd hate to see him made into a snob and he has all the ingredients that, plus prep school would make him into a good imitation of one.

We saw Margaret off for London yesterday—that is, we pushed a pile of equipment we presumed was Margaret into a 3rd class carriage and waved it a sad goodbye. I am meeting our new crew member tomorrow—unfortunately the arrival of her train will coincide with the arrival of John Barbarolle[20] on the stage of the local concert hall. I <u>was</u> going to hear him, but instead, must play my heavy new rôle of captain. Jimmy, our driver, has just phoned and given me the glad news that the doughnut machine has broken down. Nuts.

It's still beautiful here—and at night, there has been a wonderful full moon that makes the little dimmed-out streetlights seem almost infinitesamal. The British really appreciate that moonlight when not so long ago, they feared it so terribly. That's in this region, anyway. The Londoners are still hurting, but it doesn't matter what the weather is for them. Poor Margaret—she hates the buzz bombs so and spent her last stay under a grand piano—I hope she's found something more satisfying to stay under this time.[21]

Mother, you asked about a watch. I bought a $15 job in Washington and it's been doing a good job—better than the Elgin which caused me so much trouble. Thanks anyway for thinking of it. It's good to hear that John is still the All-Marine boy. For Pete's sakes, don't worry about Sue and him—those things always work out and usually without any help from we, the spectators. I'm eagerly anticipating those packages and at this rate, they should be in time for the jolly Yuletide season.

I think I can tell you now our very small part in the invasion of Holland. We were at the field when they took off before and long after, sweating out each and every mission with our coffee and doughnut brigade. That's when we lived in the rough, if you remember. The first time was still-born and I'll tell you about that later—when I see you. I wish I could describe adequately that green field, the air strip, the atmosphere of waiting, the anxious eyes cocked at the ever-changing weather. And our boys, sweating under their equipment, though it was a cold morning. It was an awesome sight, which I'd just as soon not see again. First, the planes, then the planes with gliders joining the armada overhead. As for now, we are working hard yet, still and so on. Last night, Aileen and I did manage to go to a Halloween party at the club and Saturday I had another with an adolescent Captain—one of the Air Corps ground boys—they stay young in that branch.

We're listening to Bob Hope—all the way from America! Ah! Radio! It's the same one that brings us Lord Haw Haw, to whom Mrs. Tipper listens in Sotto Voce—she doesn't think the neighbors would approve. He makes _me_ mad, idiot that he is. No "Time" yet—please tell Henry Luce for me "Peuy." Be sure to have Johnny Bodle tell you about the places he was near, especially where he stayed with Mrs. Roal-Raoul. (sorry, speeling).

Love to all of you—Butch, dogs, everything except the chickens. I take that back. You may give my regards to the eggs.

Elizabeth

[p.s.] Thanks so very much for mailing Ernst's Christmas package. I know he'll appreciate it—he'd better!

In the pile of mail that arrived on November 1 was a letter from John Richardson, which prompted an immediate reply full of interesting detail. Liz wrote more about military matters to her marine brother, then stationed at Quantico, Virginia, including sharing her observations of good and bad officers and her challenges of being a young woman among so many lonely guys.

November 1, 1944

[Leicester]

Dear Johnny,

Today brought a big pile of delayed mail, which I devoured hungrily, including your letter of September 18th. It was awfully nice to hear from you, especially since I've been thinking of you a lot and wondering how you were getting on with your Marine career. Anyway, you _are_ a Pfc which is only about 14 steps from a full general, so upwards and onwards, she screamed! I wish I had more details on your training—we can see how they train them for the toughest branch of the army—and it would be interesting to compare the two. This afternoon in a damp English field under a perpetual glowering English sky, we watched the new members of our division do 50 push-ups before a 5 mile run and when I expressed sympathy for them, one of the lieutenants just back from the front said, "That isn't anything to what they get in combat, and if they don't have it now, they'll be hurting later."

So it's all to make it easier later on and the more you have, the better. It's all a pretty fearsome business—I've seen our fellows in full gear just before they hopped off for Holland and I've seen the fear in their eyes—not for the unknown—but because they know what's in front of them. Also, while I'm on the subject and since you might get your commission, I want to tell you how important it is for you to be a <u>good</u> one (officer, I mean) whom your men trust, respect and have confidence in. We're in the peculiar position of being able to observe good and bad alike and there is nothing sadder than an officer who has not secured these things, for his is an empty title and a wretched life. Thus ends my lecture for the day[. . . .]

Anyway, I'm still here and working hard. I'm Captain of our merry clubmobile and tomorrow, I get another crew member—a rookie, I hope—if she proves to be an old ETO veteran, I will have to retire shrinkingly behind my greasy WAC raincoat. Our evenings are interupted by many visits to our parked clubmobile, where our cook, Mrs. Freeman, holds forth, badly in need of supervision. This is further complicated by the fact that we live about 3 miles from the center of the "city" and our means of transportation is either bicycle or G.I., which might be anything from a jeep to a 2 ton truck.

The English are still an enigma to me and I imagine they'll always be . . . they certainly live in a beautiful and time-mellowed country, but God knows how they became an empire with such a climate. If you could see us of a morning as we face the new day, you'd be amused and incredulous—feet, paratroop booted; RAF WAAF style slacks (Red Cross issue) GI shirt, RAF battle dress top, combat jacket, the famous Richardson red nose and those awfully Kraut-style hats that the Red Cross has chosen to adorn us with. How the men refrain from whoopsing when they see us, I don't know, but instead of that, we're treated like Miss America in a Wolf corale. By now, I know not all the answers, but I certainly have improved my stock of evasive tactics. And you should see me jitterbug, with proper, Red Cross decorum, of course.

Mother & daddy have certainly taken Sue to their heart! Well I hope things work out as you and she would want them to, as they will—everything does—so why worry? I'm sitting on top of the fireplace, writing on my lap and waiting for a Special Service Lieut. who is dying to have somebody laugh at his shaggy dog stories. And I'm the lucky girl, so I must go now and climb into my laughing clothes. Keep writing, Johnny and I think of you often. Be good and don't work hard—

Lots of love,
Elizabeth

A new crew member had arrived, Betty Goit from Philadelphia. This was the first letter in which Liz referred to the given name for the Clubmobile, the *Kansas City*. The bigger news is the first mention of a possible love interest, Larry Pickard, an officer from New York. But as much as she would like to "burn toast" for Larry, Liz knows from observation, at least, the strains of wartime love.

November 5, 1944
[Leicester]

Dear mother and daddy,

How do you like the way I rotate my letters—first by rural delivery and then via industry? I rather think that they arrive in your hands a little bit sooner when I address them in care of the BALL BAND [her father's employer]. Anyway, I am once more crouched by the fire, having just returned from a Sunday session with the doughnut machine. We gave it a bath and if you've never given a doughnut machine a bath, you haven't lived. A fine clump of letters have arrived, including one from Butch. Thank you, old goat—I'll answer soon.

I find my new duties as Captain not too arduous, but complicated. We have a new crew member, fresh from home and bubbling with enthusiasm—but she's never made a doughnut—and that's rough. She is a very attractive divorcée all of 24 years of age and she completes our happy family, as they say in the women's magazines. We have our work divided up so that we're able to extend our social life, which is not too hard to take. I heard a wonderful symphony conducted by John Barbarolli, which I enjoyed immensely—this with a G.I. who used to be a radio announcer, specializing in "better music"—who added to my somewhat limited store of music lore.

What else? Well, last night, Larry took me to the local civilian dance. Have I told you about him? 2nd lieut. from Yonkers, N. Y. and under happier circumstances and better years, I can imagine nothing better than burning the toast for him. He is a darling, really, but I've seen too many ETO involvements to let myself get intense about him. Anyway, these civilian dances are quite amusing, enlivened by the usual very drunk Americans, fox-trotting Britains (mostly with horn-rimmed glasses) and the local feminine population between the age of 14 and 44. We hooked a ride home in a Colonel's large, black Buick and sat in front of Mrs. Tipper's fire watching it die a lingering death. Today, we were invited (we being the crew of the Kansas City) for dinner with the local M.P. force, complete with ice cream and fried chicken. Afterwards, we sat around, singing to the tune of an accordion and Aileen sang some of her bawdy songs. Otherwise, the weather has been its usual wet, damp self, enlivened by a damp wind. God knows how, but the flowers are still blooming and though the trees are drabber, the leaves are clinging. Egad, what a country.

I'll try to write a long letter later on in the week—I <u>can't</u> write a letter with a conversation about internationalism going on about me. So this member of the lost generation will sign off for the evening, with love and little red crosses to you all—

Elizabeth

With most of the 82nd now fighting on the Continent, the Clubmobile prepared to move too, leaving behind Mrs. Tipper's tarts and icy bathroom. There was sadness over news of one death among the many, that of Ed Kennedy, the decorated officer they called "Ken," who reminded Liz of her brother John. And there was the inevitable parting from Larry Pickard, off to France. Integrating Betty Goit into the unit proved difficult: she was a "fast worker," but not at making doughnuts. In fact, as Liz later learned, Betty and the guy she met on the boat coming over did get married. Betty remained part of the *Kansas City* crew until mid-December, but Liz never warmed to her, though they later had a drink together in Paris.

November 9, 1944
[Leicester]

Dear mother & daddy,

Daddy's letter of October 30th arrived today and I'm sorry that the mail situation is as bad over there as it is over here—though nine days isn't bad timing. However, that letter is just one that happened to slip in between Christmas packages and ballots and I, for one, will be glad when Santa Claus goes back to the North Pole and the last traces of the election die down. Everybody over here was terrifically interested in the results of the election, meaning mostly the English, who I guess believe that the war would be lost unless Roosevelt won. I guess I told you that my ballot arrived last Friday, which was a big help all around. But I mailed the thing anyway with the date extra big and black.

This has been a bad week—all the little puddles have coatings of ice, it has rained constantly and taking a bath is a Trojan deed. We are leaving Mrs. Tipper, very reluctantly, I assure you, in spite of her icy bathroom, for other pastures where it will be, no doubt, even colder. Today was our last run and tomorrow we spend cleaning our local deity, the !@#$@% doughnut machine. Our boys, as you know, are occupied elsewhere and the stay-behinds are moving up, and how we hate to leave even the remnants! We have to pile the entire contents of our storeroom, plus our personal luggage, on the Clubmobile. As said storeroom contains 11 barrels of doughnut flour alone and we each own a footlocker, a barracks bag and a suit case, this is going to be an interesting experiment in ballistics. I think we ourselves will end draped artistically about the engine hood. My APO <u>does not change</u>.

Do you remember me telling you about watching one of our friends get the Silver Star just before Holland? He was killed on patrol, along with his Sgt.[22] It only seems yesterday that I was dancing with him at a division dance and he gave Mrs. Tipper his soldier's medal ribbon and told her to pray for him, but I guess you need more than prayers in this war. He reminded me so much of Johnny and it seems unbelievable that anyone so alive and good could have gotten it. Larry (I think I've mentioned him before) left here this morning and I am very sad, needless to say. My affairs always end in farewell scenes controlled by elements far out of our hands and I hate to think of him going into what he is going. We both know that we'll meet again some place—I hope so—for he's a wonderful guy, and I am quite infatuated (probably owing to farewell scene). Mrs. T. likes him more than any of the other characters we have lured into our den and we had a gay time (while it lasted). I can't shrug my shoulders over this, as has been my wont, because it isn't like seeing somebody off for a week's stay in Chicago—there are so many other implications—and anyway I shore like him and he shore likes me. Or maybe he likes the odor of doughnuts that clothes me like a shroud. He says that when he arrives in France, a flash will go out from Radio Paris—translated from original, it is, "Frenchmen! Have no Fear! Pickard has arrived!"

So much for my love life, which as you see is at a stalemate. Otherwise, Betty, our new crew member, has proved to be most interesting. She entertains us with stories about events leading up to her divorce and is at present engaged to a Russian jew lieut. whom she met on the boat coming over. The trip was a short one, but our girl is a fast worker. The G.I.'s stand around and smile at her in a gooey sort of way, while Aileen and I have to project our personalities like crazy in order to compete. This bothered Aileen at first and being a basic and fundamental person, she went into a spiritual decline and sulked for 2 whole days. Old Dr. Richardson had a long talk with her and now, Thank God, Aileen is calling Betty "Honey" too and everything is sweetness & light. Mrs. Tipper, however, does not like her and while she killed Larry with kindness, she treats Betty's admirers with a coldness that would make a polar bear go south.

I will write as soon as we are located—no doubt in an old thatched roof hostelry with plumbing dating back to William & Mary. Margaret writes that she is billeted in a hotel where a bath is something that nice people don't take. So I guess we've been darn fortunate.

My teeth are chattering so that I must retire. At least in bed, I'll be warm by 4 A.M.

Love to you all,
Elizabeth

Among the few comments in her diary as she looked back on this time in November was the memory of Larry Pickard.

Diary, January 10, 1945

One night, Larry called up and said that his turn had come—he was going in as a replacement. He came over and we sat in front of the fire until 2:30 in the morning and I watched him walk into the misty English night. I wished that was all he was walking into.

Liz experienced military field dentistry and missed Larry Pickard as the crew prepared to move.

November 16, 1944
[Leicester]

Dear mother and daddy,

This is the last letter you'll get from Mrs. Tipper's—we are off tomorrow to new and more northern fields. I don't think anything could be more damp and dank than the midlands in November, but the Clubmobile dept. and other circumstances have made it possible for us to find out for ourselves. It will be just that—we have the name of our base, a roadmap and Jimmy, who is strictly London and vicinity. So if you hear from us from the Bonnie highlands of Scotland, you'll know that it wasn't because we were sent there—Jimmy and the Clubmobile did it. So this letter is just an interlude between packing and I'm sitting in front of the electric heater, listening to the Allied Expeditionary Forces program and casting a bleary eye at the weather, which is like a Sherlock Holmes mystery.

Betty has gone off in a jeep as of yesterday afternoon to say goodbye to her love of the moment and the atmosphere is so Farewell to Armish that you could cut us up in little pieces and call us Hemingway.

I wish you could have seen me getting a cavity filled yesterday—Army style. The chair is a collapsible job, comfortable enough, but you never know exactly what to do with your arms. The grinder is pedaled by the PFC who is the dental assistant and you spit resoundingly in a largish tin can. As for the dentist, clad impeccably in an O.D. sweater and jump boots, he orders you to open, close and spit as if he were commanding a battalion. The work was done in record time and with a minimum of ouching—silver filling, too. I think I'll stick to the Army for the rest of my life. (Probably it won't be a matter of me sticking to it, but the other way around.)

We have been making the most of our time, having gay times. Aileen's brother was here as on a 48 hour and we had a very nice party, getting Mrs. T. slightly tipsy. And a G.I. took me to a very out of the way pub where we played darts with an assortment of locals. Then we went to a dance to the tune of the music of a RAF band. I miss Larry terribly, but I guess there's nothing I can do about that.

The mail situation smells. We aren't even getting our £ sterling from headquarters and I have cashed my last two traveler's cheques at Thos. Cook's. However, I did get a V-mail from Anne [Bodle] Schuknecht, which was gladly received. And now, I must get dressed and down to the Kansas City. The poor old bus is about to clank and give up the ghost. It doesn't like the weather and the other day, thanks to a call to Maintenance Hdq., we had not one, but seven Red Cross Maintenance men laboring on it. Being British, they took all day (and all our cigarettes) and naturally, although it moves now, it threatens to stop entirely any moment. You know where it will stop. On a damp deserted lane, far away from human dwellings.

All my love to the Patch and the contents thereof—
Elizabeth

98

[5]

Into the English Provinces

Loaded with doughnut flour, coffee urns, phonograph records, cigarettes, magazines, chewing gum, and their personal belongings, including Liz's bicycle, the *Kansas City* departed Leicester on November 17, 1944. The crew stopped along the way for food and a sampling of English characters as they moved northwestward. Liz found the trip so interesting she wrote this short essay, which appeared in *The Sinker*, the Clubmobile newsletter, on January 5, 1945.

Huzza for the Open Road

We of the Kansas City love her with a passion that surpasseth all others—but after this, thanks we'll travel long distances by 20 mule team or even dog sled. We didn't think that way the morning we optimistically rolled flour barrels, coffee tins, etcetera, etc., ad infinitum, into our passion's hungry maw and then topped it off with what London refers to in telegrams as "luggage": not to count ourselves, dainty little folly girls that we are. Thus burdened, the "K.C." rolled on the road with a motion faintly reminiscent of the third day out from the P.O.E. [port of embarkation], and her crew—doubled up like pretzels between flour barrels—gritted their collective teeth and remembered with regret the dead days when doughnuts were something to eat.

At intervals along the way meerie Jimmy, the pilot, navigator, and turret gunner, stopped to unbend the pretzels . . . but we still walk as though we'd been born on the side of a hill.

Liz, Aileen Anderson, Betty Goit, and Jimmy Saunders arrived at their new home in Biddulph that evening, although Liz could not reveal their location to her family. Set in Staffordshire 25 miles south of Manchester, Biddulph was a small town, "certainly not on the map," Liz wrote. Its people struggled to earn a living in potteries, mines, and small factories. Yet in her short stay, Liz came to like the place and its people, including their new landlady, Annie Greenhulgh.[1]

Once settled, the *Kansas City* began making daily runs out to the men in area camps, this time those of the 87th Infantry Division. Only recently disembarked from the *Queen Elizabeth*, the 87th had not yet seen combat, unlike the 82nd Airborne the Clubmobile had served in Leicestershire. The 87th had arrived in the Biddulph area on October 25. A month later they were on the Continent and soon in battle. Liz would see many of those who survived combat again in France in July 1945.

Nov. 19, 1944
[Biddulph]

Dear mother and daddy,

Two more letters came through from you just before we left Mrs. Tipper's—the last one dated October 30th. Now, of course, it will probably be another three weeks or so before the mail catches up with us and I can see why. Although I don't quite feel like a character out of "How Green Was My Valley,"[2] I come darn near it. We are not exactly near any pulse of civilization.

Our trip up hear (egad, even Olde Englishe spelling) here, I mean, was a wild experience. The clubmobile bulged with our assorted equipment, plus bicycle and I had to sit like a pretzel up front with Jimmy. We stopped at an inn en route, supposedly for lunch and were greeted with such enthusiasm by the local harpies that our trip was delayed by at least 3 hours. We finally ate at an officers' mess, served by Italian prisoners, one of whom spoke enthusiastic and bad French. I conversed with him in like tone and we got on quite famously.

Our next stop was for tea in a wayside inn that was like a scene out of Hellzapoppin'.[3] The proprietor was half farmer, half inn-keeper and spent most of his time changing his coat to suit his profession of the moment. His wife, a woman with a voice like a trumpet, talked continually from the time we stumbled in to the time we wafted out. An assortment of animals wandered in and out of this remarkable stage set and it was with difficulty that we pried ourselves loose from the north country hospitality. We ended up at a dance, escorted by some of our new G.I.'s. As for our billet, it is very nice. Our landlady is a sweet old thing whose husband just died and we go about at night with candles (no electric lights) and she puts hot bricks in our beds to warm them and wakes us up in the morning with tea. We are veterans, compared with our men—a slight change from our combat wearied men in Leicestershire. Last night, a group of the officers took us out to a few local inns huddled against hillsides and we spent a very pleasant evening. The last place we went to was especially charming—lovely china, antiques, and lady proprietress who lives all alone and manages the pub. We eat in the local Officers' Mess and start our doughnut slinging tomorrow, goody, goody.

The country is beautiful, slightly reminiscent of West Virginia, even without sun. The weather is milder than the midlands—Thank God—I was beginning to creak when I walked. The people are most cordial, much more so than the Midlanders. I wish you could see this house—a perfect example of Victorianism from the flowered pitcher in our room to the steel engraving of two dogs by the seashore. I am sitting by the stove this morning—a remarkable built-in sort of contraption enclosed in a mantle piece. Betty has gone off to London (not ordinarily a weekend project, but she is In Luv) and Aileen and Mrs. Greenhulgh have gone to church—Church of England, of course. And I must get dressed in preparation for chow 3 miles up the road. We are called for very grandly for every meal in the Red Cross Field Director's Hillman [automobile] which has 10 horsepower and 5 of the horses have the colic.

Mother, your views on the international situation are very sound and true and I will try not to put a flaw in our Anglo-American relationships and I hope that I never have an opportunity to even look at Russo-American relationships.

Love to you all, including Topsy & Freckles—

Your
Elizabeth

Liz later described the new home in her diary.

Diary, January 10, 1945

We loaded up and moved northwest towards Liverpool. Our new home was in a cold, drafty house made pleasant by a charming old lady—Mrs. Annie Greenhulgh. We had a new infantry division, the 87th, fresh from the States. We ate all our meals in the officer's mess at headquarters and at night, went pubbing in the field director's Hillman, along with the Colonel and assorted officers—all very pleasant and southern. It was a nice, impersonal sort of relationship. The country was beautiful and bleak—Biddulph is at the corner of three counties— Shropshire, Cheshire and Staffordshire and the center of the pottery district. The little villages were built on the side of the hills and with my bicycle, I discovered Biddulph castle, partly destroyed by Cromwell's guns. More than 500 years before. A Dr. Murphy, an Irishman took us out to dinner to a beautiful English home.

Liz wrote her second letter from Biddulph the day after Thanksgiving, a time that has always been especially hard for an American so far away from family. The food had declined to K rations. The army designed these rectangular boxes to fit in a paratrooper's pocket. They contained canned and processed foods high in calories but with minimal flavor or appeal.[4] Liz expressed her concern for the very young and untested men of the 87th. Both the demanding social life and work continued.

November 24, 1944
[Biddulph]

Dear mother and daddy,

Once again, you may picture me crouching by the fire, only in slightly different surroundings than those of my last letter. I'm in the parlor this trip—a fine, sturdy room, lighted by a central gas jet. We expect to move again Monday—don't know where, don't know how, but we have had a good week of work and fun, terminated by the usual goodbyes and good lucks. Our mail hasn't caught up to us as yet, and I can see why. Our hamlet is certainly not on the map and sometimes we wonder if London knows exactly where the "Kansas City" is. The country is strangely beautiful and the sun actually came out for a few hours the other day, so that we could see it in all its glory. Ask Mr. Wood about the "potteries." Last night, we attended an Officers' Dance in the local town hall—a very proper officers' dance, attended by the local gentry, including the Lord Mayor with a seal. The band, a GI divisional one, was wonderful and we had a grand evening, coming home afterwards divided up in three jeeps with a heavy escort of shavetails. We've also been to a GI dance, not counting several exploratory journeys in the countryside to wayside inns. As a result of all this, plus our work (which begins at 7), we have here tonight three very weary creatures and I won't mention our dear sweet landlady, Mrs. Greenhulgh, who just stands by open-mouthed.

Life over here seems to consist of one long series of goodbyes—nothing is permanent, nothing is sure, not even tomorrow's mail. At present, we are subsiding on K ration and the novelty has worn off. Before that, we were eating like Kings and yesterday, being Thanksgiving, Uncle Sam came through with Turkey and all the fixings—even pumpkin pie. It's funny, but though these boys have been over here for a comparatively short time, they were much more conscious of the distance between themselves and home than our old wards, the Paratroopers. They are so young and have so far to go yet, but we try not to think of that, although comparisons are unavoidable. The veterans are stoical about the whole thing—they've "'ad it."

Thank goodness, the weather is milder up here, although it's just as damp. But it does make it easier to get up in the morning. However, it is with Spartan courage that I face my daily ablutions in water that can only be called tepid.

Well, Mother, Daddy, Butch—I thought of all of you yesterday as I gazed into my mess kit overflowing with turkey—a small symbol of home. I hope yours was a wonderful Thanksgiving and that our thought waves met somewhere in mid-ocean. It suddenly seemed strange to be sitting there surrounded by those boys, each with their different memories, in an alien land, while the sun did try to come through the dampness. Holidays are bad for the morale.

We had a good volley ball game the other day—a pick-up team of a colonel, 2 majors, 3 captains, 2 lieuts., and an assortment of G.I.'s. The field was a bit damp and by the time we were through, we were well camouflaged with mud. But anything for sport!

So my next will be from some other spot of the isle. At least I'm seeing England, although not the England that the peacetime tourist usually sees. This particular spot is especially isolated so we feel as if we were really a part of it. I can't describe the country, other than it sometimes reminds me of West Virginia, sometimes of northern New York, sometimes of Wisconsin. Farming is important, but not as important as the industries which are grimy and dank. The people look as if they'd seen some lean years and every little hamlet has its own atrocity of a factory. The pottery industry is of course the mainstay—but there is also mining (the hard way, with pony carts hauling the coal through the streets) and the whole is spread out over the whole area, blending into the sodden landscape. This sounds horrible, but it isn't really—lots of color, glowering hills and a certain charm. The people seem to enjoy themselves and we had a gay evening in one of the inns singing with the regulars—slightly bawdy songs which sound best when sung by people without any teeth. Nobody over 20 has teeth.

On this cheerful note, I shall leave to brush mine. My love to all of you—Freckles & Topsy included.

Your
Elizabeth

Liz's memory a few weeks later of that Thanksgiving Day far from home, as recorded in her diary, was grim and succinct.

Diary, January 10, 1945
It was with the 87th that we spent Thanksgiving. I ate my Thanksgiving dinner in the enlisted men's mess out of my mess kit. No one was very thankful.

The next day the *Kansas City* crew started saying goodbye as the 87th began to depart for France. Biddulph grew quiet, with a few days for a curious Liz to explore the countryside and get "far away from doughnuts and a more total war." There was time to meet some lovely local people, especially Dr. and Mrs. T. C. Murphy. In response to their kindness, Liz gave Mrs. Murphy two pair of silk stockings, a wartime gift of immense value.[5]

November 27, 1944
[Biddulph]

Dear mother and daddy,

It seems to me that I'm always afraid that I won't be able to write to you for a while and as a consequence, I'm getting to be a better correspondent (in some ways). Anyway, here we are on the brink of another odyssey via Clubmobile and just as we were more or less settled with the gas lamps. We hate to leave this nice little town and the friendly people, especially our nice landlady, Mrs. Greenhulgh, but c'est la mobile. These last few days, we have been more or less at loose ends and have had an opportunity to share in the life of the community. Sunday, Aileen and I escorted Mrs. G. to the local church, a lovely picture postcard place of Norman vintage and I took communion and felt quite up-lifted by the beautiful surroundings in spite of the penetrating cold, accumulated, no doubt, from the 14th century. The service was very low—first morning prayer and sermon and then communion—and a visiting fireman did the honors since the local vicar is "with the forces." Then we were invited by the doctor and his wife to visit some friends of theirs. The doctor (Murphy) is Irish, as is his charming wife and therefore more or less lacking in the traditional English reserve. "You know, we <u>like</u> Americans," he confided to me. The friends proved to live on a semi-estate and gave us a heart-warming welcome and a wonderful dinner on lovely china . . . you know, civilization. Mr. Arrowsmith has something to do with the pottery industry and fancies himself as a collector of pedigreed Guernsey cattle, antique figurines and old chests. So we had whipped cream and I admired both the figurines and the chests which were truly magnificent.

It was the kind of English home I always knew existed but haven't met up with and a most pleasant evening. The Murphys have a son in medical school in Dublin and a daughter in Italy and take a delight in bringing in the poor Americans and I on my part, take a delight in being able to know them. They have invited me down for Christmas and perhaps I will be able to make it—at least some time during the Yuletide season.

Today, I was doing a bit of bicycling which I find rather wearing considering the number of hills, and I was investigating a charming old mill when a lady, two children and two dogs came along the path through the dusk and asked me if I had seen the castle. A castle! My ears pricked up as she told me the history of the place—16th century, slightly pre-Elizabethan, destroyed by that bounder Cromwell with a big cannon that he had dragged from a nearby stronghold.[6] We walked up what once had been a driveway and there in the twilight was a breath-taking sight—a broad lawn and a stark wall with gaping Gothic windows and portcullis door, and the indentation of the moat—just as Cromwell had left it. There were two other walls, one with the huge fireplace and climbing over the edge of one wall, you could see (if (a it wasn't foggy (B it wasn't rainy) way into the next shire. One tower rose up from the remainder of the castle, which was occupied by a descendant of the original owner, whose name adorns this village. We entered through a little door cut into one of those same big fireplaces and I was as entranced with the interior as with the ex. You know— oaken beams, floors that slope, little steps and the traces of generations of occupants, each with a different idea of what to do with that corner—or that window—or that beam. My guide was the wife of a convalescening (sp.) British officer at the local hospital and very nice and charming. Finally, she introduced me to the mistress of the Castle—in the room that King Charles occupied when the roundheads besieged him.

So I pedaled home through the wet lanes living in a different century, far away from doughnuts and a more total war. The wonderful part about finding a place like that is its air of being part of the land— none of our commercialism, although of course it exists in such spots as Stratford & Westminster. I do like the people in this district—they are hospitable and kindly. Today, Jimmy & I drove the Kansas City to a neighboring town to get diesel oil (how this differs from "petrol" I don't exactly know) and I found a beautiful church there and a William & Mary Unitarian Chapel. I also bought you a Christmas present, Mother, which I might as well tell you about now as it will no doubt arrive in time for Easter, at least. It's a Wedgwood cookie jar with the typical blue Wedgwood background and little figures representing some biblical allegory—has a silver lid and handle and I know you'll love it. It's the first thing I've really bought, because I don't think we're over here to buy—but I couldn't resist it and it's a memento of this pleasant section.

The next time you'll hear from me t'will be the northland, but it couldn't be chillier than this. We have had two days of globby snow— great big flakes that make everything very Christmasy, if you could see—but when we get up it's night and when it becomes daylight, there's an enveloping fog which drifts away in time for a light drizzle which is immediately followed by night again when all hell breaks loose—snow, rain, fog, wind, sleet. My nose drips constantly and is always a bright cherry red. Our new base is in nice country and will no doubt be interesting—shades of Wordsworth & Hazlitt!

My love to you all,

Yr chilly daught,
Elizabeth

Next stop for the *Kansas City* was Barrow-in-Furness, located on Morecambe Bay on the northwest coast of England and near to England's Lake District. Barrow-in-Furness was the home of a major ship builder, Vickers, and thus a very busy place during the war. It was also a target for German bombers early in the war and suffered considerable damage. During spring 1941, as one resident recalled, "it seemed as though the planes were over and dropping bombs every night."[7] Because of its port facilities and nearby airfields military personnel from many Allied nations were stationed in the area or traveling through.

Liz, Betty Goit, and Aileen Anderson were delighted to find their new home in the Imperial Hotel, located in the center of town. They had single rooms for the first time and far more luxuries than they had had with Mrs. Greenhulgh or Mrs. Tipper. There were other guests to savor leisure time around the fire in the lounge, including British naval officers and civilians, giving Liz opportunities to continue her observations of the natives.

The early mornings and late nights resumed, with darkness extended by very early sunsets in northern England. An exceptionally harsh winter brought cold, rain, and snow that grew cruel by mid-January. The weather challenged the Clubmobile's diesel engine, the doughnut machine, and the crew's health. Most days, before sunrise, the *Kansas City* crew had finished preparing their coffee and doughnuts at one of the nearby American camps. With Jimmy Saunders in the driver's seat the bus rattled off to other camps to serve, stopping at as many as a half dozen a day. The crew often ate their meals at the mess in whatever camp they worked, so they had plenty of food. It was warmth they lacked. Absence of heating in the *Kansas City* and in many other places in which they spent their days made shivering a fact of life. Absent too was news from home; again and again Liz lamented the lack of mail.[8]

The three women bonded quickly with the men, most of them fresh from the States. Liz and her colleagues knew what the men were facing better than they did. Many of the GIs were from a recently arrived New York National Guard unit, joined by others from Pennsylvania and Massachusetts. Margee Main, who joined the *Kansas City* crew later, thought them "a lot cleaner and higher type of GI than we had before." Indeed, the Americans seemed better behaved than their British counterparts, to Liz's satisfaction.

In her diary Liz recorded the trip from Biddulph to Barrow, with a depressing stop on the way.

Diary, January 10, 1945
[Barrow-in-Furness]
Two days after the division moved out, we were on our way again, this time further north to Lancashire:—Barrow-in-Furness. We drove all day, stopping at Warrington to see Margaret [Morrison] and at a rehabilitation camp for chow. These are the camps where men, made

psychologically unfit for combat by combat, are retrained for more combat. It was a depressing experience. From Warrington, we struck northwards over beautiful and rugged hills, different entirely from the hills of Staffordshire. We followed the coast and in the late afternoon, passed over the most glorious country I have seen so far. By 5 o'clock, we drove into Barrow and to our new billet, The Imperial Hotel, in the shadow of the shipyards.

The Imperial is our most comfortable home so far. We each have a room and a small electric heater. The beds are heaven and the bath water hot. At Mrs. Greenhulgh's, bathing was like some sort of Spartan conditioning exercise. The clubmobile lives in the Imperial garage, along with my bicycle and our stores. We have, or I should say, had quite an assortment of troops—Signal Corps., artillery, Ordinance and stray companies of Medics. We did have two troops of Calvary Reconnaissance (mechanized), but they have been shipped to southern England, preparatory to France. Barrow is a comparatively modern city, strictly Victorian in origin, and therefore essentially unlovely. Besides the big Vickers-Armstrong works, it boasts about 5 cinemas and at least three hotels. The ruins of Furness Abbey are up the road—nice well kept ruins they are. The lake district begins at Ulverston and on clear days, we can see the snow covered hills beyond our own local hills. Otherwise, we are more or less isolated, as we found out when our doughnut machine broke down on Christmas eve. We are eight hours from Edinburgh and the same from London and the trains are habitually late.

In her first letter from Barrow-in-Furness, Liz described the new luxury of the Imperial Hotel which had "hot water and American biffies." There wasn't much ready amusement in Barrow that winter, contributing to the "serious drinking that so many of the men indulge." There was plenty of alcohol everywhere Liz went. She was certainly no teetotaler herself, but she tended to drink in moderation, if perhaps more than she reported to her parents. Neither her letters nor diary show concern about the policy stated in the American Red Cross manual, that "personnel in uniform are requested to refrain from the use of liquor."[9]

The *Kansas City* crew, standing near their Clubmobile, December 1944, Barrow-in-Furness, England. In addition to their "Clubmobile clown suits," Liz is also wearing the fleece-lined leather vest her brother John sent for Christmas. Left to right: Aileen Anderson, Elizabeth Richardson, Margee Main.
Courtesy Charles Richardson, Jr.

December 1, 1944
[Barrow-in-Furness]

Dear mother and daddy,

Enclosed is the bank business—sorry that this ink is so stinky. If you get me an occasional $25 job—say once a month—I will be quite happy. I'm referring to bonds.

The mail is vile. I did receive a Christmas package from Anne Schuknecht which pleased me to no end—Aileen had to practically tear it from my clammy little paws to keep me from opening it. Mother, could you get a little something for Judy from me? Maybe a book—she loves to be read to.

We are now billeted in a hotel—a very modern hotel, we think, with hot water and American biffies, although I still grope for a chain. I have a room to myself and an electric heater and the best bed I've had since hitting the United Kingdom. The "Kansas City" lives in the hotel garage and the countryside is out of this world, although still draped in mist, rain and fog. The work is hard—or I should say, was—because the doughnut machine broke down yesterday and we are awaiting first aid. Meanwhile, we sit in the lounge, toasting our feet and writing letters in this horrid ink. Hope you can read it. The navy rules here—not U. S., but everything else. Today at lunch, which we eat with a full supply of silverware (they serve Spam and brussel sprouts as if it were ambrosia), I was fascinated by four young British Naval Officers who after acting like four Butches [Liz's teenaged brother Butch] on an outing, calmly ate the centerpiece with bovine satisfaction. Usually, the British are so busy looking down their noses at those ill-bred Americans that it was a pleasure to watch somebody else make fools of themselves. . . . In fact, the Yanks haven't exploited this territory at all and they are very well behaved, compared with the other nationalities. The other night, what looked like an entire RAF squadron, all very tanked up, played a football game in the lobby, while we looked on with glazed eyes. The Dutch are more stoical—they get drunk and stay drunk. Alas—the local brew leaves the Americans untouched and unsmiling in the corner.

This is a heck of a time to see this part of England, although we do see it au naturel. However, it's not nearly as cold as the midlands—not even as cold as Staffordshire and if the sun ever comes out, I contemplate many bicycle expeditions in the countryside. I like this hotel life—no shivering by a half-hearted fire and our beds are even turned down at night! We are lucky clusters.

The G.I.'s are very fresh and new and you don't have to be amateur psychologists to work with them. If you only knew what combat does to these boys—not in the physical sense, although that's bad enough—but mentally. You have to be very stable indeed to come out without too many wrinkles.

As for amusement, there's not too much, except sitting over a glass of bitter. One is plenty for me, thank you. I can't see the point of this serious drinking that so many of the men indulge in—there are other ways to escape reality that aren't so hard and the best way is to face it instead of running away.

Tea-time, so I must stop—naturally. Food. Keep on writing. Butch, study hard. My love to all of you,

Elizabeth

On this very late evening, Liz rushed to get a monetary Christmas gift in the mail home, but she was exhausted, even to the point of only abbreviating her name in closing this short letter. And the Imperial Hotel's hot water, which had been such a blessing, had vanished.

December 7, 1944
[Barrow-in-Furness]

Dear mother and daddy,

Just a hasty note in order to get the enclosed Christmas remembrance on its way—divided four ways it t'aint much, but I hope, Mother, that you will go out and get them what they want—especially John. I think I mentioned another Christmas present for you, Mother, and one for Butch that is on the verge of being on its way. Your Christmas letter arrived yesterday, Mother—a bit previous, but it was well received.

We are busy as beavers. It's now midnight and this was going to be my night of beauty rest. The water in this hotel either doesn't come out of the faucet or else when it comes, it's liquid ice. Sorry, too tired for energetic letter-writing—will write in a few days—

Love to all,
Eliz.

Liz forced herself to write a Christmas letter, a wistful one with a few touches of humor, including a proposal for a "pubmobile" and more observations on English social class. And she mentioned Frank, a frequent dance partner, but, unlike Frank Pickard, not a romantic interest: she described him in her diary of January 10, 1945, as "a big, red-faced lieut. From the Ordinance with a perfectly good wife in Minnesota." She never wrote his last name.

Liz's lament that the *Kansas City* had been "forgotten up in these hills" was not unusual. The challenges of Clubmobile work often included supply shortages and infrequent communication from London headquarters. Clubmobile crews worked with very little direct supervision, which allowed for independence but made them feel all the more isolated. Only those with initiative and flexibility and those able to work for goals other than pleasing a supervisor succeeded. The organization's selection process seems to have been reasonably successful in identifying such exceptional women.[10]

> December 11, 1944
> [Barrow-in-Furness]

Dear Family,

This, I hope, will arrive in time to wish you all a very wonderful Christmas. Certainly, I will be thinking of the Patch festively alight, Christmas tree and other years from the time that I first remember—all of them very happy memories—as you who share them know. We are working Christmas eve and Christmas day, but will have 78 hours over New Years, so while you are gathering about the tree, I will be slinging doughnuts at homesick G.I.'s and there could be worse ways to spend Christmas eve. I'm writing this in the camp kitchen in front of the stoves, while at least 20 people tred back and forth on my numbed toes and two cats frolic somewhere in between. Outside, it's a bleak Lancashire day, with anaemic snow on the ground and a sad sun trying to break through. I still find the countryside beautiful, though, in spite of my perpetually running nose and my ETO hack. We have been kept awfully busy and our social life has become an overwhelming thing, all of which is strange considering that there is practically nothing to do, other than pubbing and pubbing again. In fact we have a wonderful idea which we are anxious to present to the Red Cross—a pubmobile—ingredients: one London double-decker bus, the top devoted to a complete pub serving bitter, mild, nut-brown and Guinesses, the bottom to the doughnut and coffee racket.

Last Friday, we went to a very formal dance given by the local golf club (so you can see that the black lace is getting a work out). First, we were invited to a cocktail party at the home of one of the local dignitaries. We arrived rather late, so the host & hostess were quite stewed in their own scotch and my opinion of them can really not be formulated until I see them sober. During the course of the evening, a dance was announced for "members of the American Forces and their guests" and clicking our heels, Frank and I got out on the floor awaiting the call. The Yankee music proved to be the Star Spangled Banner in Waltz time, Old Black Joe and Sewanee River. I think the yeomandry think that back home we sit around listening to old negro mammies plunking away on banjos.

Yesterday, we took out a young English naval sub-lieutenant (equivalent to our Ensign) on our Clubmobile. He looks just like Alan Wood and is a dear. After our work was over, we all had dinner at the camp in our mess kits and he enjoyed it very much, although I think he's recovering today. The well-educated Englishman is certainly delightful, but there is such a chasm between a boy like Peter (Eton & Cambridge) and the man on the street. I am so amused at the lounge in our hotel where everybody sits about like well-bred sticks, until our peasant-like Aileen bursts in—or 2 or 3 G.I.'s from Brooklyn. Then the funeral like silence is shattered and I think everybody feels happier.

Betty (our newest crew-member) is going down to London tonight to be interviewed about some other branch of the R. C. I'm going to have her drop in to remind headquarters that we exist—we haven't gotten any supplies for 3 weeks and I can see how we'd be forgotten up in these hills.

This is not a very good Christmas letter, but it's put me in a Christmasy mood, writing it and thinking of all of you—even Topsy. You can be certain that half of me at least will be with you, that I will be just a little bit homesick for the warmth and security of Dragoon Trail—and St. H. playing Silent Night—and Butch being grabby over the presents—and CMR sitting back and gathering up the tissue paper. Let's hope that in another year or so we'll all be together again.

Love to you all and a Merry, Merry Christmas,
Elizabeth

In a Christmas letter to her brother John, now in Marine Corps officer training, Liz provided more detail about Barrow and the active social life and allowed just a touch of the hardship of war to seep in.

13 December, 1944
[Barrow-in-Furness]

Dearest Johnny,

If it weren't for the fact that the clubmobile gave up the ghost yesterday (spectacularly, on the main drag) I wouldn't be writing this, for the luxury of letter-writing appears to be a thing of the past. However, a whole beautiful day stretches in front of me—plenty of time to wish you a most Merry Christmas and a New Year that will put all the others to shame. I knew you'd get to Quantico, so although I'm very proud and happy for you, I'm not surprized. Have you forgotten what the word leisure means?

Since I wrote to you last, we've changed bases again—this time to a beautiful spot—hills and all that. Do you remember your English poets? We are billeted in a hotel where we are most comfortable, although I imagine we'll be evicted very shortly. Our fellow inmates range from stuffy business men to young British naval officers to American G.I.'s on a 48 [hour pass]. The navy is especially interesting— they always get quite drunk before their ship leaves. And if there's anything I gloat in—it's a Britisher drunk. Last night, one came in to dinner in his tin hat and kept on shouting at intervals—"I'm a most meticulous man, sir!" He also gave forth with a ditty about "Oh, my uncle, Sylvester! He's got 40 metals on his chest!" All of which sounds admirable when sung in the best Harrow accent.

Americans are treated rather like the extinct dodo bird, which is a treat and I enjoy being a curiosity. And when you're a female of the species—especially a large female—the ovation is terrific! We work hard and always smell like doughnuts and beside that, we play hard too which is wearing. I wish you could have attended the supposedly "posh" dance that we went to last week—the officers were guests of the local golf club and for once, the Americans were well behaved, while the chosen people forgot their centuries of accumulated dignity. We do have fun, though, although there is nothing to do but go pubbing, go dancing at a slightly ill reputable dance hall frequented by gentlemen in Gilbert & Sullivan sailor suits, or go to the movies—all of which are antiques. But the more I live in this strange isle, the more I like it and understand the British and their foibles. We Americans are loud and gauche and have much to learn from them.

Our G.I.'s are a nice bunch—they always are! They certainly take good care of us, see that we are well fed, have clean mess kits, have G.I. gin (cough medicine) for our coughs and all that. The difference between them and our paratroopers is appalling (pardon spelling—it's still early in the morning) and it makes me very sad to see what combat can do to a man.

Don't let me get started on that—I started out to write you a jolly Christmas letter. I'll certainly be thinking of Dragoon Trail and my absent little brother come Christmas eve. God knows it will be a long time before we are all together again, so here's hoping that you have a merry one wherever you are. We are working Christmas eve and Christmas—but we have a 3 day leave over New Year's, which sounds good to me. Give my regards to your love—how is she? Did her brother visit Butch? How do things stand? Why in the hell don't you two stop dashing about the bush and acting coy? Life is too short for the finer things of courtship. (I don't really believe that).

Write soon, old dish and be good—and merrie yule tide—

Love,
Elizabeth

[p.s.] Rassle up a good picture of yourself, will you?

Christmas brought presents from home, some to be shared. And Jimmy Saunders emerged as a poet, just as crew member Betty Goit prepared to leave.

Dec. 15, 1944
[Barrow-in-Furness]

Dear mother and daddy,

Christmas packages have been coming through like mad—but none from Dragoon Trail, darn it. Otherwise, the mail situation remains notoriously bad except for a letter from daddy written November 24th, I believe. Sorry that mine haven't been coming through,[11] but as you can see I am still fat and sassy—in fact, so fat and sassy that it's almost chronic. Have received a package from Anne Schuknecht, Mrs. Bodle, Aunt Gertrude and John—also 1718 No. Prospect. The latter leaks confetti and undoubtedly contains a rat killed by Twine's own fair hands. The return address was "Women's Christian Temperance Union, 1718 No. Prospect" so at least I'll get a good name with the mail clerks. Last night, 2 G.I.'s, myself, Aileen and Peter (our 19 year old British sub-lieut.) went to the local cinema and when we returned (through the iciest pelting rain that exists), we sat about the fire and opened Aunt Gertrude's package. It contained wonderful cheese and crackers, fruit cake and peanuts that went very well with a few glasses of the local brew and by the time the evening was over, we had finished everything. We were further helped by four more British Naval Officers who almost swooned over the fruit cake. Peter left today—we were lucky enough to have the Clubmobile break down on Wednesday so that we had three days of comparative freedom and we all hated to see him go, together with his Fellow Officer, Ted and Ted's wife. In the hope that their boat will stop in New York, I gave him Uncle Bill's address—it's seldom that you come across a boy like him, the product of everything good in England and we are fortunate to have been able to know him. His sister was killed in the blitz.

Our Betty is leaving us for a rest camp for flak-happy fliers, which leaves Aileen and myself—and of course—Jimmy. Jimmy has recently blossomed into a poet. Every morning, he comes through with a new one commemorating Betty's cold, or the weather, or the editorial in the Daily Mirror. I present his latest for your edification and admiration.

We give you doughnuts,
We give them free.
Please don't come up like limey's
And ask for cups of tea.
This outfit's all American,
Except for one limey,
And he likes a cup of java,
Too—with the tea.

We all have colds—snively ones. But we have had some sunny days—as I've said before, the country is lovely. I've spent this morning in the library, reading about the local ruins—a famous abbey that's been deserted since Henry VIII's confiscation of the monasteries.[12] But the wind blows so wildly that bicycle riding is courting pneumonia and blindness. It should die down one of these days and I'll visit them or it. (Is a ruin singular or plural?) Otherwise, I was taken to the local dance hall by one of the G.I.'s—heavily disguised as a civilian. The place had more or less of a waterfront atmosphere and was frequented by gentlemen in bell-bottoms. I felt like a character in a Gilbert & Sullivan operetta—a badly done performance of "Pinafore," perhaps. By the way, I received a card from Mr. Wood from Chicago and you can tell him for me that it's still cold and still damp in his country, that even my BALL-BAND synthetic Rubber Boots don't keep it out and that I suspect an ice-age is originating somewhere in this region.

And now I must depart in the faint hopes of getting a bath. Rumor has it that the pressure is off again and anyway, it doesn't matter, because the water is cold even if the pressure were on (Rumor is confirmed, alas). Keep on writing, in spite of the mail situation and lots of love to you all—

Elizabeth

Soon after Betty left, the *Kansas City* acquired a new crewmember, as Liz noted in her diary.

Liz posed with a coffee urn and a smile in the very cold winter of December 1944, Camp Dane Ghyell, Barrow-in-Furness, England. *Courtesy Charles Richardson, Jr.*

Diary, January 10, 1945
[Barrow-in-Furness]

Betty Goit has transferred to the Rest Home Department and we now have Margee Main of Cleveland, Ohio, who knows how to make doughnuts. She has been over about three months and has been based on the east coast with the 8th Air Force.

Marjorie Main was delighted to join Aileen and Liz. She wrote home that "there never were two sweller gals to work with and have fun with."[13]

119

Writing two days after Christmas, Liz thanked her marine brother for a fleece-lined vest and touched on the strangeness and loneliness of the holiday in wartime but also on her conviction that she was doing what she should be doing.[14]

News of the German counteroffensive in the snow-covered Ardennes, to be known as the Battle of the Bulge, began to reach Barrow. The 82nd and the 87th were heavily involved and took large causalities. What little news there was from the front was not good. A troubled Liz could guess what was happening. She repeated again her frustration with those at home who since D-Day had thought the war was nearly over.

December 27, 1944
[Barrow-in-Furness]

Dear Johnny,

Here sit I, well protected from the northern breezes in a very stunning leather vest—you are most original, old goat, and strangely enough, you picked out something that I really needed, because not even three layers of Brooks Brother's sweaters can keep this northern wind, laden as it is with moisture and cold direct from the Greenland ice cap. In fact, I have a cold right now that is the granddaddy of all colds—my pore little nose is stuffed up, my pore little throat feels like a new piece of sandpaper, my pore little head is twice as big as it is normally—I am most unhappy!

Well, old goat, I wondered how you spent your Christmas and I hope it was a merry one. The whole idea seems pretty alien over here, but we had our clubmobile decorated with holly and a small version of a Christmas tree and we attended Christmas eve services in a beautiful parish church before the donut slinging began. On Christmas day, we were out bright and early again with two G.I.s aboard equiped with guitars. They twanged away at what I presumed were native ballads (native, that is, to West Virginia & Ky.) but the fellows loved it and our Christmas was quite a success. We have a 2 day leave over New Years in which to recuperate and I intend to sleep 24 hours a day, except for long intervals in a hot tub.

Butch sent me some snapshots taken while you and Sue were at

Dragoon Trail. She's an attractive girl, Johnny, old meatball, and I hope things are progressing swimmingly on that front.

Things don't look so well over here, as I guess you've read. It's too bad that people at home expected such an early end to war in this theatre, because it's not anywhere near the end, as I saw as soon as I arrived. The hardest part is still ahead of us, so I imagine this will not be our last Christmas in the ETO. Home seems far away, but I still would much rather be here than there, in spite of everything (including this cold). By the time you get this, you'll probably be over O.C.S.—be sure and keep me posted about what happens, your life, your [illegible] plans for the future and all that. And lots of love to you, sorghum.

Elizabeth

That same day, Liz wrote Betty Twining and other friends from 1718 North Prospect days in Milwaukee. Her reference to "my pore little hands" referred to the red and raw condition caused not only by the winter weather but by mixing the doughnut flour with water. The process quickly removed nail polish.[15]

December 27, 1945
[Barrow-in-Furness]

Dear B-bub and Ladees,

Your package arrived, leaking confetti and an aroma of holiness and temperance thanks to the return address (Women's Christian Temperance Union, if you remember) and I opened it with trembling fingers come Christmas eve; as we sat about the one fire in this charming hotel where we do not hang our barrack bags. Kiddies, Youse are wonderful! Everything—Kleenex, Stockings, Handcream, soap, was as they say in the books, just what I needed and it was all so attractively wrapped that I seemed a little nearer home as I nervously tore them open. Really, it was darling of you to think of me, especially in such a nice material way and with such nice luxuries (and that includes the Pond's lipstick at 49¢). She's lovely! She's engaged! She was almost down to using mercurochrome in the first aid kit as a substitute!

We are now in the north and I am not just joshing when I say it. God knows how Wordsworth lasted the winters out. The countryside is beautiful and bleak and cold, filled with ye olde ruins and ye olde are billetted in a hotel that is the last word in modern conveniences—it has hot running water at least 3 times a week, and biffies that flush in the American way rather than via chain. Not only that, but we get butter once a day for breakfast so it's only enough for 1 slice of toast, but what the hell. We eat most of our meals at the camps, so we're not really suffering—in fact—well, I'm still the same bouncing girl, plus. On Christmas morning, the employees were almost hysterical—they were going to have grapefruit and fresh eggs for the first time in two years. The hotel is frequented by many British naval men all of whom are quite Gilbert and Sullivanish and inclined to the goldfish-swallowing school of thought. On the other hand, maybe it's tradition that compels them to eat floral centerpieces.

Otherwise we work madly turning out unmentionables (donuts to you) and my pore little hands look as if they should belong to the ladies who scrub Schusters after hours. Also have infection and horrible cold, which doesn't make me too happy. Do write, ladees.

Letters are ammunition and I'm fresh out. Or can't I interest you with propaganda? Write soon and love to all of you and your lucky mates.

Liz

Liz's nasty cold continued, but she went dancing with Frank, mentioned as a dance partner in her letter of December 11. The long-held desire to receive *Time* magazine had still not been fulfilled.

December 28, 1944
[Barrow-in-Furness]

Dear mother and daddy, (AND BUTCH)

Your pore daughter writes this from her downy cot where she has retired due to a case of the sniffles. And sniffles in this country are different from sniffles back home. I've had this cold for about three weeks and it's getting progressively worse, so it's bed until I shake it off. Unfortunately, it's rather like going to bed in Grand Central Station as a procession of visitors parade through, varying from Jimmy, our driver, who reports that he has moved 10 kegs of doughnut flour with his own hands—to one of the hotel maids, who has a telegram for me—something about the doughnut machine.

The package containing socks, currants, T-shirt and soap arrived the day before Christmas. Owing to the breakdown of our d. machine, we were forced to make doughnuts the old-fashioned way which is no fun, but when we returned from our labor over the hot stove, we sat in front of the fire in the lounge, decorated a tree with streamers of Kleenex and opened our Christmas boxes. 1718 North Prospect came through with a good one—all sorts of luxuries like lipstick and hand cream and John sent a beautiful leather vest—at last I'm able to send my uniform top to the cleaners! Before this time, I haven't been able to because I didn't have anything to wear in its place. Then I opened Butch's Christmas letter and admired the snapshots—only Butch can produce more unhappy expressions on his subject's faces—but John and Sue looked very nice and they were a nice addition to our Christmas celebration. Then we all went to a Christmas service at the local parish church—a lovely church, beautiful music and long enough to keep me going for at least 3 or 4 months. We were well escorted by miscellaneous G.I.'s and Jimmy took his wife. And after church, we served coffee and doughnuts until three o'clock. On Christmas day, we were up at nine and eating the hotel's piece de resistance for the year—grapefruit! The maid was almost hysterical with joy when she brought it in. We served, smiled until our faces cracked and had dinner in the Officer's mess— turkey, cranberry sauce, oranges, mince pie, cake—in other words—the works! And then we went to another camp, picking up 2 G.I.'s who played the guitar and who entertained the fellows all afternoon. It was a good Christmas, all in all, though all of us felt far from home, but you can't feel too lonely when you've been surrounded by your fellow countrymen and God knows we were surrounded.

On boxing Day [December 26, a traditional holiday in Great Britain], Frank and I went to a country club dance. The course looks pretty good (though a trifle sodden), dominated by wonderful hills and the glowering north country sky. As for the country club and inmates, they are very much like any small-town country club crowd in the USA—the successful butchers, bakers and candlestick makers of the town—all of whom are having smorgesborg while the Americans are about.

I received the gift from Dean Groton and the parish—also the pledge card. Mother, would you take $20 out of my bank account and make out a pledge card for me? I could send it from here, but I think it would be easier and safer if you did it. I'll let you know when the other pkgs. arrive. I'd certainly write to Time and tell them that I have received no copies since the subscription went into effect and that my APO is 413, not 887.

Love to you all,
Elizabeth

In her catch-up journal, Liz recorded events of the Christmas holiday, a heavy work day. The doughnut machine broke down, necessitating a move to the Red Cross kitchen in town and making sinkers by hand. "Some of them looked more like pretzels and dollar signs," Margee Main wrote home, "but we carried on." For the special holiday the crew wore their dress uniform. It was the first time most of the GIs had seen them in skirts, which caused considerable comment and wolf whistles. Margee explained that it "makes you realize that guys just aren't particular about what they whistle at."[16]

Diary, January 10, 1945
[Barrow-in-Furness]

We spent Christmas eve and Christmas day working—after first cooking our supply of doughnuts in the doughnut dugout's kitchen—by hand. Jimmy, our driver and an Americanized cockney, got drunk and fell asleep during Christmas eve mass, but otherwise everything went off normally. Before going out Christmas eve, we decorated a small wizened tree that ordinarily decorates a corner of the lounge, with torn shreds of

Kleenex. Then we opened what boxes had arrived from home. And the next morning, the hotel came through with genuine grapefruit for breakfast. It was quite an event. In honor of the day, we wore our dress uniforms rather than our doughnutty battle dress and as a result, I am still sniveling and sniffing.

Liz spent her New Year's weekend of leave fighting her ongoing cold, but she was well enough to enjoy social life with a variety of men in uniform.

In her reference to reading and enjoying *The Story of Philosophy*, Liz revealed something of her intellect and herself. Will Durant's book became a bestseller when published in 1926. It was the sort of publication sometimes labeled "middlebrow." With sparkling writing and an idealist framework, Durant made Aristotle, Plato, Kant, and other philosophers accessible to the intelligent general reader, the person who wanted to know for the sake of knowing the general outlines of philosophy.[17]

December 31, 1944
[Barrow-in-Furness]

Dear mother and daddy,

Believe it or not, this seems to be the last day of the year—a very bright day in this part of England—as if the sun was trying to make up in brilliance for its failure to appear the rest of the year. My cohorts have all gone to London; Margee to spend the New Year's at the Savoy, Aileen to meet her brother who has completed his missions and has a 7-day leave. And that leaves me holding down the Hotel Imperial, along with a lot of very staid natives, all of whom speak in a low undertone and stop talking completely as soon as I come in. I think they're discussing some delicate aspect of Anglo-American relations. I do not lack companionship, however, for I have my favorite cold and an assortment of G.I.'s to keep me company. Last night, myself and an ordinance Lieut. went to one of those squadron dances that sometimes assume a wearying sameness and tonight, a PFC and myself have been invited by our English Army friends to somebody's home. The English Army consists of Denis, a major, plus Jimmy, Eddie and Wacker—all lieutenants. I can only tell you their first names as they insist on being typically American and introducing themselves in the most informal manner. When I was in bed with my cold, they all came in one night with fish and chips and beer (fortunately, I had lost my sense of smell) and with Aileen and another G.I. and a passing chambermaid, they proceeded to have a minor party. Jimmy Stroud was sent to the States for four months, so he is the local authority on things American. We are not considered as authorities as "you Yanks always exaggerate."

Because I've spent so much time in bed, there's not much I can tell you, except that apparently, my cold is temporarily under control and my finger has assumed normal proportions. I am reading "The Story of Philosophy" and enjoying it very much, in fact I'm rather glad that I didn't attempt to go somewhere on my leave as I'm so comfortable here as I could hope to be in any spot in England. New Year's doesn't appear to be the big occasion for revelry as it is at home, one reason being that there isn't too much to revel with. The news [about the Battle of the Bulge] which is now coming over the air via BBC seems to be better, but still not good. We are all relieved that Norman, Aileen's brother, has completed his combat missions, but apparently, he won't be going home for a while.

This will arrive a little too late to wish you a Happy New Year, but you know that I'm thinking of you and hoping that 1945 will be the year.

Love to you all,
Elizabeth

Aileen Anderson continued to provide proper English citizens with glimpses of brash American culture. The weather grew even colder. News of the Battle of the Bulge was better, though Liz remained concerned about the men of the 82nd, including her special friend from Leicester days, Larry Pickard.

January 5, 1945
[Barrow-in-Furness]

Dear mother and daddy,

The mail situation still is something we don't discuss—I do hope that you haven't stopped writing or something, but the last word I had of you discussed Thanksgiving and that's quite a way back, but I guess that is part of the game. I'm writing this in the lounge during tea time—several dour looking Anglo-Saxons are making smacking noises over their tea and Aileen is embarrassing me by opening a Christmas package in front of the whole assemblage. She is also chewing gum. The other day she called the Colonel "Baby," so you see that she is in fine fettle.

We are enjoying the warmth of the common fire before going out on a night problem. Today was glorious—sun and all—but colder than Greenland. However, we are in no position to quibble about the sun— we take it as it comes. Norman Anderson, Aileen's brother, left this morning—could be that he will be home shortly, and for once, we were glad to say goodbye to him under these new circumstances. It was different when we knew that he had to go back to flying. Our English Army friends also departed, but not until after we had properly celebrated. In one of the Royal Armored Corps' lorries, we drove to a trés moderne inn called the Fisherman's Arms, had dinner and a few Irish whiskies. Our party was a motley crowd—the Major, the 3 Lieutenants, plus Norman and a PFC (American) and a T5 (also Amer.). Last night, we took them to an Ordinance dance given by the G.I.'s, including a royal Navy lieut. and his wife. They enjoyed it a lot and we even taught Jimmy a few basic jitterbug steps (Jimmy, the lieut., not Jimmy, our driver).

Otherwise, nothing stupendous has occurred. I suppose you've read about our old division, the 82nd. They were in a rest area and were sent in as ground troops and held one corner of the German salient. It seems hard that they were sent into combat so soon after being taken off the line in Holland. When I last heard from Larry, he was settling down for a nice rest, but things move much faster than the creaky mechanism of the army mailing system.

We all have colds—mine is practically my oldest possession. I gulped down quantities of G.I. cough syrup, but no sooner do I spend one day in our wind-filled Passion Wagon than I'm right back where I started.

This has been written with at least 10 interruptions. I might as well give up and try again sometime when I YAM ALONE. Keeping on writing and love to you all,

Elizabeth

Bad weather, bad cold, and bad mail service continued. But more packages arrived, including one containing the journal in which Liz began keeping her diary, writing the first catch-up entry on January 10, while sitting in the Imperial Hotel lounge. Red Cross officials at London headquarters had recognized Liz's administrative and writing skills and offered her a position at headquarters that included editing *The Sinker.* She turned down the promotion in order to remain "on the slinging end of the doughnut business"—and away from London's V-2 rockets.

Liz introduced Bernie Levine, who would become a good friend and her traveling partner to Edinburgh and who two weeks later she would describe as "a fine boy with a wonderful sense of humor and a good mind." Her friendship with Private Levine is evidence that Liz was not afflicted with "officeritis." Bernie was the guy she planned to see in Paris on July 25, 1945.

January 10th 1945
[Barrow-in-Furness]

Dear mother and daddy,

[. . .]Egad! It's cold! I was just able to taste food again, when low, another case of exaggerated snivels have descended on me. So I am being stoical and expect to have a case of arrested pneumonia until the first daisy, which I strongly suspect will not rear its golden head until middle August. The other day, London called me up and offered me a job as editor of the Clubmobile publicity sheet together with a supervisional job about the London area. I was not at all interested, first of all because I feel much more useful at the slinging end of the doughnut business and secondly (and this I didn't admit right away) because I have a most healthy respect for those things that explode in and about London. I'd probably be shaking so that I couldn't wield a very mean pen. (A Norwegian gentleman just came in. His name is Olaf Evard Johanneson of the Norwegian Navy. He asked me to whom I was writing and I said to my parents. "Give them my regards," he said. So I'm following instructions.)

Have I told you how pleased we are with our new girl, Margee Main? She fits in very nicely and does her share of the work, which is important. Our gay divorcee [Betty Goit] called us up the other day from her new base—a rest home, where I feel sure her manifold talents can be better used. We now have an admirable arrangement (not approved of by headquarters) wherein one of us stays in every third day—it gives us a chance to take things to the laundry and bask in the music of the BBC. Last night, Bernie and I saw "Dragon Seed" at the local cinema. This town had its own little blitz not too long ago and yet, the audience snickered over the bombing scenes and I found the whole picture most depressing.[18] Otherwise, we have a long weekend coming up and if I have to ski, I'm going to Edinborough (I'll probably have to ski). This last Sunday, myself and bicycle saw a rugger match, very colorful but pointless, I thought. The locals think our variety of football equally pointless.

It's good to hear about the Luzon landings [in the Philippines] after all the bleak news from this theatre. We do a lot of worrying about our boys, needless to say, but they know their stuff and will come out on top if anybody does. I do hope that tomorrow brings a big bundle of mail— by the way—your nice Christmas card came through. And thanks for the nice journal—I'll inaugurate it tomorrow.

Love,
Elizabeth

A wonderful trip with Bernie Levine to Edinburgh, "a great leave town," included dances, tourist sites, and men in kilts. They found accommodations at the Red Cross Club, but Liz made clear to her parents that Bernie stayed in the enlisted men's rooms while she slept in the women's officers' quarters.

Liz used military style to date this letter, one of numerous examples of military vocabulary and jargon that crept into her writing. She closed with an interesting list of toilet articles, necessitated in part by the challenges of bathing.

15 Jan., 1945
[Barrow-in-Furness]

Dear mother and daddy,

Your wondering daughter has just returned from her <u>very</u> short trip to Edinburgh and in spite of no sleep for 24 hours, I shall say, again and again, "WOW!" and again, "WOW!" The Scotch are wonderful people, and they have a beautiful city. We (myself and Bernie—a PFC) started out early one morning and went through wild and snow-covered mountains enroute. We finally ended up staying at the Red Cross Club—they have a grand club in Edinburgh, with accommodations for G.I.'s and Officers both male and female. It cost Bernie 2 shillings for his, 4 shillings for mine in the Officers' part. And we had dinner in a very swank restaurant off Prince's St. and afterwards, wandered from hotel to hotel—finally, to a big public dance hall, where the dancers look like the league of nations—kilted Scotsmen, G.I.'s, jitterbugging sailors of all nations, British Tommies, ATS girls, WRENS, American WACS, Army nurses, Canadians. Edinburgh is a great leave town— therefore, the conglomeration. We went back to the club at 10:30 when everything closes up in preparation for the dour Scottish Sabbath. They had a nice dance with pretty Scottish girls—much more attractive than the English equivalent. The next morning after a good Red Cross breakfast (1 and 6 including ORANGES), we walked up to the castle which dominates the city from its high craigs. The guards—Gordon Highlanders and Royal Scots Fusiliers entertained us in their antique guard room and we wandered about, gulping in a beautiful vista of the entire city. Fortunately, the day was sunny, although colder than a Frigidaire. I love men in Kilts—particularly the Stuart Tartan which is bright red, but they're all pretty glamorous as far as I'm concerned.

The only building open to the public was the Scottish War Memorial, built very recently, with tablets commemorating the various Scottish regiments—very impressive and dignified. Then we walked the Royal Mile to Holyrood Castle, too early to get inside, but it's a charming place and certainly more deserving of royalty than the heavy Hanoverian inspired equivalents in London. We finished up our day with tea and crumpets and another Red Cross meal, 2' 6" for the works. And after a walk in the twilight down George St. where the shops are, we finished up with a Red Cross dance and sadly took our train. After 5 changes, and the coming of dawn, we finally reached our home destination and I am quite exhausted. Therefore, the sloppy letter, but I'm too tired to even hold the pen firmly. And now, I have to go out to catch a truck to camp where my co-workers are grinding out our product. I'll write a better letter later when I recuperate.

Mother, I need some toilet articles which I can't get here—namely:
Dorothy Gray Deoderant (Dept. Store)
or Arrid (Dept. Store or Drugstore)
Eau de Cologne
(I think you can get a non alcoholic kind in Lenthiric—or solid cologne)
Handcream
TOILET PAPER
(and I ain't fooling)
Amolin (a powdered deodorant)
I hope you don't mind this—but it's the only way I can get them.

Love to you all,
Elizabeth

Mail brought a picture of her little brother, a V-Mail letter from her mother, and the long-awaited subscription copy of *Time*. The weekly newsmagazine was an important source of information, along with the radio. Margee Main wrote on January 17: "Last night we all sat around the fire having a big long talk about war and politics. I just have to devour my little copies of Time from cover to cover in order to sound half way intelligent."[19] Another dance gave Liz opportunity to note the attractions some local women had for the American officers.

January 20th '45
[Barrow-in-Furness]

Dear mother and daddy (and Butch)

In the first place, Butch, old boat, your picture has arrived and occupies a place of honor in my leather frame. It's very nice and natural and you are growing to be hideously handsome. By the way, who cut your hair? Bernardie? All joking aside, I am very proud of it. Secondly, "Time" arrived at long last and has been devoured—it was addressed to APO 413, so the mix-up must have been over that, although I don't see why. It was wonderful to get comparatively recent news—we get magazines for the Clubmobile, but by January, an August "Time" has lost its flavor. Thirdly, your Jan. 2nd V-mail arrived today, Mother, so I'm more or less up on news[. . . .]

It is now the next morning—Sunday and there's lots of snow and bright sun. Last night, Frank took me to an Artillery Officers' party, which by now have begun to assume a set pattern. This one was in an overgrown Victorian estate, surrounded by beautifully landscaped gardens which were at their best in the snow and moonlight. First, everybody jockies for position around the fires and then on with the dance, sandwiched in with a few mugs of bad beer. The local belles are always border-line cases (not quite professionals) and then home, Thank God, in a Weapon's Carrier. Today Bernie and I, Margee and Dick [Best] (Cpl.) and Aileen are going to hear the Hallé Orchestra conducted by John Barbarolli—I heard them in Leicester and it's a wonderful symphony orchestra and we're lucky to have them here in the back woods.

The weather is cold! Our Passion Wagon has no heat at all and yesterday, we cleaned it and almost froze ourselves in the process. It's rather like house cleaning in the barnyard. We have a huge kitchen all to ourselves. It's occupied by nine cats, six steam vats, 12 ovens and innumerable sinks—but there's hot water and every morning, Jimmy builds a fire in one of the many stoves and we take turns huddling about it. As you can see by empty kitchen, I don't think we'll be here much longer and how we hate to think of leaving! Our beds are so comfortable, the water (when it's working) so hot—and we've made a lot of good friends. We should be used to these partings but I guess we wouldn't be human if we were.

I'll write more in a day or so. Meanwhile, do the same—

Love to you all,
Elizabeth

Sunday evening Liz recorded in her new journal that she had attended the John Barbirolli concert, which included Antonin Dvorak's New World Symphony. Margee wrote that "when they played that part about 'Going Home' I guess every American in the audience had tears in his eyes."[20]

Diary, January 21st, 1945
[Barrow-in-Furness]

This afternoon, we heard John Barbirolli conduct the Hallé Orchestra, a great treat for Barrow and a greater treat for us. They played a Mendelsohn violin concert beautifully, plus the Eine Kleine Nachtmusik and Dvokacs (it's late, but that doesn't pardon my spelling) New World Symphony—all expertly done. The concert was in one of the local cinemas, which was naturally without heat and everybody listened with coats on. It took me until intermission to warm up. Then Bernie and Dick joined us in tea and we spent the evening playing bad bridge on Margee's footlocker and shooting the breeze.[21]

Saturday, we cleaned the clubmobile. We cleaned it as it's never been cleaned before and considering that we have no heat inside the bus and that the outside elements were most uncooperative with snow and a wicked breeze, we did a fairly complete job. Jimmy brought us lunch in our mess kits—we ate huddled about the one fire and then back to our scrubbing. In the evening, Frank, Aileen, Mr. Ho Hell (a warrant officer) and I went to the Artillery Party, held in the extremely chilly and Victorian house of a Mr. Ramsey who at one time not only was Mayor of Barrow, but made a pretty penny with Vickers-Armstrong. Mr. Ramsey, of course, was not around and the house was quite deserted, with all the good 19th century atrocities under sheets. We had the use of three rooms and as many fireplaces. Dancing, to the tune of an aggressive trumpet player and other instruments (identity submerged by trumpet's enthusiasm). The estate looked beautiful in the moonlight, its carefully landscaped lawns and gardens under snow. Hollywood couldn't have done better.

Liz's next diary entry reported on the departure from the Barrow area of newly made friends, a now familiar routine. This entry showed her efforts to follow the military course of the war as the Battle of the Bulge finally came to conclusion (with over 80,000 American casualties) and the concern about those they knew in the fighting, from the 82nd to Frank's brother with the 75th.

Diary, January 26, 1945
[Barrow-in-Furness]

Once again, we're ready to move—the Signal Corps leaves tonight and Margee and Aileen are out at camp cooking. There's a soft mushy fog outside and it's bitterly cold. Yesterday, the Clubmobile refused to budge and we took a Weapon's Carrier over to Dane Gyll—my feet lost all feeling and my hands were like over-cured hams. As usual, we hate to see them go, especially Bernie, Dick Best, Bill Karos—but this time, we have the satisfaction of knowing that they won't be going into combat. Bernie and I toasted bread over my heater and drank pineapple juice—he's a fine boy with a wonderful sense of humor and a good mind. Last night since they were restricted and it was the Ordinance's last night out, Frank took me to the Victoria Park Hotel's Allied Officer's Dance. He also took a bottle of Johnny Walker and managed to get quite numb. The music, furnished by the Royal Artillery dance band, was good and we had a wonderful time. Capt. Robert's WAAF got very sick and had to be taken home—otherwise no casualties.

Yesterday, we rode up to chow in a fur-line jeep. The A.P.O. officer from Blackpool belonged to it and not only did it have doors, but it was carefully covered with fleece and most luxurious. Everybody is a little bit encouraged by the Russian offensive—today they are almost in Breslav. But on our front, progress is very slow. The 82nd was taken up the line in trucks in middle December during the German breakthrough. Frank's brother with the 75th infantry division, said that the confusion was horrible. He was wounded by shrapnel on the 26th and is almost the only survivor of his company. He's now in England and hopes to go home. All the outfits in the Ardennes Sector were pretty badly cut up.

In spite of the cold which penetrates like a drill, the countryside is beautiful in the snow. These bare hills always looked neat with their hedges dividing and subdividing them so carefully—now the pattern is emphasized and the contrast of hills and sky is like a Bruegel landscape. The children have funny home-made sleds and do a lot of coasting. We wear paper in our boots and blow our noses constantly.

The cold weather continued, but the compensation was a weekend trip with Margee and Aileen to the Lake District, just to the north of Barrow and one of the loveliest spots on earth.

Sunday evening late
January 28, 1945
[Barrow-in-Furness]

Dear mother and daddy,

Your very chilly daughter is sitting in front of her little electric heater (15 shillings per week) and shivering. It is cold. And I am tired of hearing people say, "This is the worst summer we've had." And "This is an unusually wet fall." And now "This is a most unusual winter." Well, it is unusual and I'm still working on that ice-age theory. But I can't really put my heart into it, on account of my teeth chattering so. The only alternative is going to bed—and that bed is too @!#~$+* frigid!

Our hostelry's hot water system—always temperamental—sighed and gave up the ghost on Wednesday, so as soon as decently possible, we packed our musette bags and took off for the lake district. Our pilgrimage was by bus and we were clad in our Clubmobile clown suits and the buses (plural, we changed at least 3 times) were (of course) unheated. But we climbed upward through the most beautifully breathtaking country I have seen since hitting the island. It has snowed quite consistently and everything was white—the trees outlined in white and the shiny green holly sparkling through the hedges for contrast. The sun was out, the sky blue and the scenery too beautiful for words. We finally landed at Keswick where we got good rooms and eureka! Hot Water! Keswick, you know, is where the poet Southey lived in the shadow of Skiddaw and by Derwentwater. Our room, by the way, was once occupied by no less a personage than Edward VII. It said so on the door. I hope for the sake of the royal goose pimples that he occupied it during the Wednesday they call the English Summer. We were the only Americans in a sea of Englishmen and the food and service were almost up to pre-war standard. Keswick is a charming town, built rather on White Horse Inn standards. We felt as if we should have alpin sticks and shaving brushes in our hats. The habitants went out for plus fours and knotted canes in a big way. In the light from a full moon, Margee and I walked down along Derwentwater to Friar's Craig—the moon lit up the mountains and the reaches of the lake. It was a wonderful sight. The next day, Aileen went off to church and we escorted her to the door, but got entangled in the Churchyard (one gravestone to Robert Richardson and Elizabeth and John, his children) and then walked for about 3 hours. Skiddaw was crowned with clouds and people were skating on Derwentwater. We left most reluctantly and it was a perfect weekend. Why, we even had a REAL egg for breakfast!

I certainly can see why the lake poets were so prolific. The whole region would be perfect for the literary life. And colors! I do hope that I'll be able to spend a longer time there with my bicycle. Can't do that now as I don't believe they make tire chains for bikes.

Otherwise—we are still where we were, but I don't think we'll be lingering much longer. By the way, only two packages have arrived so far: the one with the socks and red shirt and the Journal. But I did get a nice Christmas card from you, Mother. Thanks a lot. Also, a nice newsy letter from Aunt Gertrude. Also a book from Aunt Lily. Also Bob Hope's "I Never Left Home" from Miss Julia.[22]

My teeth have stopped chattering for a moment. Guess I'll take advantage of the lull and retire to icebox haven (alias my bed).

Eskimo kisses to you all,
Elizabeth

[p.s.] There's a big gap in mail. None for 3 weeks and then a V-mail. Ugh.

The last days in Barrow were not pleasant, as Liz noted in her diary.

Diary, February 1, 1945
[Barrow-in-Furness]
We were supposed to leave for Warrington, near Liverpool, this morning. Aileen went off most reluctantly on her leave and Margee and I had footlockers locked and duffle bags packed—then Jimmy's landlady arrived with the news that he was flat with an overdose of nut-brown ale. We finished our last run yesterday in a pouring rain—Greystone and Dane Gyll where there are still a few medics and Ulverston. Warrington, our new base is not exactly my idea of perfection. But maybe we'll be able to get baths—our last one was Sunday afternoon in Keswick. It is now Thursday.

[6]

From the Gray Midlands
to Sunny Cornwall

The *Kansas City* crew left Barrow-in-Furness on February 2 bound for
Warrington, a smoky, industrial town on the Mersey River. They had
stopped at Warrington on their move to Barrow in late November, when
Liz had found so depressing the rehabilitation center full of men with
combat fatigue. She recorded in her diary the uncertain prospects of the
new location.

Diary, Feb. 2, 1945
Warrington, Lancs.
    Warrington, from our doubtful point of vantage, is a sprawly city of
dowdy English suburban homes, punctuated by many tall factory
chimneys belching smoke. We are about 20 minutes bus ride from
Liverpool and not much further from Manchester, two cities of dubious
charm—and I am writing this from the parlor of Mrs. Whittle, 405
Manchester Road. The parlor is decorated by three overstuffed chairs of
flamboyant design, a rug designed to make one dizzy, a picture of two
English settlers and another of a lady of the flaming 20's, and one
anemic coal fire. We occupy one room—all three of us. The third one is
Sunny Hagenbeck of Cleveland, Ohio who is taking Aileen's place
during her leave. She also will initiate us into the mysteries of our
routes, which so far include an Infantry Rehabilitation Camp ("We's
recuperatin'" a negro boy explained to Margee this afternoon as we

unpacked our stores), an Air Force Replacement Center, a hospital, and others of a more or less transient nature.

We left Barrow this morning in a light drizzle. The outskirts of the mountains were beautiful through the rain and the whole countryside looked sodden. We stopped in Preston for a wretched meal at the British Restaurant[1] and then at the Rehabilitation camp to dump our stores. It seems that we are to eat across the road in the Air Force Replacement Center's mess, which is quite all right with us. The mess hall is big and jarringly cheery—murals of luscious females and red tables. Evidently, the men don't do anything but sit around waiting for orders—either sending them home or to an operating base in England. Viva Warrington!

The new billet in Warrington was the least comfortable of the accommodations Liz had in England. The three women shared one room with lumpy beds. And Mrs. Whittle, the landlady, Margee Main agreed, was "truly a spook." The only compensation was hot water for baths.

The work in Warrington was hard because of the quantity of men to serve and because of the emotional demands. The largest numbers were at the air base at Burtonwood, but harder were the war casualties at Haydock. Liz had seen the effects of combat on the veterans of the 82nd Airborne in Leicestershire, but some of the men they worked with at Warrington were so severely affected by combat that they had been pulled from their units for rehabilitation. Margee Main wrote that "It is so pitiful. . . . The whole spirit of the place is so nervous and tense—they argue and fight over anything— but even worse are the dear little kids who just sit and gaze off into space."[2]

No wonder that Liz began to think about her upcoming leave and a possible trip to Cornwall, a place very popular with tired Red Cross women eager to get far away from war.[3]

February 3rd, 1945
[Warrington]

Dear mother and daddy,

We are settled once again this time in one of those horrid English houses that appear only in rows. I can't even say anything nice about the countryside, because it consists of miles and miles of similar rows, relieved by black sooty masses of brick which I presume to be British Industry. All three of us share one room and we have the use of a stark little parlor which represents everything in the way of English bad taste, including stained glass windows, green, blue and red electric plush overstuffed chairs and a fringed chandelier. Our landlady (I secretly think she's batty) charges us 11 shillings a day for this misery—we eat our meals at any Army Mess, Thank God. In fact, the whole atmosphere of the place is not exactly pleasant. By the way, we each pay 11 shillings and why we can't have a similar house of our own, I don't know—we'd own it outright at the end of six months. However, our work should be interesting.

We have an Infantry Rehabilitation camp which depresses me enough under ordinary circumstances, a hospital (which depresses me even more)[4] and bases of like nature—also a replacement center (where we eat) which appears to be in a happier frame of mind. All the men have been over too long, are too fed-up, are too weary, are too worldly wise and we see the patches of almost all the divisions that have been and are now active in France. Yesterday, a little negro helped me unload our stores—"We's recuperatin', M'am" he told us, which I think we'll be doing when we're through here.

I go on leave next week. So far, I think it will be Cornwall, although I'd like to see parts of the Devon Coast. Perhaps I'll be able to stop and see Mrs. Young's relatives when I'm in London (at which place I have no intention of staying longer than absolutely necessary). Well, I know that [Barrow-in-Furness][5] was too good to last, but we did have a wonderful time. This will not be too bad when we're here for a while, I know. The weather is milder at least, but we almost froze en route. Jimmy brought along a thermos jug filled with tea, which we swigged at intervals.

And now, I must bicycle over to chow—5 o'clock on the head. My love to all of you—

Elizabeth

Life in Warrington improved slightly, as Liz contemplated leave. She still thought of Larry Pickard, the guy she said goodbye to in Leicester.

In a brief comment on the "negro outfits" at Warrington, Liz raised the subject of race, one she noted only occasionally in her diary or letters home. America's Jim Crow patterns of discrimination crossed the Atlantic in the form of segregated, all-black military and nursing units. The presence of African Americans on British soil was a special challenge because the British were so unfamiliar with or unsympathetic to American racial prejudices that English women were quite happy to date black GIs. To many white soldiers such a sight was an abomination and often led to outbursts of violence as well as objections from home. In 1943, after some U.S. publications ran photographs of English women dancing with black GIs, the War Department ordered censors to prohibit distribution of such disturbing images. Liz must have known a good bit about these tangled racial matters, including something of the serious racial violence between her much loved 82nd Airborne and an all-black transport unit in Leicester in early 1944, prior to her arrival there. In the months before her arrival in Warrington the military assigned an all-black nursing unit at the 168th Station Hospital to treat German prisoners of war. Both POWs and the black nurses moved elsewhere just before the *Kansas City* arrived.[6]

There were large concentrations of African American GIs at Warrington but no Clubmobile to serve them. Whether the *Kansas City* ever served African Americans is unknown. The American Red Cross felt obliged to follow the military's policy of segregation and claimed, as one administrator reported in September 1944, that "generally white and negro military personnel preferred to be served by their own race." The organization declared on February 11, 1944, that all its Clubmobiles were open "irrespective of race, colour or religion." That spring at least one Clubmobile, the *Houston*, staffed by three white women, served black GIs. The Red Cross also printed one of its promotional post cards showing a Clubmobile serving blacks, but the Clubmobile woman has her back to the camera so that her race is not clear. Black soldiers continued to report that they were usually discouraged and often turned away from white facilities.[7]

There were separate Red Cross clubs and Clubmobiles staffed by black personnel and located near concentrations of black troops, but the shortage of black crews and facilities was severe. At the end of 1944 there was only one "Negro-staffed" Clubmobile in Great Britain. Such shortages meant that here, as in so many other aspects of the war, black soldiers received the short end of the stick.[8]

Black leaders challenged segregation and caused considerable difficulty for the American Red Cross. Walter White, head of the National Association for the Advancement of Colored People, complained in late 1942 that the organization's practice of segregated facilities in Great Britain "more accurately fits a Hitlerian than a democratic way of life." Black Red Cross workers complained too, with some support from their white colleagues. Meetings of African American personnel in Manchester and Bristol in November 1943 burst with anger and threats of resignation and attracted the attention of the black press back home. Attracting even more attention at home was the Red Cross policy, again following military requests, to keep blood from black donors separate from blood given by whites. Not surprisingly, the Red Cross had great difficulty recruiting talented African Americans to overseas work.[9]

February 11, 1945
[Warrington]

Dear mother and daddy,

The above date is no doubt incorrect, but it's somewhere around there. Today brought two letters from you—one dated January 13th and the other January 21st from Chicago, the first I've heard for a couple of weeks. In fact, almost the first mail I've had. But my co-workers are suffering from the same lack, so we blame it on the chronic mail situation.

It's good to hear that Johnny and Sue are at last announcing their engagement, but in Washington? Where? In the Pentagon or on the White House Lawn? Or in the Potomac basin? I'm sure Washington Society will be agog. I haven't heard from the future groom since early December, but I gather that his military career is taking up most of his time.

Leave on my leave tomorrow and, needless to say, although I am not anticipating a wild, hilarious time, I am looking forward to it with growing joy. As Margee says, a Clubmobile in this spot is like running a hash house in Pittsburg. First, Margee and I are going to Chester, then I am going on to London, Bristol and finally Torquay. I'd like to get into Cornwall, but time and the admirable English Railways prohibit that.

We are eating well, though.[10] Not only do we consume piles of fresh fruits, but being fed by the Air Corps, we gulp down sulpha pills, plus most well balanced menus. Not a trace of my cold remains, Mother, so don't worry about that. As for the sniffles, well, everybody's doing it tra-la-tra-la. Our billet is still what it was, but we finally broke open one of the carefully sealed bedroom windows, so that at least we have fresh air. Fresh air is evidently taboo in this kind of English household.

You'd be interested to know that our new bases include several very black negro outfits. I don't feel one way or another about them, but I'm glad that we don't have the granddaughter of an old Confederate veteran with us. Aileen, as it is, is most unhappy. I'm practicing up on my southern drawl—think I'll have Jimmy call me ole Massa. Our hospital is a rather pleasant interlude—mostly ambulatory patients, and our pschopathics aren't too bad. I've been listening to one of them all evening and, as a consequence, feel as if I were a veteran of 100 horrible incidents from Holland to Luxemburg (Got a little bit ahead of even Ike Eisenhauser for a minute). Our home base has everything from movies every night, permanent party club with beer to very smooth bicycle racks with roofs. What more could you want?

Had a nice letter from Ernst [Kuenstner]—he was most pleased with his Christmas gift and is now somewhere above Florence. Have some round-about news about Larry [Pickard]. One of the fellows in a hospital Aileen visited said he was o.k. when he left the line. That was about 3 weeks ago, though. The Division is still in the line.

"Time" is coming through very nicely at last—but no packages from Dragoon Trail or from the Farmer's Club.

Margee and I kneel every night on either side of our horrible lumpy bed and silently pray that hdq. will see fit to send the "Kansas City" to a newer and greener base—Land's End, John O'Groats, but please, great White Mother, don't keep us too long here!

Love to you all,
Elizabeth

P. S. I have odd looking bites. Could it be our new billet? NEVER!

Liz finally got leave, resulting in a trip via Chester and Wales to London, where Red Cross facilities provided excellent recuperation. She had time to get her hair done and to see a film. The danger of "the newest variety of Krautism," the V-2 rockets, was less terrifying than the V-1s had been during her London days seven months earlier. As the *New Yorker's* Mollie Panter-Downes wrote about the V-2s, "they arrive so abruptly you don't have time to get scared—you're either dead or simply startled."[11]

February 14, 1945
[London]

Dear mother and daddy,

This is being written from smokey, foggy London town on a nice misty night—it's a different London than the one I saw last July—the lights are partially on and the old lady looks as if she'd taken some vitamin pills. I must say I don't miss the sirens and I sleep so soundly that I don't hear the newest variety of Krautism, so my outlook is untarnished. Why am I in London? I'm on leave—so there. And I need a permanent and I got it. As a result, my head is a mass of curls and British curls at that. Having accomplished my one objective, I'm leaving tomorrow for Cornwall which I've been planning to visit for these many months. [...]

I'm staying at the Red Cross Club for Red Cross people— wonderful beds, good food and better service than can be found in most hotels—plenty of hot water and RADIATORS WITH HEAT IN THEM. There's one thing I must say about Wales. It's cold and nobody seems to do anything about it. The chief inmates are girls who are waiting to go back to the States for their 30 day leaves (you get this after 28 months and then only if you've been under combat conditions.) After listening to them, I feel that my small experiences are tame indeed[. ...]

Not wanting to go sightseeing in the wet, I went to a movie this afternoon. It was "Since You Went Away" and don't see it. Hollywood gave it the works and misery oozed out of it. God knows there's enough in the world without paying 3 and 6 to see more.[12]

Well, family, old cheeses, I wish you were here so that we could do this town together—

Love to you all,
Elizabeth

In Cornwall Liz opened her diary, the day after writing her parents, though misdating either the letter or diary entry. She looked back on her trip to Wales, her short visit in London, and a stop to catch up with her good friend from Leicester days, Margaret Morrison. She was now in St. Ives, on the Atlantic coast in the far southwest of England, and staying in the Porthminster Hotel, which was populated by Londoners who had left the city during the blitz of 1940. Her opening paragraph described the seaside town, which she also captured in a charming watercolor.

Diary, Feb. 14, 1945
St. Ives, Cornwall

It smells like spring in Cornwall. Outside, I can hear the roll of surf and if it weren't for the blackout and an uncooperative moon, I could see it. This is a beautiful spot, but like some toy village on careful tiers, beginning with the reflected and brilliant surface of the sea, decorated by infinitely tiny boats, then the toy railway, miniature houses in grey stone, more substantial houses in white, all outlined by green hedges and trees that bend cheerfully in the wind. I am staying at a comfortable but tomb-like hotel, decorated by numerous living corpses, but my room looks out over the half moon bay and the corpses don't really count.

My leave began officially when Margee and I took the train for Chester. We meant to spend an educational day (this was last Friday) looking at Cathedral, Roman walls et al. Instead, we found ourselves in Wales. Friday night as we counted sheep in a horrid little Chester hotel, we were aroused by insistent knockings on our door. The Knockeés, obviously G.I., finally gave up, but we met officially at breakfast when they persuaded us to forsake the joys of Chester for those of Wales. They had a command car, an English driver (female) and a Captain— all of Air Transport Command, headed for Valley, Wales. We drove to Llandudno, on the Irish sea through story book country. Llandudno itself proved to be a sort of Junior Atlantic City enclosed by eroded sandstone cliffs. We had lunch, visited a shooting gallery, ate tea, drank, had dinner and Lou, the British driver and myself attended some Hollywood attempt starring Jean Arthur and a baby. Margee and I enjoyed a good bed and in the early morning hours, she left, bound for Warrington and work.[13] I stayed until noon, shivering under the

Northwest Hotel's hospitable roof. (They were out of coal). The solution was obvious—and myself, a G.I. and 2 RAFers found it in the bar. By 5 I was in Chester, eating buns in the Red Cross with another G.I. named Sparky and by 10:30 I was in London enjoying a bath at 103 Park St. London looked revived—there were lights and no sirens, although I was sure that at any moment a V2 would streak down on me. Somebody said that there were two during the night, but if there were, I didn't hear them.

Monday morning, thanks to the Staff Room at 12, Grosvenor Sq., I had a permanent at Charles', in the P.M. I raided the London Officers' PX and did the usual London errands. And Tuesday after a good meal at the Consolidated Officers' Mess, I took off for Bristol. It drizzled in London all during my stay, but by the time I reached Bristol, the sun was out and the countryside looked glorious. Bristol still looked horribly scared from the '40 blitz (but nothing compared to Plymouth today where whole streets are gone), but I liked the neo-classical houses and the taste of the sea. Margaret [Morrison] and her crew are billeted in a school of some sort near the Avon—they occupy the entire top floor of what once must have been a mansion. We had a good evening and this morning, Margaret saw me off for Cornwall—a wearisome trip involving at least three changes and all my patience. But St. Ives is worth it. These people, who look like stuffed dolls, who eat (at the same tables, decorated by their own personal jams, sauces, and patent medicines), read (in the same chair that they've sat in since they moved out of London back in 1940) and take constitutionals (in tweedy plus fours for the males, mousy fur pieces for the females) I have discovered inhabit all out of the way and liveable resorts and I have to restrain myself from screaming "Viva Tolstoy," or "Up, Dublin!" when I see them. On the other hand, perhaps I should. It would give them something to think about. The St. Ives variety don't even listen to the 9 o'clock news. At least the ones in Keswick did that!

Back in Warrington, Liz reported on her wonderful trip to Cornwall and her forthcoming move. To get by the military censor, she slyly hinted to her family that she was soon off to France by referring to her French teacher and to Mother Sill's seasick pills.[14]

From the Gray Midlands to Sunny Cornwall

February 18, 1945
[Warrington]

Dear mother and daddy,

The fruit cake and cookies arrived while I was on leave—thank you so much but what a time they picked to arrive! In fact, right now I wish I'd paid more attention in Miss Rosenberger's class. Needless to say, I'm terrifically excited and a little bit scared, but we have been expecting it for the last few months and there's really no danger involved that Mother Sill's can't remedy.

My leave was all that a leave should be[. . . .] The weather was mild and I even went wading during low tide. In fact, there was a palm tree in front of my window—that, the screams of the seagulls and the roar of the sea made me completely happy. I won't talk about my return journey via my favorite means of transport, the British railways. But I have learned to take advantage of those numerous delays at every other station. You pile nervously out of your compartment and rush for the tea canteen where you grab a pile of dubious looking sandwiches and buns and, of course, the tea. This you gulp still nervously, with many glances at the waiting Iron Horse, which of course, emits much steam, not counting the Station Master who blows his whistle obviously to confuse you. Then you sprint back to your compartment, preferably just as the train moves out, warmed spiritually and physically.

Don't worry if there's a slight gap in letters—I'll write as soon as possible. Anyway, this battered little isle will always have a warm spot in my heart.

By the way, FLASH! Chris [Hanson] has resigned from the Red Cross (an impossibility in our theatre) and is returning to the States to get married—to a Navy Flight, I mean Flyer named Edward Watson. What do you think of *that*? [. . .]

Love to you all,
Elizabeth

With very short notice Liz moved from Warrington to London in preparation for her new assignment in France. Among the details she recorded in her diary was selling the bicycle she had taken with her through England and a fond backward look at the seven months there. The *Kansas City* acquired new crew members. After the old Green Line bus finished its war service it returned to carrying fare-paying London passengers until sold and scrapped in 1958.[15]

Diary, Feb. 21, 1945
London

I returned from St. Ives Saturday night after a wonderful three days, climaxed by an unending train journey back to Warrington. And when I walked in the door, Sunny [Hagenbeck] greeted me with the news that Aileen and I were to report in London Monday. We're going to France—so Aileen and I packed up Sunday night after our last days work at the Recovery Center at Haydock and Monday morning, Jimmy and George (a slightly combat-happy veteran of the 9th Division) took us, our two footlockers, four barracks bags, 2 suitcases, a bicycle and a radio down to the LMS [train station]. At Euston [London] the Q's for cabs were so unending that we finally wangled a truck from the RTO [Railway Transportation Officer] and arrived at York St. in style.

Yesterday, we spent going through the same vague motions that we went through last July in Washington. We are loaded with equipment— sleeping bags, dowdy looking battle dress, G.I. rain coats, blankets, bedding roll ad infinitum. There are about 30 of us, including Margaret, Lindsay Rand, Mary Read and a lot that came over on "The Elizabeth" in July. It seems strange to be sitting in London this fine day when I should be cleaning up the doughnut machine preparatory to an afternoon's doughnut slinging. I've done as much as I can do—P.X., Quartermaster and all the rest. One of the porters sold my bicycle for £6—it's been many a good mile and I hate to see it go. But I'm sure a bicycle plus my faulty French would be too much of a handicap. Now that the time is near for leaving England, I've forgotten the many little inconveniences and remember only the softly rolling hills, the strangling hedges, the days when the sun did shine. St. Ives was a good way to terminate my seven months stay (although I didn't know it at the time)[....]

Now, Aileen and I are on the second floor of 103 A Park St.—a room which we share with 4 others, piles of equipment, barracks bags and general confusion.

A quick letter home reported on the move to London and preparations for the next stage. Liz and Margaret scheduled a portrait sitting. During these days Liz also made several watercolors of London street scenes. One showed the bustle and the variety of people walking past a Red Cross Club, including a young boy likely asking a GI for gum.

February 22, 1945
[London]

Dear mother and daddy,

This is London calling, as Ed Morrow used to say in 1940.[16] I'm sitting on my bed—one of six in the room—along with as many foot-lockers, bedding rolls and accumulated junk such as only females can collect. London, as if to leave a good impression, has been basking in a warm sun, a blue sky and better still, quiet nights. And in this magic city, we have been running about like agitated chickens. It's been a grand reunion—some of the people who came over with us in July (Naturally, all R's), plus Margaret, our old Captain. And I'm now a Captain First Class, with a raise which I'll get here.[17] However, I'm going to start sending money orders home—and the first one is for you, Mother and Daddy. I hope you'll go to Chicago, take Uncle J & Aunt G. out and see a good play, on your dear daughter who thinks a lot about you both and misses you, too. I'm lousy rich, having sold my bicycle (sob)—felt as if I were parting from a near and dear friend.

Margaret and I are having our portraits drawn tomorrow at Selfridge's, so keep an eye peeled for the resulting masterpiece.

To tell the truth, there's nothing much I can tell you (don't believe it for a moment). Somebody's leaving for the APO, so I'll have to terminate this quickly with my love. Daddy, the vitamins arrived today—awfully nice of you. I'll need them more than ever now.

Your
Elizabeth

[p.s.] Seeing the International Ballet tonight—tomorrow "Laura," a play.

Liz painted this watercolor of a bustling London sidewalk in February 1945. Civilian and military personnel, including Yanks, pass in front of an American Red Cross Club. At the right, a boy calls to a GI, likely the ubiquitous question "any gum, chum?" *Courtesy Charles Richardson, Jr.*

This "rotten letter" to Milwaukee friend Winifred Wood summarized recent adventures, Liz's reluctance to leave England, and eagerness to get to France.

Feb. 23, 1945
London

Dear W.W.,

Today's mail not only waddled in with Mr. Caesar's Christmas money order for $15, but also your Christmas card and ditto V-mail. The mails, as you perhaps have gathered, STINK. And they are about to stink more. (Ungrammatical, but true.) Needless to say, I'm still goggle-eyed about Clarey's marriage. She did write me a casual little note that she was about to resign from the R.C. and wed and so I was forewarned by a few days for your later bulletin. Alas, in the E.T.O., resignation and marriage are not so easy. If you do get married, it's over

On February 22, 1945, just before leaving London for France, Liz wrote home: "Margaret [Morrison] and I are having our portraits drawn tomorrow at Selfridge's, so keep an eye peeled for the resulting masterpiece." The result, she wrote the next day, was "terrifically flattering." The artist softened her face, emphasized her curly hair and blue eyes, and clearly showed her Clubmobile Captain status. *Courtesy Charles Richardson, Jr.*

here and you work as a volunteer (hard on bank account) or else, zip! You're yanked out of the theatre and sent to another (probably where they have cobras and stuff). I know if Chris married the lad, he must be absolutely tops, and he'd have to be tops for Clarey. My only regret is that I was not on hand to scatter flowers during the ceremony.

We had been transferred—a horrible place with rows of chimneys and grimy little windows. Then I had a leave and a wonderful one it was—Chester, Llandudno in Wales and then London and St. Ives in Cornwall, the virtues of which I have neither the space nor the time to extoll. Anyway, it is on the North Cornish coast with a doll-like bay and white stone houses climbing up the side of the hills. When I returned, I was ordered back to London with all my junk (including bicycle and radio). And here I am, surrounded by foot-lockers, sleeping bags, bedrolls, steel helmets, etc., etc., preparing for the journey ahead. You can imagine that I am both eager to go and reluctant to leave. I've grown attached to this sunny island, the haphazard provincial villages, the neat hedges, the lousy food. But we're more needed elsewhere, and I imagine we'll look back on our days in England as an idyllic prelude.

Naturally we're making the most of London. Saw the International Ballet last night—very colorful with Schumann's "Carnival" and a ballet version of "Twelfth Night" which was charming. Today, a friend of my family's took me to lunch at the Cafe Royalle and tonight we see "Laura"—a current play. This is a rotten letter but I promise to come through with a better one when things are more settled and I don't have to write sitting on top of a barracks bag with my feet on a gas mask.

[7]

Across the Channel and into France

Slinging coffee and doughnuts continued to dominate Elizabeth Richardson's life in the spring and early summer of 1945, but France offered a different experience from England. While her housing and food were generally better than they had been in England, the job in other ways proved harder. Often she worked nights in cold and rain, serving coffee and doughnuts to thousands of men, so that there were fewer opportunities to get to know individuals as closely as in Leicestershire or Barrow-in-Furness. Liz could usually joke about the challenges, as on June 12, when she wrote to a close friend: "I'm turning into a doughnut and if I see less than 15,000 men at a time, I feel lonesome." Her letters and diary show more discontent and restlessness among people around her as the war wound down and especially after the Nazis surrendered in early May.

The war itself remained the central context of her life, never far away even as the Allies moved into Germany. By spring 1945, everyone was desperately eager for it to end, yet the Germans kept fighting. There had been too much brutality and death, too much time so far from home and loved ones, too much cold and mud, too much waiting, too few hot baths, too few cold beers.[1] Even after German surrender on May 8 the work continued and, indeed, intensified. Sometimes the burdens got to Liz, especially as the prospect of going home seemed so distant even after V-E Day. "The weeks . . . ," she wrote in her diary on July 3, "have a sameness that gives time a certain dateless quality."

Active social life continued, with dances, dinners, parties, trips to the beach and to Paris and Reims. Most important, Liz began a romance with Lt. Frank Policastro, who quickly became the most serious boyfriend she'd ever had. There was fun, too, in the house she lived in with a dozen or so other Red Cross women. Turnover among these housemates was rapid, but Margaret Morrison from Leicester days was there most of the time and Liz always made new friends quickly.

Liz departed England early Sunday, February 25, 1945. She and a motley group of passengers crossed the English Channel to the port of Dieppe in Normandy and then traveled by train to Paris. That same evening she made a long diary entry and wrote a short letter home. Both compared France with England. She continued observing people and places, often with the wonder and delight of John Keats on reading Homer and sometimes with the cold impatience of a hardened combat veteran.

Diary, February 25, 1945
Paris

The "all clear" has just sounded. Outside, Paris is bathed in moonlight, but my judgment of the city is not very clear as what little I've seen has been from the back of a 2 1/2 ton truck. We are staying at the Ex-hotel Normandy, now a Red Cross Club for women officers which after England is sheer luxury. The only thing that spoils the general effect is the siren, which disturbed us, trained as we are by London where an alert is usually followed by a too audible bang.

Our week in London (from Monday night until last night) consisted mostly of several visits to [Red Cross] headquarters, several journeys to the Quartermaster's and P.X. and fevered packing and sorting. Our footlockers remained behind and we set out with one barrack bag and one musette bag—also a bed roll and sleeping bag. We saw the International Ballet, part of the 1st act of "Laura," and Hollywood versions of "Arsenic and Old Lace" and "None But the Lonely Heart"—the latter an excellently done film on cockney life.[2] About Thursday, lists were posted and people started to leave—my name, owing to a slip up some where along the line, never did appear—

so I'm here as Nancy Richardson. Saturday night, we were driven to Victoria [Station] and left in a bewildered little group at the boat train gate. By eleven, we were in New Haven, as far as we were concerned a long shed dimly lit, British officers going over our AGO cards (rather carelessly as I got by as Nancy) and a pint-sized boat beside the quay. We straggled up the gang plank and were assigned berths in a sort of steerage. And the next morning we moved out into the [English] channel past the sad little fortifications of 1940. The boat pitched around considerably—although I wasn't really sick, I was awfully sleepy and after gazing at the fading white cliffs and the closer white foam, I retired to our hold where I slept until 12:30 when we arrived in Dieppe. Our fellow passengers, besides the Red Cross, were three correspondents plus a female correspondent (this war will be well reported), two disgruntled looking WACs, four G.I.s in steel helmets (one with a dog) about five or six British army, as many navy and half a dozen miscellaneous Frenchmen, all ages and all talking very rapidly.

Dieppe was a theatrical little town—rather like a stage setting, the buildings pockmarked with bullet holes. From the boat (named "The Isle of Guernsey") we boarded the train for Paris. We all were much impressed with the cleanliness of the carriages after those of England and we were further impressed when we invaded the dining car, ate a fairly good meal along with vin ordinaire and good cognac. You could even see out of the windows and that was an impossibility on the LMS. We sat in Dieppe until 3:30, goggling at the usual children, the few adults and especially two little girls with bare bottoms who played oblivious of exposure. The train took us up past Beauvais, through calm rural countryside strangely reminiscent of home. The destruction of the towns was different than that of England, the difference between bombing—and artillery plus house to house fighting. We passed shattered freight cars, the steel twisted and rusted with the stenciled letters "Deutch" on the side. Otherwise, it could have been any countryside.

My French is impossible. I've tried it tentatively on the lady downstairs in the coffee bar. But it really wasn't fair at she speaks excellent English. We are all dead tired, but we know our trip was luxury. The Boat-train has only been running about a week.

A V-Mail to her parents announced her arrival in Paris and her expectation of being sent close to the front.

25 Feb., 1945
[Paris] France

Dear mother and dad—

This is Paris and a very comfortable Paris it is, after a good trip from London and a comparatively calm crossing. All very civilized. Needless to say, we weren't disappointed. Haven't the slightest idea where I'll be sent but I know it will be eastward. Don't worry though. Nobody could find a shelter quicker than I in London and no doubt it will be the same way with foxholes. We're staying in a hotel taken over by the Red Cross—no doubt you know it well. As for the city, I haven't seen anything of it as yet and I'm hoping we'll have a few days before the business at hand begins—so I'll have time for some sightseeing. The French look well fed and well clothed and the city is clean—even the windows of our train were clean and that would never happen in England. The destruction here is different—a little more pulverized and the scars haven't had time to heal. I'll write at more length when I have more time. Daddy, could you write Time a change of address—as above? Love to you all—

Elizabeth

Liz's diary entry the next day presented her first sights of a glorious Paris. A long walk sparked her observations on the seeming abundance of food, clothing, and shop goods compared to London. Paris was a beautiful city in early 1945, and many Americans quickly fell in love with it. Wartime suffering was far less obvious than in London, where Liz had seen the bombed-out buildings, the terror of the V-1 and V-2 rockets, the dinginess of dress and food. Such physical ravages were harder to find in Paris. Instead, there was good food and drink, shops filled with dazzling goods, and well-dressed, chic people strolling the boulevards, as Liz often noted. Some Americans doubted if France had done its part in resisting the Nazis, if the nation had surrendered too quickly in 1940, and if too many French citizens had then collaborated with the enemy. American reporter Ernie Pyle, who was in Paris to celebrate its liberation in August 1944, later wrote of his "rather low opinion of Paris." "I felt as though I were living in a whorehouse—not physically but spiritually."[3]

But Paris had suffered. The German occupation had begun in June 1940, just as Liz graduated from college. Nazi flags hung from hotels, government buildings, and the Eiffel Tower. Increasingly harsh rationing created real food shortages and growing malnutrition. Restrictions on freedoms tightened and matured in Nazi atrocities against any form of resistance. The Holocaust swept through the city as the Nazis rounded up foreign and French Jews. Always for French citizens there was the moral and practical challenge of deciding whether and how to resist the conqueror or how much to comply or even collaborate with the enemy. The four years of occupation left a great darkness in the city of light.[4]

Americans came to Paris with high expectations, especially GIs on leave who sought wine, women, and song. The army guide to the city, prepared prior to D-Day, advised Americans that "one of the first ideas you should get out of your head is that Paris is a city of frivolous and wicked people." Liz's prejudices never went so far, but in comparison to what she had seen in London and across England, the French seemed not to have suffered. Like most Americans, she arrived in Paris after the Germans had retreated. She was not there long enough to see the very deep strains below the gleaming surface of cafés, boulevards, shops, and fashion. Perhaps she did not see that the Parisian women wearing the large, colorful turban hats that so amused her had often sewed them from scraps of cloth and wore them to hide their straggled hair.[5] Keeping up appearances of French chic may have been nothing but frivolous fashion. Or it may have been a gesture of contempt toward the German occupiers, aimed, as one Parisian wrote in late 1944, at the "fat ugliness of those overgrown trouts packaged in grey."[6]

Diary, Feb. 26, 1945
Paris

Paris was grey today—no sun—but it looks wonderful with or without. Jo Banacer and I walked through the Tuilleries garden, past the

Place de le Concorde and across the Sienne to the Quay d'Orsay, avoiding bicycles, army trucks and civilian cars. The people looked normal enough, the women with towering turbans and platform shoes the men bereted and theatrically dressed in scarves and wide bottomed trousers. Paris appeared well-groomed and passive. Off in the distance were etched the Eiffel tower and the Arc d'Triumphe. It was wonderfully unreal.

We eat in a restaurant off the Place d'opera and it is complete with bar (only cognac) and hovering waiters. It differs from other restaurants in that only Red Cross personnel can eat there and we pay only for the liquor—but it's far more splendid than anything I saw in England, including the Savoy and Claridges. There's a sign in the door— "American Red Cross Mess." And only in Paris will we find a mess like that. The shops are full of luxury items, things that you can't get at home like fountain pens, portable radios, jewelry, perfumes etc. etc.—at terrific prices, but no coupons, no limit on quantity. Lots of G.I.s on leave, mostly from the front. The women are smartly dressed.

Business of the day consisted of a token visit to headquarters (a building occupied not so long ago by gentlemen of the Wehrmacht)— our first assignment will probably be ranging[7] in Le Havre or Rouen. After dinner in our beautiful mess, Margaret [Morrison] and I saw "Wuthering Heights" in French. We left before it was through—too much French is an exhausting thing.

Liz's second letter home from Paris noted again the upbeat side of the city and its fashionable women, "mostly spared the ravages of war," and the pleasure of a first-class hotel, the Normandy, located near the Louvre Museum. In Paris, as elsewhere, Liz was the eager tourist finding her way around a new place. Many GIs struggled to do likewise, including Clarence Davis, who wrote his wife from Paris at the time Liz was there:

> I used the subway but you can't see much from it and I did not know how to find places I wanted to see. And it seems none of the GIs I met knew either. There is not any use to ask any of these frogs

anything for they will just chatter for about ten minutes and you do not know any more than you did before.[8]

Liz hoped to see Larry Pickard, the special guy from the 82nd Airborne she had met in Leicester, England, and would have liked to "burn toast for." He was well and close by, she'd heard.

February 27, 1945
Paris

Dear Mere et Pere,

Alors! A few moments before dinner in our very glamorous Red Cross mess and I'm sitting in our hotel, this time one taken over entirely for Red Cross female personnel. I can look out on a narrow little street filled with homeward bound Parisiens, all of whom look quite well fed and normal, except, AWK! You should see the ladies' hats! They are momentous affairs made of yards and yards of material and crowned with feathers, or bangles or what have you. And under these atrocities are coiffeurs piled high and long. The shop windows are filled with luxuries, which are good to see after Britains' but the prices are out of this world and as I own just about 1000 tattered francs, I'm not indulging. The main Red Cross Club is in one of the erstwhile finest hotels and not so long ago was filled with little Krauts, as they took it over for their enlisted men, too. My lousy French is serving me pretty well (in fact, some people consider me quite a linguist). We have received our assignments and we'll not be fox-hole girls for a while yet, which is just as well.

What can I tell you about Paris? Well, I imagine it's very much as it was when you last saw it and it's good to see one city that hasn't scars. Every once in a while, you see a bullet hole in the stone, but that's all. And beautiful! You can imagine how I felt as I stood in the Place de la Concorde and saw off in the hazy distance the Eiffel Tower and the Arc d'Triumphe! Tomorrow, we take a tour, but Versailles will have to wait until another trip which will no doubt be soon.

The best news is that Larry [Pickard] is O.K., is not too far from here and naturally, is off the line. Hope to see him soon if all goes well.

I'll write more very soon, but it's chow time and alas, food comes first. I must tell you about the Red Cross mess (we're not allowed to eat any place except there). It is a very elegant restaurant near the Place d'Opera, complete with excellent service, table cloths, bar and everything except the bill. Our room at the Normandy was a huge suite and I occupied a huge divan covered with some sort of tapestry—and there I slept in my G.I. flannel p.j.'s, dog tags and bobby pins. Margaret thinks that Goering occupied the same room, but we don't fall in with her. There are better suites over at the Ritz.[9]

Love to you all,
Elizabeth

From her new base in Le Havre, Liz wrote her parents about the trip from Paris the previous day, after a last night on the town. She settled into new accommodations, which promised some comfort, including hot water and, because she had officer status, generous liquor rations. Even though she no longer had to face the frustrations of operating the doughnut machine, the work ahead appeared demanding. It certainly was to be done on a larger scale.

March 2, 1945
[Le Havre]

Dear mother and daddy,

We finally left Paris—in a fine cloud of dust and amid much tooting of horn. Reason: a French driver at the wheel of a British ambulance, now an A.R.C. carry-all (including six of us and luggage). Our homme's idea of good driving consisted of sitting on the horn and trusting in God—and although at first I felt rather imprisoned in the completely enclosed back of the vehicle, I finally became philosophic and fell asleep, draped artistically over the duffel bags and bed rolls. The roads were horrible, the countryside wet—alongside were the rusted and stripped corpses of vehicles that had met their end in 1940. And destruction such as I have never seen, far surpassing anything in England—destruction, too, that left me feeling not so self-righteous, as it was mostly ours. When we passed the shell of a famous cathedral [probably Rouen], I felt pretty small. Our base is on the fringe of similar ruins all more or less recent.

But the set-up is ideal. 12 of us live in a house on a hill overlooking a wonderful view. We run a fleet of four clubmobiles, 2 jeeps and a sort of enclosed station wagon. We also run our own mess (with rations from the army), seven French servants, a doughnut kitchen and an attached G.I. detail. How we run it, I don't know—it's all a mystery, but it better unravel itself quickly as the pioneer group is about to leave we newcomers to the fruits of their labors. Our doughnuts are all cooked for us and we just have to give them out—sounded like a snap to me, but after a day of it, I take it all back.

Our house is really nice—a sort of junior chateau. Right now, the Navy is painting the interior and it's rather messy. Because of overflow, Aileen [Anderson], Margaret [Morrison], Mary Rea and myself live in a neighboring house in our sleeping bags. But they are very comfortable and all in all we couldn't have better living conditions. Water is always froid[10] in our house, the Navy has installed a portable shower and 3 times a week, we have ice cream. We can't drink the local water unless we put pills in it, but we have a liquor ration—1 bottle of champagne, 1 Scotch, 1 Gin, 1 Cognac or Benedictine, per month—520 francs. Everybody is very congenial and the Army and Navy, thanks to the pioneering of the first group, take awfully good care of us. They (our predecessors) came in when things were really rough—this house, for instance, had as furniture one baby's crib—now we have everything, including the new paint job. It's especially nice, because we thought of course, that we were going to be roughing it in the worse way—and it's 10 times better than Mrs. Whittle and her bugs!

But I didn't describe the destruction—the woods are still full of mines and our kitchen is on top of a temporary graveyard which the French are now rearranging. Thank God most of their rearranging was completed by the time of our arrival. But I gathered that donuts and opened graves didn't mix.

We might as well be at the South Pole as far as mail is concerned. It just isn't. However, it gets to us eventually, so don't stop writing. It's supposed to come from Paris via courier, but this seems to be only theory.

We had a wonderful last night in Paris—3 G.I.'s took Margaret, Mary and myself via Metro to the Montmartre region and we enjoyed ourselves with the assistance of much white wine. You can imagine how I felt the next day in the back of that ex-ambulance with our friend Pierre at the wheel.

My love to all of you,
Elizabeth

Liz sent her parents a letter through a friend traveling to New York, which bypassed the censor. She took the opportunity to indicate her current location and the places she had worked in England. And she offered a short description of Le Havre, which she would expand in future writing.

Located where the Seine River flows into the English Channel, Le Havre had long been a major European seaport. Transatlantic passenger liners and cargo ships had entered its deep harbor where they had eight miles of quays for unloading. Railroads and the Seine provided quick access from the port to Paris and the rest of Europe. The Nazis bombed the city in May 1940 and in mid-June began their occupation. Because of its strategic location the Germans heavily fortified the area, which led the Allies to begin their aerial raids in late 1940. In the weeks following the D-Day invasion, the Nazis blew up most of the docks as the Allies moved toward the city. They scuttled several hundred vessels in the harbor and mined entrances. At the same time, the Allies, mostly British RAF, heavily bombed the city and destroyed as much as two-thirds of the business and residential areas. The first troops, Canadians, entered Le Havre on September 12, 1944. The Americans arrived six days later and joined in rebuilding a port that was one of the most devastated in Europe. Ships began to unload equipment and men in October.[11]

Mile after mile of wreckage and debris still littered the harbor and beaches in early 1945, but Le Havre had become the primary troop debarkation point in Europe. Ships unloaded cargo and men night and day. By V-E Day more than a million troops had moved off ships at Le Havre, part of the massive supply of men and equipment that destroyed the Third Reich. In March alone 247,607 soldiers disembarked. For

Americans just off the boat from home, Le Havre was the first sight of the war's terrible destruction—a "giant, decayed corpse," as one described it. The work at Le Havre required large numbers of personnel. On duty in April 1945, were 12,601 U.S. troops, 3,785 employed French citizens, more than 6,000 prisoners of war, mostly German, and, of course, a small contingent of American Red Cross women.[12]

The people of Le Havre paid a heavy price for their strategic location. German occupation and harbor destruction followed by Allied bombing left 5,126 dead, most homes destroyed or heavily damaged, public services closed. Unknown numbers of bodies lay under the rubble when a writer for the *Atlantic* magazine profiled the city in early 1945. In one square mile of the city center, she noted, "the only object . . . that had not been destroyed was the 1914–1918 war memorial, now flanked by the fresh graves of bombed civilians." Those who had fled in September were now returning to smells of decay and shortages of food, coal, housing, and electricity that in the coming months made their lives very hard.[13]

By contrast, the Americans stationed in Le Havre had an abundance of nearly everything—"les fabuleuses richesses de l'Oncle Sam," as Le Havre citizen Pierre Aubery wrote. They had more butter, eggs, and meat than the scarce rations available to civilians. The Yanks represented a new world, one confusing to older citizens especially. They surged through the streets and into the cafés and bistros. They gave children chewing gum, as they had English children. They shared their jazz and took young women off to jitterbug at dances. Their trucks and jeeps ran over bicycles and sometimes pedestrians. Of course, thousands of young foreigners in the city meant trouble in cafés and bars, with drunks, with local women, sometimes between black and white. And yet there was American generosity too. In late May 1945, for example, a unit of GIs put on a big party for 300 Le Havre children whose fathers had been taken away by the Nazis. And doubtless there were citizens in Le Havre and across France who would have agreed with Louis Gullioux, a French civilian interpreter for the American military in northern France: "I admire the Americans' democratic spirit: even in uniform, they never stop behaving like civilians." Above all, the Americans offered high-paying jobs to French workers.[14]

In her five months in Le Havre, Liz came to know the city and something of its people and their suffering. Although she developed her own frustrations with aspects of French cultural ways and with individual French citizens, she also sensed, even at the beginning, why the French might have had mixed feelings about the Allies who liberated them. She came to see how they might even doubt that it really was necessary to destroy the city in order to save it and why they might suspect that the answer depended in some degree on whether it was your own hometown that had been destroyed.[15]

March 4, 1945
[Le Havre]

Dear mother and daddy,

This is rather illegal, but it's an opportunity for you to get news via New York. To tell the truth, now that I've had the opportunity, there's not too much really to tell you, except that I'm in Le Havre and will probably be here from 3 months to 3 weeks before moving forward. It's a beautiful city—or rather, it was a beautiful city, because the bombing damage is so terrible. We understand why the word "liberation" means nothing and why the French don't exactly drape us with bunting and flags. You'd be interested in knowing that we came over via boat train, one of the first one's, and landed at Dieppe, thence via train (with dining car) to Paris.

As for England, you know that I was at Leicester, Biddulph in Staffordshire in the Potteries and Barrow-in-Furness, ending up with Warrington, near Liverpool. I was called in to London the night I returned from my leave and was there from Monday until Saturday night.

We have a terrific amount of work to do and the place is fascinating—the Germans moved out of here quickly, leaving what hadn't been bombed intact—the pillboxes named "Schranhorst" and "Barbara," numerous land mines, neat graveyards, munition dumps and all the rest. Our billet is most civilized, as I've told you. And we're having a good time when we're not working.

I hope this reaches you intact—the courier is here and in 10 days he'll be in the U.S.A. Mail is worse than ever.

Love to you all,
Elizabeth

[p.s.] Keep the contents of this to yourself—not that it's anything important, but it ain't exactly right.

In this long diary entry Liz described the trip to Le Havre and the war damage she saw. More directly than in her letters, she questioned the destruction brought by Allied bombing, which French people had told her was more heavy handed than necessary. At the same time she was troubled by French antagonism toward the British and Americans. In less than two weeks on the Continent, the war had become more complicated, more ambiguous, more terrible.

France offered work very different from England. Men were coming and going on schedules that frequently changed at the last minute as ships and planes arrived or failed to arrive. Facilities were makeshift, although the Red Cross eventually established three permanent clubs in Le Havre. Most men were spread far out from the city, however, which required the Red Cross women to scurry after them in their Clubmobiles and various other vehicles. Much of the time Liz worked at the Le Havre docks and train depots serving troops arriving and departing at all hours of the night and day. Sometimes she and her colleagues were so busy there was little time for more than a perfunctory "hi, soldier," as the women concentrated on moving doughnuts and coffee in huge volume. French civilians joined the work as paid employees. The Red Cross hired I. M. Velter to set up and run a Le Havre doughnut kitchen. Monsieur Velter soon had two shifts of French workers turning out 135,000 doughnuts a day. The frustrations and smells of the doughnut machine were now for Liz a thing of the past.[16]

When there was less activity at the docks, the women drove out to the anti-artillery units above the city and to the "cigarette camps" beyond Le Havre, many on a bleak, flat plain. Named for popular brands of

American cigarettes, these assembly and staging areas were massive tent cities that held thousands of men. Hastily made gravel streets ran between the tents, with traffic that a French visitor to one camp compared to Paris. In early 1945 most soldiers in the camps were en route to the battlefront. After V-E Day they were more often on their way home and, for many, on toward the Pacific where V-J Day seemed far away. The conditions in which the men lived as they waited transportation were better than foxholes, but still far from the comfort of home. Boredom mixed with an eagerness for those going home to be moving to the docks at Le Havre. The cigarette camps offered some entertainment and recreation, including Paris streetwalkers who moved into adjacent areas. Only a small percentage of the hoards of men were permitted to take leave because French authorities greatly feared their cities would be overrun by drunk and violent GIs, a fear with considerable basis in fact.[17]

This diary entry included Liz's visit to Camp Herbert Tareyton in the forest of Montgeon above the city and also to the most famous of the cigarette camps, Lucky Strike, a "desolate dusty place." Liz was preparing to assume leadership and decision-making responsibilities more demanding and complex than her modesty suggested. The large scope and scale of the Le Havre operations required well-coordinated teamwork. Liz proved to be a superb administrator. Her leadership skills were such that her colleagues were "crazy about her," as one of them, Mary Haynsworth, recalled. She was "the boss," and yet she was "just one of us." Her sense of humor, Mary thought, was especially important, for she was a really "funny gal."[18]

Diary, March 6, 1945
Le Havre

We left Paris on the first of March in an ex-British ambulance now owned by the Red Cross. The driver was a bereted Frenchman who could not speak English and he drove in the traditional French way— on two wheels and a horn. The back was without windows and we draped ourselves on our duffel bags and prepared ourselves for sudden death. The roads were poor, the evidence of war everywhere—in the shelled towns, rusted vehicles alongside the road pock marked with bullet holes, destroyed bridges. But the countryside was beautiful in the rain, the fields meeting the horizon as they always have. Our first stop was in Rouen in the midst of terrible destruction. For the first time, I felt not so sure of our part in this war. It was nothing like London—or Plymouth—or even that single block in Barrow, because it was fresh and looked like a horrible wound. We reached La Havre in the rain. Our temporary billet was in the transient officer's mess, a white empty house overlooking houses falling down into the misty sea.

The crew here have been in Le Havre since November, two months after the Germans moved out. Thanks to them, our billet is a pleasant house. Well staffed, with good food—our routes are worked out and things are pretty civilized. In September, the AAF and RAF bombed the city, after the Germans had moved out, the people say. Thousands upon thousands of citizens were killed—a lot of them are still under the uncleared rubble. The harbour is a mess—sunken ships, concrete piers blown to bits, surrounded by block after block of devastation. The LST's land on the beach and larger vessels use a sort of pontoon pier. The result of the September bombing, besides wholesale destruction is whole sale antagonism—the civilians of Le Havre don't like us and they hate the British. The situation is improving now, but I still get the impression that the French don't give a damn who has their country as long as they can live as they always have. The Germans evidently let them do that in this region and we are just another invasion, more violent than the last one, which must be tolerated like bad weather or excessive cold.

The evidences of German occupation are everywhere. Their pill boxes are huge massive things with numerous underground passages. The hills are still mined—mostly anti-personnel affairs. Above the town is the forest, now a huge replacement center [Camp Herbert Tareyton]. The region is pretty well cleared out, but it's advisable not to wander about. The civilians of Le Havre are beginning to trickle back into their town and little shops are opening. The terrific job of clearing up the damage is being tackled by little men in blue denims.

Our work is everywhere—on the beach, in the forest, above the town where the Ack-Ack [antiaircraft artillery] boys sit on top of the German fortifications. Yesterday morning, Nancy Fiske and I took the carry-all and coffeed and doughnut-ed the men sitting on the beach, waiting to go on the LSTs bound for England. Then we found a convoy of trucks filled with replacements and after that a negro truck convoy. Sometimes, it's a train pulling out or men leaving by ship—or the replacements in the west. The other day, we drove up to Camp Lucky Strike, a huge replacement tent city (they're all named like that: Camp Twenty Grand, Camp Old Gold). We drove through Fécamp, a charming village on some sort of inlet—nice church, not too much damage and what there is looked as if artillery had done it. Lucky Strike is a desolate dusty place. Two Red Cross girls were in a tent trying to organize a club with almost no equipment, although they do have the use of our M. Velteur [I. M. Velter] who runs our doughnut kitchen.

Recreation: troop movies, free in various ex-civilian cinema houses. Occasional dances, cognac drinking in little spots. Although this is a base area, the army is more relaxed than it ever was in England. Beaucoup negro troops, nice individually, sullen in large groups. In this area, we have Ducks (amphibian trucks), Ack-Ack, Engineers, Sea-Bees, Navy Flag (but the admiral & his flag are about to depart), plain Navy, and almost everything else including a general. The Admiral lives with his aides in a terrific chateau with a swan stolen from Cherbourg, tapestry wallpaper—on the other hand, the boys in the forest live in tents with no washing facilities and certainly no recreation.

This morning, Cush[19] and I were on O.D. That is, Cush was—I'm learning how. We make up earth-shaking reports about how many doughnuts were consumed and how many transient troops were served. Then we call the various numbers to find out when the trains leave, when the boats come in etc. etc. We also answer the phone and have endless discussions on how many girls it will take to serve 15000 men in half an hour. Finally, we come forth with the schedule which sends us off on our various missions.

Liz wrote to her parents about the more positive sides of life in Le Havre, including good accommodations and food, dances, and movies. The veteran Red Cross workers had moved on, and Liz and the newcomers were now responsible for operations.

March 9, 1945
[Le Havre]

Dear mother and daddy,

There's a minute or two before our jeep picks us up for morning operations, which, as you see, I shall spend writing to you. As can be expected, I haven't heard from you for about four weeks and your last letter was dated somewhere around middle January, so you can see that I'm a little bit behind on the news. What has happened? Is John still at Quantico? Etc., etc.

There's not too much I can tell you, except that we (all 10 of us) are working hard, are most comfortable (when we're not working) and we're awfully well fed. The chief reason is that beside army chow, we get extra goodies sent over nightly by the gold braid. We newcomers are now in complete possession of Chateau Hysteria and so far, things are running smoothly enough, although I still can't tell the maid of a morning that I don't want cereal, but will take an egg if it's the real thing. In the morning, my French, always more or less unoccupied, is not functioning at all.

Social life is a galloping thing. Last night was the first time I managed to retire to my little cot at a reasonable hour. There really isn't too much to do, except a lot of talking, but the boys are an agreeable lot and we have a lot of fun. The other day, I picked up the phone to call a number and discovered that the operator was one of our boys from Barrow—almost like finding a long-lost cousin! Tonight, we're going to a dance, although what I'm going to wear is a moot question. All my civilized clothes were left (per instructions) back in England and—

And at that point, the Jeep arrived, so what I was going to say remains lost and unwritten. It's now after lunch and we have a short time before going out again. This morning was a beautiful day—much sunshine, a mild wind and a blue, blue sky. Although we no longer smell like doughnuts, we do have dust to contend with—one ride is enough to cover you with a fine film—but the bathing accommodations are excellent.

Have I told you about the movies? They are taken over by the Army, are free and only Allied troops can attend. Therefore, we never lack American films. We saw "Janie" the other night and the night before, walked out of a Wallace Beery opus.

Keep on writing—that mail will catch up to me eventually. Lots of love to you all—

Elizabeth

In her diary Liz reported on a twenty-four-hour day that began with Margaret Morrison driving the Bedford Clubmobile to one of the cigarette camps. The Red Cross women who mastered driving these huge British-made vehicles on European roads were rightly proud of their skills, especially since this was traditionally men's work.[20] Liz seemed uncertain about Margaret's skills and was not yet herself a comfortable driver. After a day working from the Clubmobile, there was a social evening, followed by night duty at the docks, where she served long lines of troops until dawn.

Liz provided a description of the house in which she and a dozen or so other Red Cross women lived. They called it "Chateau Hysteria." Located at 10 Rue Chef de Caux, just next to the old Fort de Sainte Adresse, the house was set among other villas built in the mid-nineteenth century and offered a spectacular view of the harbor and English Channel. Later Liz painted watercolors of the house and the harbor. Though it was hardly a grand chateau, this billet was among the best Liz had had, and included hot water, good food, and plenty of room. The Red Cross women cultivated good relationships with mess sergeants and officers and they were experienced scroungers, so there was often fresh food. Because the women were coming and going at all hours the kitchen was always open. French civilians did the cooking and housework and were also a source of some amusement and frustration. Liz was the group leader, the person the staff and her colleagues came to for solutions to problems.[21]

Chateau Hysteria was the center of an active social life as well. One of Liz's colleagues, Nancy Nicholas, later remembered that "we entertained everyone in Le Havre in our big blue living room with its lovely view over the harbor and danced to the Magnavox radio."[22]

The most important visitor to Chateau Hysteria for Liz was Frank

Policastro. This diary entry was her first mention of the man she had seen "almost every night since being in Le Havre." Policastro was born in New York City of Italian parents. He earned a business degree from Rider College in New Jersey, entered the military soon after Pearl Harbor, and graduated from Officer Candidate School. He was with the 818th Amphibious Truck Company, in charge of a unit of Ducks, or more correctly DUKW's, the Army's designation for 2½-ton amphibian trucks that moved over land and water as they unloaded cargo and men from ships anchored in the harbor. Lt. Policastro's men were African American soldiers, one of many segregated units with a white officer in charge.[23]

Diary, March 12, 1945
[Le Havre]

This is my day off and I had intended to spend the morning in bed until the two little femmes de chambre [maids] descended on me and bed and literally drove the sheets from under me. It's a gray day, the harbour is misty and you can hardly see the toy ships further out, waiting to be unloaded. We've had good weather otherwise—sun that is warm after England and out in the country, there's a green haze over everything.

Saturday morning, we were up in the forest with long unending lines of replacements [at Camp Herbert Tareyton]. In the afternoon, Margaret drove the Bedford (with me sitting nervously beside her) to a little town [Balbec] on the road to Rouen where there's a big P.W. camp and some combat troops going home for 30 day leaves—the catch being that they have to act as guards to the P.W.'s who are going home with them. In the town square, we picked up two lieutenants who volunteered to direct and drive us to the camp. The Bedford complained mightily and we tied up traffic while Margaret turned it around—the hill was worse. The place looked like a concentration camp with high barbed wire fences and observation posts maimed by machine guns and French soldiers. The prisoners themselves were digging at something. Our troops were living in tents on the side of a hill and after we finished serving, one of them drove the Bedford for us to the bottom of the hill.

171

The engine stalled once, but we finally got back to Le Havre intact. Frank Policastro of the Ducks came to dinner with his Captain—their whole unit was leaving for Marsailles Sunday. Afterwards, we went to the Troop movie and then to one of the few civilized cafés. Being on permanent dock detail, I had to work at 1:30, so Frank drove me down to the platoon pier where there was a big U.S.-Porto Rico Steamship. We served long lines—all going back to England—it was chilly and damp, although the stars were out. By 5 o'clock A.M. we were at home and I slept until noon next day.

Last night, we served the Ducks going by train to Marsailles. The enlisted men are all negroes and looked very military. I'll miss Frank—mostly because I've seen him almost every night since being in Le Havre. After we finished, we were carted off to an Engineers' dance—all Majors, Lt. Colonels and eagle Colonels—mostly drunk. There was a good negro band and it ended with three bosomy French girls squealing the Marsallaise with background accompaniment by the boys from Harlem.

We have discovered three graves in our yard. Somebody has been decorating them with green leaves and little pathetic bunches of flowers. The one by the wall is the grave of a "Sgt. Shropshire—U. S. Army." And his serial number, printed on a slab of wood in pencil. Our house is a four story affair, with much iron work in front of the tall windows. The wall hides it from the street and another wall apparently keeps the hillside from sliding down on top of it. The front windows over look the north end of the harbor, the side windows our yard, with a v-shaped drive, a fir tree and what must have been flower beds. At one corner, there's a round Norman tower and little steps and gateways. But exploring is not the thing to do because of left-over land mines. Even poor Sgt. Shropshire can't be touched because of the possibility that his grave might be mined. Our furniture is scrounged from the Navy and Army Special Service. It includes a very grand piano, radios and two baby cribs. We even have rugs.

Liz described some of the countryside near Le Havre and let her parents know of the very special guy but without any girlish gushing. Frank

Policastro later wrote that "we spent every possible moment together." Just to be together, he said, "I would ride along and serve doughnuts with her."[24]

There was still no mail from home, a problem exacerbated by the confusion over several Richardsons in the ETO. In an unusual closing to her parents, she signed her name "Liz" rather than "Elizabeth."

March 13, 1945
[Le Havre]

Dear mother and daddy,

Tonight, I'm O.D. and am spending the evening acting as a sort of social secretary, phone answerer, schedule-maker-out and bouncer. We rotate at it and it gives me a good opportunity, between activities, to try some letter writing. You'd be surprised how hard it is to write at all when mail is something we just don't get. The other day, some came through by devious ways (not by the approved army method) and to my horror, headquarters only sent the alphabet up to M or N, thus neatly cutting off the tail of the alphabet and me. And right when I'm in a position to keep an eye on at least one Richardson's mail. Her name is Nancy and she comes from Hartford, Connecticut. When I get Elaine cornered, my life will be complete.

For once, I didn't have work this afternoon, and got to take a long walk over the local hills. We investigated several interesting battlements and if I had a passion for souvenirs of the ex-conquerors, I could have quite a collection. The French graveyards are fascinating—very gaudy, with artificial flowers, but they don't seem so prone to give the life history of the deceased as are the English. Alas. Talking about graves (again) we thought we had a few in our yard belonging to G.I.'s. Our maids decorated them as only the French can and we called in the Graves Registration, who arrived today, escorted by gendarmes. The Captain of Graves Registrations investigated and diagnosed them as ex-Latrines. We haven't told the jeune filles yet. The decorations are too beautiful.

My social life who managed to keep me busy every night since my arrival in this place, departed temporarily. We served his unit, little negro boys all slicked up for the occasion, and bade him farewell #5,000,000. The night before, we went to the Allied movie, then to some small café, then I had to work (at 2:00 A.M.) and finished at 5:00 with the local roosters crowing to welcome the new day. Since then, thanks to Frank's departure, I've caught up on sleep.

Keep writing and love to you all—

Liz

A diary entry in mid-March focused on the beauty of a spring day amidst the reminders of war.

Diary, March 14, 1945
[Le Havre]

This is a beautiful day, such as we never saw in England. Our front yard is being worked on by a detail of negro prisoners and it's gradually beginning to look well groomed and less shabby. The sun is very warm and bright—I'm sitting on our front steps, without coat—or gloves—or hat—or any of the other necessary accessories to out-door life across the channel. As for the sea; it's a dazzling blue and one almost forgets the rusted hulks the retreating tide reveals or the crumbling rubble that once was the city.

This afternoon, Aileen & I, Al (G.I. driver) and carry-all went up to the Ack-Ack boys, located on the high north arm of the harbor. Then we went down to another company located on the other side of the beach. They are ready to move forward and like everybody who hasn't had too much of a taste of action, are anxious to have it. They live in tents in the sand, bounded on one side by the huge blasted piers of the Trans-Oceanic piers, on the others by miscellaneous twisted pill boxes and sheds and by their own radar instruments on the others. The dust is blinding, especially when kicked up by convoy after convoy of trucks, Ducks still dripping water from their trips out to the ships and anything else the army provides under the name of transport.

Nancy Nicholas remarked today how incongruous this all was— Sunday we were sitting in our living room with its newly painted blue walls and the Admiral's grand piano, listening to Brahm's piano concerto number via B.B.C. Outside down the hill lay this crumbling wreck of a city and its accessory tale of suffering and terror. However, nothing can diminish the beauty of the countryside, the sky, the sea, the silhouettes of trees against that background. Man's persistence in building and destroying is small indeed compared to the calm persistence of nature.

A quiet Sunday afternoon, after a night of hard work, offered time to write home and to be homesick. The clean-up of war's debris was beginning to take effect. At a tent warming party there were black "servants" and even fresh milk to drink, the first for Liz since leaving the States.

Liz sent home an interesting list of requests for American phonograph records, particularly the last one. Gertrude Niesen was a sultry singer known for her song "I Wanna Get Married," which had a chorus line that asserted "I'm a big girl now." With Frank Policastro, Liz was moving toward love, yet she always insisted that marriage in wartime was foolish.

> March 18, 1945
> [Le Havre]

Dear mother and daddy,

This Sunday afternoon finds your weary daughter sitting on her side porch looking out on our front yard which at present contains one beat-up jeep (ARC 2433843) and much sunshine. I have just gotten up—mainly because I got to bed at 8:00 this morning after working from 3 A.M. until then in a fog enshrouded atmosphere through which I couldn't see the doughnuts in my hand. Ha! London fog, indeed! During the course of our wanderings, we lost a jeep that was following us, almost drove into a Body of water, not mentioning several man-created craters and I think I lost my sense of humor. Tonight we do the same thing, I hope without benefit of fog.

Before going out, I went to a tent-warming party. The tent's owner had dinner ready, by candlelight, wonderful steaks, biscuits and one of the guests brought the most precious contribution of all—a quart of Borden's milk—the first I've had since July 14th 1944. You'd be amused at the pride of our host in his new home and how nicely he played the part—Scotch highballs, red wine with dinner, champagne afterwards, soft music from radio Allemagne [Germany]. But a tent is a tent and the soft footed servants were just pore little black boys who's draft number had come up.

As you can see, we are working hard, but because we have our pleasant billet to come home to, warm beds and good food, it isn't hard in the sense that it was in England. The countryside is so like home, it makes me quite homesick—the same stretches of newly plowed ground and woods against the sky. And our particular house against the hill is in a charming setting overlooking a tremendous view. We've had negro prisoners working on the yard and it's becoming very attractive— Mother—you'd love it. Some German gentlemen have carried away the accumulated trash left by their comrades and the same thing is happening to this sad city that is happening in a miniature scale in our yard.

We have inherited a beautiful grand piano and a Magnavox combination [radio and phonograph]. [Y]esterday a boy named Tom Edwards from the Navy, a graduate of Oberlin and the Juilliard School of Music, came up with his music and practiced for four solid hours. He has a glorious voice, beautifully trained and was thrilled with the piano—almost as much as we were thrilled with his voice.

I daresay my friend, Mr. Kaltenborn [U.S. radio commentator] is full of sunny optimism these days and you can tell him for me—"Nuts." Our current house joke is, when we hear a shout from the street "The War's Over! Only two more years in the ETO!" There's a long way to go and we might as well face it.

Mother, could you have some record albums sent off to me? First of all, I'd like the "Oklahoma" album, one of Eddy Duchin's and if there is such a thing, one of Glenn Miller's or Tommy Dorsey's. We need records and when we go, succeeding generations of ARC Dock Rats can use them. Also, if you can stick it in, Gertrude Nissens recording of "I Want to Get Married."

You can imagine how I'm awaiting any news at all—I have an awful lot to catch up on.

Love to you all,
Elizabeth

The same Sunday, after a cancelled troop departure, there was time to make a diary entry, one in which Liz showed the wear of the hard work.

Diary, March 18, 1945
[Le Havre]

The shank end of a Sunday afternoon and we are waiting for Helen, our French cook to announce that "deenair is raidee"[. . . .]

At 3 A.M., Mary Rea, Steve (G. I. driver) the Bedford [Clubmobile] and myself started out for D for Dog battery of the Ack Ack boys—leaving for the front. Our guide was a lieutenant in a jeep. The dock area was shrouded in a dense fog and the jeep led us into two blind alleys before we finally took the lead. When we finally stopped, hemmed in by fog, we had lost the jeep and after another half hour of groping, we gave up D for Dog and climbed the hill to B battery. By 5 o'clock, we had them all fed and their convoy rumbled off, leaving us to return to number 10, Rue chef de caux. At 7:30, the other clubmobile returned after a rough time feeding the other three companies at the marshalling area. We were in bed by 8:00 o'clock. It was a beautiful day with blue sky and sea melting into the horizon.

This evening, we had a train leaving at 10:15 and another at midnight. The whole thing is off, after we arrived at the station. Now, we have 15,000 men to feed embarking LST's at midnight in Area I. Maybe I won't have to go.

Liz expected to be sent closer to the front, as soon as she mastered driving the big Bedford Clubmobile. War news continued to improve as the Allies had crossed the Rhine and moved farther into Germany to meet the Soviet Red Army coming from the east. Liz carefully followed these movements in the Stars and Stripes, the U.S. military's daily newspaper.

Lining up for Red Cross coffee and doughnuts were all sorts of the war's people, included prisoners freed by Allied troops. The stream of liberated prisoners coming to the Le Havre camps would continue to grow. And Frank Policastro had returned.

March 27, 1945
[Le Havre]

Dear mother and daddy,

There was something too nice about our set-up here—5 of us leave at the end of this week for the front and I was to be one of them, but owing to my inability to drive the English Bedford, I'm excused for a week or two. I'm still in the Jeep stage and I curse the day in my youth when I didn't learn, as do my co-workers, seeing that I'm the only one out of our group of 12 who is in the learning stage. Otherwise, we are working madly, all night and all day in shifts. And Frank, my little Duck Lieut. has returned, which increases the tempo of the vie sociale.

The news is wonderful and everybody is terrifically encouraged now that the end is dimly in sight. The weather seems to be on our side and by the time I get up there, we at least won't have to live in mud. You would have been amused at the line we served the other day—Indians (with turbans) and Scotchmen just released from a German PW camp where they had been since Tobruck, Negroes and Italians in G.I. uniforms dyed green. We also had a bunch of Polish girls just released from a Concentration Camp—unfortunately, owing to the usual language barrier, not many words were exchanged between us[. . . .]

Our mail man is here (he also brings the Stars & Stripes)—so love to you all—

Elizabeth

This diary entry captured some of the scale of troop movements in Le Havre and the demands placed on the Red Cross women. Perhaps Liz declined the chance to move closer to the front because Frank was back. By this time they were very much in love, though Frank would later write Liz's mother that "we were very level headed—we were biding our time"—not rushing into marriage, perhaps not into premarital sex.[25]

Diary, March 29, 1945
[Le Havre]

We've been working at all hours and at all times—especially in that damp cold hour before dawn and I'm able to go to sleep whenever I find the place. Thousands upon thousands of troops have poured into Le Havre—a somber sight when we pass them silently shuttling into the station where they're loaded on 40 and 8's [French rail cars]. But no matter what the hour, they always have a come back and a smile that makes it worth while. According to Eisenhower and the BBC, the war is in its last phase, but these boys are still being poured in an endless stream to the Reinforcement centers near the front. Three days ago, Paris called with a list of five of us to go immediately to the front, myself included. Why I declined, I don't know—anyway—I have 2 or three weeks now until I do go. Margaret and Aileen have gone down to Cherbourg to meet Aileen's Jim—they left this morning in an open jeep as I was coming in from our 5:15 shift. Tomorrow, I go on the "President Garfield" up to Rouen, back on Saturday. Frank is back from Marsailles, which partially accounts for my excessive weariness.

It's been raining for three days—almost a steady drizzle. Yesterday, we served in the rain—rain that almost reduced the doughnuts to pulp and ourselves to a sodden mass of irritability.

A diary entry two days later reported on a pleasant trip up the Seine River to Camp Twenty Grand, another of the cigarette camps. Liz enjoyed the spring beauty, observing as she often did the colors of the landscape, and the luxury of a stateroom, all a change from dock work. On this trip she acquired a German helmet, which she later sent to her brother Charles, who long kept it among his prized possessions.

The troopship *President Warfield* was an American passenger vessel before the war. She joined the navy in 1944 and served off Omaha Beach and then on the Seine River. Acquired by the Jewish group Haganah and renamed "Exodus 1947," the ship gained world attention when Jewish refugees on board attempted to land in Palestine in 1947. Leon Uris took the ship's name for the title of his bestselling 1958 novel.[26]

Diary, March 31st
[Le Havre]

It wasn't the "President Garfield"—it was the "President Warfield" which used to ply between Baltimore and Norfolk. Now it's painted Navy grey and carries troops from Le Havre to [Camp] Twenty Grand, below Rouen on the Sienne. We came aboard at 0800 to a neat ship moored by the quay and a good breakfast (fresh eggs) in the Ward Room. The troops were in the lower decks, where we stayed until 1200 and chow. The countryside was lovely—Cezanne colors, hills that rose on the bank, unbelievably picturesque cottages and chateaus—set in a hazy green setting in which the colors intensified themselves. The apple and plum trees were in bloom and the hedgerows were green enough so that you almost couldn't see the rusting equipment of the Wehrmacht, left there since late August when the Canadians pushed them to the river.

The troops disembarked to Duclair (I think that's the name) in bright sunlight, lining up in formation and trudging off down the dusty road beside the musical comedy shops of the town. The "President Garfield" with the aid of a puffing Army tug, turned in the river and went down stream to a makeshift quay where we tied up until morning. We were welcomed by the populace, who stood in tight little groups bartering cigarettes and candy bars for German equipment. I got a helmet, very big and full of leaves. The sailors, having acquired their fill of helmets, bartered for bayonets, field caps and rifles. Some of them had shore leave—a 5 mile walk to the nearest pub. After dinner, we had a movie and by 10:30, there was a round orange moon looking down on the shattered buildings near our mooring and the glassy surface of the Sienne.

This morning, against the tide, we went back to Le Havre, passing three LST's loaded with troops and two dirty British freighters. The ship pitched about a bit in the channel and we threaded our way into the confusion of the harbour, with Ste. Addresse high above us to the north and the wreckage of Le Havre in front of us.

We each had a stateroom to ourselves, with hot running water and an inner spring mattress. The bathroom was pure Americana—the first one I've seen for nine months. As for 10, Rue Chef de Caux, Aileen &

Maggie aren't back from Cherbourg (broken axel the reason), Nancy Richardson, Cush, Beth McCoy & Mary Rea have all left for Paris via Navy courier. And I am O.D. tonight, with a 13:30 session of work to look forward to.

The mail was complicated by yet another woman named Richardson. Red Cross officials attempted to sort out the problem, but Liz's mail service continued to be sporadic.[27]

As Nazi defeat seemed closer, Liz held to her conviction that the work would continue far into the future. Evidence of the value of that work was the touching way in which GIs recognized her and she them. Men from England not only remembered her but her American hometown when they called out "Hey, Liz! Hey, Milwaukee!" Clubmobiler Margaret Gearhart wrote her parents "they call us by our state name— 'Hey, California.' They very seldom forget where you're from if they have seen us before." Acknowledging connections to a particular American place was part of coping with the long distance and time from home. Clubmobiles carried a register for the men to sign, which gave them opportunities to see names of others from California, Milwaukee, New Jersey, or Atlanta.[28]

Even with the large numbers of troops they served in Le Havre, the men were more than anonymous faces to Liz and her colleagues. Nancy Nicholas wrote, "We would argue as to which men we liked the most, the tired, often bitter veterans of many campaigns returning to their outfits after being wounded, the happy men going on leave, or the newly-arrived from the States. Your heart goes out to them all."[29]

There was little doubt about the importance of the work to the men on the ground in Le Havre. In late spring, as Atlantic supply lines clogged and food supplies in Europe dropped below needs, experts in the War Department back in Washington proposed a 50% cut in shipment of the lard, evaporated milk, sugar, and coffee allowed for Red Cross operations. Army officers in France quickly protested that Red Cross coffee and doughnuts were essential contributors to army morale and stymied the proposed cutback.[30]

Liz reported, without revealing her feelings, that Larry Pickard, the guy she had met in Leicester and had imagined "burning toast for," was missing and had been since the Battle of the Bulge. She and Frank planned a weekend in Paris, a trip they never got to take together.

April 2, 1945
[Le Havre]

Dear mother and daddy,

The mail situation is this: one V-Mail dated February 4th one Air Mail of February 9th and a V-Mail of March 7th, which arrived yesterday with the good news that Mother was embarking on an eastward trip. Now, I'm anxiously awaiting further news—of John and the New York relatives and spring in Indiana. Perhaps some day, the mail situation will clear up, but things have been further complicated by a new character with the 7th Army named Elizabeth I. Richardson. Nancy Richardson has left us and is now with the Third and Ruth Richardson is with the 9th—and Elaine is still in England, where I hope she stays. I could do better with the name of Smith.

Egad! Things look rosy at this stage of the game—rosier than they have ever looked—but we are figuring on a few years more of hard work, without added destruction, on the large scale, that is. Remember, when I told you that I might see Larry soon? A bit premature—he has been missing since the Ardennes. Guess I rather knew it all along. You know how you have feelings about things like that.

I was lucky enough to have a wonderful assignment last week—a trip up a River on a troopship and the fairy beauty of this country in the spring is breathtaking—colors that only Cezanne and Van Gogh have captured[....] Our voyage was a pleasant vacation after the work of the last weeks—I'm getting so that I sleep when and where I have the opportunity. If a bed is accessible, I crawl in, clothes and all. The good thing about this base, is seeing so many of the boys that we knew at one time or another. Last week, we were cruising past some resting troops, when I heard them shouting "Hey, Liz! Hey, Milwaukee!" It was a whole unit that we had known in England and we had a wonderful reunion right there on the road. And yesterday I met one of the cooks who had helped us brew our coffee during that week of the invasion of Holland.

It's funny how they remember you and stranger yet how we can remember them after seeing thousand and thousands of faces.

Frank and I are going to Paris together on our 48 on the condition that he takes me to the Follies. That is, if nothing happens between then and now. As for Easter—like any other day, with work at 4:30 A. M., sleep, work again and a large cake inscribed in yellow icing "Happy Easter to the Girls." Aileen's brother has been awarded the Distinguished Flying Cross and is now home learning about B-29's.

That's all—of the printable news. Hope you've received my request for shoes. Are Sue and John going to get married in June? You'd better address my mail to Elizabeth A. with ARC 42741 in Beeg Black Letters. Not CMR 42741, Mother, as you wrote last time. Tsk, Tsk.

Love to you all,
Elizabeth (A)

A quick V-Mail home included a drawing in which Liz commented on her continuing efforts to learn to drive. Though she had passed a driving test in London, she was an uncertain driver, a handicap she soon overcame in France, where it was necessary to drive a variety of military vehicles through the battered city and into the countryside.

April 4, '45
[Le Havre]

Perhaps it's just as well that your daughter is learning to drive on the sunny roads of France—the good citizens are no doubt more philosophic than those of Dragoon Trail. In the above, you can quickly spot Elizabeth A (not Elizabeth I.) and her companions, all of whom have put in for a rest cure, preferably at Cannes, but where ever the place—far removed from your

Elizabeth

Mother's Day evoked a special letter home. Liz was now learning more about how the Germans had treated their prisoners, a subject she

In this V-Mail letter home Liz depicted her difficulty learning to drive. Despite her many talents and skills it was not until after she arrived in France that she became a comfortable driver. *Courtesy Charles Richardson, Jr.*

alluded to in this letter and detailed in her diary entry the next day. Like most Americans in Europe, she had seen enough to have no doubt about the necessity of total victory over Nazism.

April 8, 1945
[Le Havre]

Dear mother,

This is a Mother's Day letter—hence the singular greeting. Sorry I can't find any ink to go with the occasion, but it's easier to write in pencil anyway, although sloppy. Enclosed is a Mother's Day gift for you which I hope you'll splurge on something terrifically extravagant and amusing, thinking, as you do it of your large daughter, who certainly thinks of you a lot. Involved, but you will be able to make sense out of it after re-reading at least three times. It seems to me that last Mother's Day, I was home at Dragoon Trail—almost a year ago, and a lot has happened since then, making me a wiser and sadder creature (the latter in itself a sign of wisdom), while you and Daddy remain as always a very firm anchor from which I can't drift too far. Comprendez?

Perhaps will be able to send you some perfume when I send Butch his Boche helmet—I bought some Russian Leather, but my swain of the moment refers to it as "untanned hide," so hereafter, I'll wait in a queue for "Channel No. 5" or nothing.

This is a beautiful day in France—air like champagne (and I speak with authority) and that blue sky that no other country has. We've been working harder than ever—12, 14 hours, finishing up at dawn or later—and recently, have seen more direct results by the enemy which make me damm mad. It will be a pretty dull G.I. who'll fraternize [after?] this war with the Krauts and when I say that, I'm not going back on my old convictions that fundamentally, the Germans are just like any other nation. But only a complete and devastating victory on our part will make the next generation realize what fools their fathers were in being misled and mis educated. Maybe we'll learn something from it, too.

Didn't mean to get in this philosophic vein—anyway, dinner is ready, it smells like steak—and I am most hungry. I'll write a longer letter soon.

Happy Mother's Day, Mother, and lots of love from your,

Elizabeth

In a mid-day diary entry Liz wrote of serving recently liberated Allied prisoners of war—"the Americans horribly thin and weak—and young." She and other Red Cross women worked with them as they arrived at the Le Havre airport and at Camp Lucky Strike. Known as Recovered Allied Military Personnel and often referred to as RAMPs, sometimes as Kriegies (after the German word for prisoner), the men were just beginning to arrive as advancing Allied armies opened the prisons of the Third Reich. There were over 2 million Allied prisoners, including about 200,000 British and about 95,000 Americans. The U.S. military made Camp Lucky Strike the primary processing area for thousands of RAMPs. There they received clean clothing, physical examinations, and a supervised diet of simple food to enable adjustment from their meager prison diets. Many had severe gastro-intestinal distress. Military doctors insisted the Red Cross keep its famous sinkers from them and serve instead juice, cocoa, and egg nog made with powdered milk and eggs. Photographs taken by Mary Haynsworth, however, show clearly that she and Liz did serve doughnuts to at least some of the RAMPs arriving at Le Havre. The snapshots show too that many were very young. The newly liberated prisoners arrived "in odds and ends of clothing, and are nothing but skin and bones," Red Cross worker Edith Steiger noted in her diary. One of them, William Cupp, weighed about 150 pounds when he bailed out over Belgium and 89 pounds when he reached Camp Lucky Strike. Another, Robert Reeves, recalled that "Lucky Strike was no paradise, but it was a lot closer to heaven than what we had become accustomed to in Munich." RAMPs had first claim on military resources, for good reason. When wild rumors circulated that conditions at Lucky Strike were worse than the German prisoner camps, General Eisenhower immediately flew from Allied headquarters at Reims to visit the camp and to personally ascertain that the rumors were false.[31]

Once settled in the Le Havre area, many RAMPs stayed put, uninterested in passes to town, content to savor simple food and thoughts of home. One who had survived the horrendous Dresden firebombing, twenty-two-year-old Kurt Vonnegut, wrote his father from Camp Lucky Strike in late May of his straightforward and simple plan for the future: "I hope to be home in a month. Once home I'll be given twenty-days recuperation at [Camp] Atterbury, about $600 back pay and—get this—sixty (60) days furlough!"[32]

The Clubmobile Cleveland and its smiling American women were a welcome sight for RAMPs arriving at the Le Havre Airport. *Newsweek* printed a letter from one returning lieutenant months later recalling that "the first thing they saw when they stepped off the planes at Le Havre were those lovely American Red Cross girls with coffee and doughnuts." Photos of Margaret Morrison from this time show her waiting for arriving RAMPs wearing her penny loafers, lipstick, fingernail polish, and, in one snapshot, a flower in her hair. An American Red Cross official who visited the airport in May found the women "most enthusiastic" as they worked from their Clubmobile and a simple wooden table set up outside a hangar. Greeting liberated prisoners off the planes was for Margaret, Mary, Liz, and their colleagues among the most memorable experiences of the war. In quiet conversations that followed their "hi—where you from?" greeting, they learned about the miseries these prisoners of the Nazis had endured. They understood quickly, as Kurt Vonnegut would later reveal to the world, that memories of those experiences would never go away.[33]

Diary, April 9, 1945
[Le Havre]

Yesterday, on our way back from Sunday morning work in the forest (15th Repl. Depot), I saw one of the German prisoners picking wild flowers in the woods beside the road. The sun shone through the trees and he looked like any other boy doing the same thing in any other country. Then in the afternoon, Marge Hillman and myself shuttled supplies to the Airport where C-47's are flying in repatriated prisoners. Italian ex-prisoners are billeted in back of our doughnut kitchen. They are dressed in Army uniforms dyed green and apparently spend all their time leaning against the wall in the sun. We passed them and drove through the promenading French families up to Ste. Addresse and to the airport. There were long lines of prisoners, the Americans horribly thin and weak—and young. These are the contrasts of war.

At about four, I remained at the airport with Maggie. Four C-47's came in, first the Americans, their long hair blowing in the wind, all alike in their cleanliness because they had just been deloused. Nobody said much, but everyone of them had a big smile, no matter how weak they were. The British looked better, some had been in German hands since 1940 and apparently they readjusted themselves to the food and living conditions. One C-47 brought British Colonials—Indians, South Africans black and white, New Zealanders, Australians. The British were starry-eyed, home lay across the water that they could see. The British officers had mostly been captured before Dunkirk, in this same neighborhood. They were dressed in their same uniforms—the Scots in Kilts. "We've been waiting five years to see you," a major told me. He had a bristling mustache like [movie actor] C. Aubrey Smith. An Army band played "Tipperary" as they walked from the plane to our

Clubmobile. "Play the Beer Barrel Polka," one of the G.I.s said. "Too much like Kraut Music," said another. Our clubmobile is named "Cleveland." One boy kept saying, "Beautiful Ohio, beautiful Ohio." I'd never really thought of Ohio as beautiful before that.

As I sit here in our garden, I can hear more C-47's coming. It's lunch time and the telephone is ringing . . .

The chateau's piano was taken away, but a ping pong table was now available. The war continued toward an end, but Liz refused to become overly optimistic. Returning prisoners were clear reminders of war's costs. Her Milwaukee college friend and roommate, Chris Hanson, who had joined the Red Cross with her, was recently married.

> Thursday
> April 10 (I think)
> [Le Havre]

Dear mother and daddy,

At present, I'm sitting on one of our new bright red lawn chairs enjoying the balm spring breeze, the insect life and a sun that can't decide to come completely out of hiding. The lawn chairs look very much as if they had come off some ship—in fact, they still have little plates on them to contain the names of whomever sat in them. Now, they adorn our front yard and add a festive touch to our lives. The Navy, who giveth and taketh away, arrived the other day and tooketh our piano, an unauthorized act of violence. As I was on O.D., my fellows are heaping the blame on me, but how could I stand in the way of one Lt.(j.g.), one petty officer and three husky gobs? Nancy says "You should have used your feminine wiles" and my answer is that it's impossible to have even a semblance of feminine wiles when you're dressed in a teddy bear suit of R.A.F. matted wool. This charming outfit was issued to us in London and was constructed to fit the British female form and not that of a polygot American. It's so scratchy that wearing it is like sleeping on a bed of nails and in contrast, our issue of last Summer (RAF Officer's material) is like a Palm Beach Cloth.

These are a few of the thousands of liberated Allied prisoners of war Liz and her Red Cross colleagues greeted at the Le Havre airfield. In her diary on April 9, 1945, she wrote: "There were long lines of prisoners, the Americans horribly thin and weak—and young." And to Betty Twining on April 22, 1945: "looking at those boys, I can work up quite a white hate against our Kraut friends."
Courtesy Mary Haynsworth Mathews.

Today's "Stars & Stripes" says that the 7th [Army] is 70 miles from Berlin—hard to believe and wonderful in its implications. None of us actually believe that there will be any out and out V-E day of the kind that the press is bleating about back home. You'd think after five years of this, people would be a little more realistic. Anything can happen, though, and the sooner the better. Meanwhile, our work goes on as usual. I can tell you that we've come in contact with a lot of recently repatriated ex-prisoners and their physical condition is pitiful. The British who have been in for 5 years are in better condition than ours, because they've managed to stabilize themselves on gruel and chicory. The shock of the change from a well-balanced diet to next to nothing is too much for ours.

Of course, I'm anxiously awaiting news of Mother's New York expedition and John's graduation—it must have been wonderful. My mail is improving somewhat—I've gotten Mother's N. Y. V-Mail and one from Butch—also a Christmas package from Schuster's, hopelessly mangled, but the thought was there. Also Chris's wedding announcement, so Mother, would you pick out a very nice wedding present for her—preferably something in silver like a sugar bowl and cream pitcher, and have it sent to her? Spend as much as is necessary and if possible, have it monogrammed—CHW or whatever is the right thing. Her address is: Mrs. Edward Louis Watson, 218 Worthington Avenue, Cincinnati 15, Ohio.

We have a ping-pong table in our stable, which has recently been cleaned of the debris left by our unworthy predecessors. We emerge from every game, smelling strongly of horses, but anything "pour le sport." Incidentally, my French is <u>not</u> improving. I'm just not a linguist and I might as well face the terrible fact. The only thing that I've accomplished is telling Odette that I want my egg boiled "dans l'eau Quatre minutes" [in the water four minutes] and this is such a major effort that it leaves me exhausted for the rest of the day.

Here's the mailman (in a jeep—he also brings the "Stars & Stripes"). More later. None for me.

Love
Elizabeth

In this diary entry Liz reported Franklin Roosevelt's death, a loss felt deeply by many Americans who had known no other president. She and Margaret Morrison heard the news along with 15,000 newly arrived troops in the vast warehouse-like building near the docks where they did much of their work. The battered building was large enough to hold two dance bands that provided music for troops waiting in food lines and for those always ready to jitterbug—if possible with a Red Cross girl.[34]

Diary, April 13, 1945
[Le Havre]
Last night, Margaret and I were working at the Exposition Building. After the long line of tired men had gone through the chow line, we listened to one of them play the piano and sing—then came the usual lecture on Calvados [apple brandy], what to wear in Paris, mines, etc. The news was good, too and the boys cheered—they all hope it will be over by the time they get on the line. Margaret and I went in back of the bandstand and sat in the jeep—when we heard taps and then the "Star Spangled Banner" we knew that the rumor that Roosevelt had died that afternoon was true. And the fact that the war in Europe is almost over makes it more tragic in its implications, for who will lead us in the peace? Such is the infallibility of a one man leadership. 15,000 then, most of whom like myself, can hardly remember another president—there in that battered building the sense of loss was acute.

A "stinky V-mail" captured details of a beautiful spring evening at 10 Rue Chef de Caux.

April 17, 1945
[Le Havre]
Dear mother and daddy,
Perhaps this stinky V-mail will get through to you when all else fails. But I always feel that I'm writing some sort of form letter, especially after scribbling two complete addresses and my own name

until I see triple. This is a beautiful spring evening—it's 9:30 and just twilight, the birds are twittering in spite of being French birds and the sea is like smoked pearl. In fact, it feels like summer and the song writers didn't know what they were talking about when they said that "spring will be a little late this year." You can tell them that it's on time in Normandy. Outside in the yard, two Naval gentlemen and two of my co-workers are guzzling their way through something obviously alcoholic. Further on three G.I.'s from some mess hall and three more co-workers are grouped about a chocolate cake and Aileen and a captain are playing a guitar (horrible) up on the hill. I am about to wash off five layers of dust in order to welcome an amphibious 1st Lieut. Hence the haste Love to you all—

Elizabeth

The delayed mail arrived in a gusher, prompting a letter to Milwaukee friend, Winifred Wood. With W.W., Liz shared more candid observations on men.

The spring weather prompted a visit to the beach, still showing remnants of war. Although extensive clearance work had begun, mines from the English Channel washed onto the beaches after every storm. On land, especially near the coast, the Germans had placed mines as close as every 1.5 meters. Unexploded shells were everywhere, as were warnings of the danger. These reminders of war remained a problem into the twenty-first century.[35]

April 19, 1945
[Le Havre]

Dear W.W.,

Your letters have arrived promptly and not with a breathtaking interval between writing and receiving. Yesterday, I hit the jackpot—thirteen, including one from Piggy, one from you, and not counting those three damn Sentinels of last fall that Schuster's is still sending to Washington. I also got a Christmas parcel from Schuster's last week. It was mangled beyond recognition, but I did manage to salvage the

Christmas tree which now graces our mantelpiece. Tell Pig that I'll write shortly and advise Mary Jane that I expect a girl (I'm torn between "Roberta" and Rosy Rhohde) and that I always knew she could do it.

This is a beautiful spot—one of France's major ports—and we live in a semi-chateau plastered against the side of a hill and overlooking a view slightly reminiscent of the rear of 1718 N. Prospect. For a week, we've been working without field jackets and our British issue is horribly itching and hot. And this winter we were cursing it for being so horribly inadequate.

I'll finish this later. I have to go to work at 3:45, but somebody just came in with a jeep and wants to go swimming. A report on the water will follow a few hours later.

Much later

The water was like ice, but the sun was there (I'm now smarting under a third degree burn), and I went to sleep beside a tangle of rusting barbed wire. The beach itself is covered with small stones that almost came under the classification of boulders, not counting other impedamenta such as spikes, discarded amo, miscellaneous sharp steel jobs, and the first question one asks, instead of "how's the water?" is "Has this area been cleared?"—or—"Any mines today?" I am fascinated by the bathing habits of the French. Little boys stepped into their trunks as we gazed blankly past them and the smaller children don't bother with the trunks. There was much speculation about our nationality and one little boy solved it. He said we were "Belgique." I haven't decided whether it was a compliment or not.

Spring is a wonderful season in France. It comes very subtly at first and not with the suddenness that we associate with ours. The colors are exquisite—I've seen so many scenes that are straight from Van Gogh. And only he has really captured the vividness of the sky and hills and trees. A few weeks ago, I took a trip up the Sienne on a troop ship—the apple and plum trees were in full blossom, the countryside a wonderful panorama. It's so different from England, which is so compact and neat—actually—it's rather like Wisconsin, except that the colors have a queer intenseness.

We have much work and at all hours. In fact, we have a crew of eleven and quite a collection of vehicles. No doughnut making, thank

God—or coffee. French help does that for us. We also have a group of G.I. drivers to supplement our driving. Mine is still rather erratic. I usually stall a vehicle on a quaint steep hillside or in front of a large bunch of Italian "co-beligerents" or pouting gentlemen of the Wehrmacht-that-was. Right now, we're working with repatriated prisoners—our own. They are a tragic sight.

As for social life, although there isn't too much to do, there is much of it. Every encouragement is given the alcoholic, but alcoholism and doughnuts don't mix, especially the next morning. If you have a club foot, buck teeth, crossed eyes, and a cleft pallette, you can still be Miss Popularity. The main thing is that you're female and speak English. It's certain that all of us will have more than a workable knowledge of the ways of men. "Men, men, men," one of my co-workers was heard to exclaim the other night, "I hope I never see another"—a rather vain hope, as she no doubt knew.

A bug the size of a B-17 just flew into our room. Screens are a luxury we <u>don't</u> possess. Do keep on writing—tell B. Twining Gleisner to prove that she still exists, my regards to your mother—

Recently liberated prisoners continued to arrive at the airport, but there was time for a trip to Fécamp, a beautiful nearby town on the sea. At Fécamp's Benedictine Abbey they purchased a supply of the world famous liqueur.

Diary, April 21, 1945
[Le Havre]

A gloomy Saturday morning with a heavy fog coming in from the channel. So far, we've had beautiful weather, almost like mid-summer. Emily and I went swimming yesterday, threading our way through the barbed wire and clumping down to the water in our G.I. shoes. The water was frigid, but the sun warm enough to give me a mild burn. We've been working at night at the airport—yesterday we had over 15,000, most of them prisoners of over a year—a lot from Kasserine Pass and Sicily, still in their sun tans. On the whole, they look a lot better than the boys from the breakthrough. A line of them coming from the planes looks like those rather blurred pictures of captured Germans on the Russian front. They are loaded with the strangest souvenirs—not only the expected swords, but umbrellas, canes, violins and most of all, stiff black S.S. hats and Wehrmacht grey field hats.

We drove up to Fécamp on Wednesday—Mary [Haynsworth], the Bedford and Paul, the G. I. driver. After serving an M.P. unit in an ex-hotel and some engineers, we drove to the top of the hill overlooking the lovely town—it was a beautiful day. A church of Gothic vintage had been pierced by a bomb, the edges of the cliff were studded with German gun emplacements and well-camouflaged trenches leading from pill box to pill box. In the bright sunlight, we returned to the town, where the Benedictine monastery is located on a shady and odiferous side street. It's a collection of well-kept buildings accented by many soaring spires and rather rococo buttresses and the procedure for getting the Benedictine involved bartering with a small boy for empty Benedictine bottles (three for a package of cigarettes) and finally, haggling over how many we should be allowed full of the stuff. We finally ended up with two large sized bottles and twenty junior-sized jobs that I imagine were given gratis to tourists in pre-war days. We paid about 500 francs for the whole business.

Fécamp itself is a charming town, comparatively unbombed, except for the waterfront. The beach, a lovely oval of yellow sand, is still covered with barbed wire and anti-tank barricades. We didn't wander about too much because of mines. Cows and people will still be running into those things fifty years from now.

A pile of mail included a much-welcomed letter from Betty Twining, now Mrs. Gleisner. Twine's news from Milwaukee sparked commentary on old romances, new marriages, early signs of the American baby boom, and Liz's own unmarried status. To Twine she could express her changing expectations in marriage, no longer content with the old-fashioned marriage expected by her old Milwaukee boyfriend, Ernst Kuenstner. She referred to her Leicester flame, Larry Pickard, and her "current swain," Frank Policastro.

April 22, 1945
[Le Havre]

Dear B-Bub,

Awk! It can't be! Not a document from B. Twining-Gleisner! Mi Gawd, when you do write, you do it with a thoroughness that puts Matthew, Luke and John to shame. More! More! Needless to say, I gobbled up each shining word with pitiful avidness and I'm glad to note that everybody is reproducing madly and that so far, none of our friends have produced Mongolian idiots. Thanks so much for the portrait of Clarey and Lt.j.g. Watson—he looks like a good fellow (naturally, since Chris married him) and that means that most of the original inhabitants of V. Villa have chosen the thorny path—except old Aunt Liz who is busy collecting war souvenirs so that she can visit old school chums. "Robert Jr., old Auntie Liz is coming today. Be good to her and maybe she'll give you an old beat-up 20 mm. shell." [. . .]

Ernst [Kuenstner] and I still correspond, he mostly complaining about la guerre and me trying to say the right thing so that he won't come through with some unsubtle Germanic crack about woman's place not being where I (obviously) am. Since the days of my unsatisfactory romance with Kuenstner, I've been infatuated enough with enough men to know that I'd never have a very good time playing Frau to his Herr. Indeed, I even met the man whom I'd wed, as you used to say, standing knee-deep in cherry juice. Then came the Ardennes and he is missing, which leaves me to start all over again, just like Laurie in "Oklahoma!." In the ETO, you have to run like hell to avoid it, so I'm not having a very hard time.

France is wonderful! Our location although in the midst of much destruction is essentially beautiful. Right now, everything is blooming madly—wisteria, lilacs, and unbelievably pink hawthorne. Appleblossom time was all that the hacks say it is. But our city has more stinks, odors, smells, and unpleasant perfumes than the stockyards. English plumbing was bad, but the French ain't! Our chateau is pretty civilized—we have johns that flush after a fashion and water that comes from taps labeled froid and chaud. Outside, we have a nice yard decorated with deck chairs that belonged to some unfortunate liner and a spectacular view. We work hard—lately we've been doing a lot with the repatriated prisoners, both British and American. I guess of all the sins of sadism, starvation is the most terrible and looking at those boys, I can work up quite a white hate against our Kraut friends. I daresay I'll be in their lair before another moon, much as I hate to leave this place.

My current swain and I are going up to Paris for our 48's. We plan to do everything that people sneer at Americans for doing—go to the Follies, drown ourselves in champagne (you can do that here, but it doesn't mix very well with doughnut doling) make much noise on the streets, and stand in a line outside Chanel's hoping to get some #5. Indeed, I'll try to get you some good stink water when the opportunity comes up.

There's so much I'd like to tell you, B-Bub, old goat, and such a time since we've really had a chance to chat. But auntie must rise tomorrow at 4:30 and I'm trying to get rid of a cognac hangover. Puleeze [write] again soon. After all, who takes care of the Red Cross's morale?

Love, Liz

A Christmas package from home arrived four months late with an evening bag that might have been more useful in England, where there had been fancier dances, than on the docks of Le Havre. Old friends continued to come and go. And Liz had news of Pvt. Bernie Levine, the smart GI who had traveled to Edinburgh with her.

April 22, 1945
[Le Havre]

Dear mother and daddy,

Merry Christmas! Your package with evening bag, mittens, soap and scarf arrived today—a little bit late but most welcomed. Whether this part of the ETO will ever provide the opportunity for sporting the bag remains to be seen—and only the fates know if I'll wear the mittens. And how I could have used them! The soap is especially wonderful, especially with a bathtub to use it in. How long I'll be enjoying the latter, remains a matter of speculation. Aileen left today for Germany—I reneged again. This war of movement on the part of R.C. is too sudden for me, but next time will be it. Margaret is still here and we have four new girls from England. That means that Maggie, Marge Calhoun and myself are the remaining old timers at the base—Marge was with us this summer on the other clubmobile attached to the 82nd[. . . .]

The weather remains beautiful—our yard is full of lilacs, wisteria and blooming Hawthorne. The countryside is a fairyland—we took a trip to Fécamp where Benedictine is made[. . . .] Tomorrow (Monday) is my day off, so Frank and I are going up there again for a picnic. The weather is quite warm enough for swimming and I tried it the other day. [. . .]

It's almost twilight—"2030," the AEF announcer just said—and I must get ready for my evening of recreation. More later.

Next day

Have just seen two of my co-workers off to the U.K. for their leaves, from there they'll go off to the so-called front (wherever that is). Plane traveling over here is not the luxurious thing it is at home and our little friends, when last seen, were wedged firmly between the London mail and some barrack bags.

Last night, we took Nancy (who left this morning) to Frank's Officer's Club as a farewell gesture. I'm sure that Nancy will never forget her last night at this base. The DUKW Officers outdid themselves in a combination "You Can't Take It With You" and "Hellzapoppin." They had a baseball game with fruit juice cans while one of them, with a box over his head, umpired. They did a high diving act from a ladder and Frank played the trumpet while the Doctor played the drums. The whole procedure was so exhausting that it's fortunate that today is my jour of rest.

On this note of exhaustion, I leave you. Love to you all,

Elizabeth

[p.s.] They've put Bernie in the infantry. He called a week ago from Belgium and one of his friends called last night to tell me he'd left that morning. Quell Domage! [What a pity!]

A long letter home reported satisfaction for the first time with mail service, new driving skills, including double-clutching, the longing to wear nice, civilian clothing, and hunger for news from home.

April 25, 1945
[Le Havre]

Dear mother and daddy,

A few moments in which to start a letter before going out to work. It's been raining all day, but the sun just broke through with its usual brilliance, which will make our doughnut doling easier.

Daddy, I saw a brand-new Continental tire yesterday on a very smooth and elongated Kraut car. They certainly know how to make things, but, Thanks, I'll stick to the Yankee variety of vehicle. In fact, I'm getting to be quite a driver-up hills, around shell holes and through gendarmes. My newest achievement is double-clutching, necessary on heavier vehicles. Two M.P.'s taught me yesterday, much to the consternation of a small gathering of natives. I think they thought I was being taken in custody.

The mail has been wonderful—got a major opus from [Betty Twining] Gleisner, who is still holding the fort at 1718. Christmas things have stopped coming through, thank goodness. There's something incongruous about writing thank-you notes for Christmas presents in April. My little friend, Bernie, has been transferred to the infantry—did I tell you he called me from Belgium? We are getting ice-cream four times a week from the CB's—wonderful organization, the Navy.

Margaret and I have inherited the best rooms in the chateau. Not only do we have ice blue satin comforters, we also have two full length mirrors, a dressing table, French windows that overlook a sea of pink Hawthorne blossoms and the blue channel—and a fireplace crowned by another rococo mirror. We also have beaucoup flies—the French don't believe in screens. But the flies are immaterial.

Our surplus junk left in London has finally caught up with us. So I'm shipping some of it home, together with some other things, including two shot glasses made out of 20 mm. shells for daddy. Hope

Liz's watercolor of 10 Rue Chef de Caux, Le Havre, known as "Chateau Hysteria" to the dozen or so Red Cross women who lived there. "Our chateau is pretty civilized—we have johns that flush after a fashion and water that comes from taps labeled froid and chaud," she wrote her best friend on April 22, 1945. *Courtesy Charles Richardson, Jr.*

he has something in which to put into them. So, Mother, would you have the coat cleaned and put in my closet—you might as well give the dress away, as well as anything else that's in there. When I get home, I'm going to start from scratch and I think it will be Bonwit Teller's. No—Lord & Taylors. Well, anyway, I'm going to blow my top. You can't imagine how we dream about clothes. But I can't cart around these civilian clothes, nice as it is to wear them. I'm still keeping my suit and two other dresses which is more than enough.

Later.

Back from work and having read the "Stars & Stripes," I'm ready for more letter-writing. To tell the truth, there's not too much to tell you, except that the news in the S & S is mostly good, but it could be better. But I suppose the Krauts, since they have to have a grave, want a good deep one. The radio is giving forth with the BBC news and the Prime

Minister has announced that V-Bomb activity over England has ceased—which brings back the moments I spent getting acquainted with the Almighty last July in London—and several times since. [. . .]

I'm getting anxious to be on my merry way, except for little Frank, whom I hate to leave behind. This will be a terrific opportunity, though. For the first time, I'll be able to say "Off to the Front" and leave somebody sitting behind in the rear echelon. However, all this rather loses its impact when nobody knows exactly where or why the front is[. . . .]

Love & much of it,
Elizabeth

Rumors of German surrender continued, as Liz recorded in her diary the comings and goings around Chateau Hysteria. She was still seeing Frank, though her last sentence suggested she might have said a curt goodbye after the lieutenant had too much to drink.

Diary, April 30, 1945
[Le Havre]

Le Havre is full of rumors—yesterday the "Stars and Stripes" came out with an extra denying the latest peace rumors—that an unconditional surrender had been offered to all three allies by Himmler. Meanwhile, the third army is the only one that continues to meet stiff opposition—the rest just walk into towns meeting not much organized resistance. Whether the strange political mechanics of this war is holding back peace negotiations for the San Francisco conference or what, nobody knows. Meanwhile, men continue to die and will keep on dying for many months. Down near Cherburg, they've been having raids from the Channel Islands. The Germans on Guernsey are getting hungry and all they are really after is food. We've had several alerts, but that's all.

Aileen is with the third army as is Nancy Richardson. Cush is with the ninth and says that in one week, they've moved five times and that she hasn't really worked since arriving at corps. hdqs. We have plenty of that. Yesterday, we served the Navy outfit who originally crossed the Rhine. We couldn't figure out what they were at first—they looked like the usual combat-weary G.I., except for an occasional navy jacket. They're all going home, after six months of army life.

Chateau Hysteria has five new girls—all from England. Margaret and I saw Polly [Haskins] and Nancy on the plane for England—7 days leave. Saturday night we spent at the Dukw Club and Frank got sick on cognac and ice cream. He also polka'd with one of his brother officers and departed into the night feeling abused.

Liz recorded in her diary the great events of the final days of war in Europe, including Hitler's death, but the work continued.

Diary, May 5, 1945
[Le Havre]

Hamburg is an open city, all German opposition in Italy and northwest Germany has ceased, the German radio says that Hitler is dead, Mussolini has been shot in Milan—the physical war in Europe is almost over.

Meanwhile, supplies and men pour into Le Havre and all these great events have little effect on us. Outside, a steady gray rain soaks the countryside, the three little French maids are cleaning the living room and Rhoda is talking to them in bad French as she waits for the 12 o'clock news. Last night, while the same rain fell, we had a jam session—one accordion, one trumpet, one trombone and a clarinet. Everybody was in a festive mood and there was much cognac and vin rouge. The boy who played the trombone was a CB who looked about sixteen, the rest were recruited from the local MP company and the band that greets the RAMP's (released allied military prisoners). Long after I went to bed, I could hear the wail of the trumpet and the squealing of the accordion, slightly muffled by the falling rain.

At the airport, we are getting many air corps men, mixed in with the infantry. One told me of being marched through the streets of Munich a year ago, while the populace spat at them, shouted invectives and generally acted like modern-day barbarians. For no reason at all, air corps prisoners were put in solitary for months at a time. Conditions only improved for them when they were under the control of the Wehrmacht.

[8]

V-E Day and V-E Blues

The celebration of German defeat had begun, at long last. It was a "sober armistice," however for, as Liz understood, "the responsibilities of the victor" meant lots of work ahead in Europe. And the war in the Pacific was far from over.

May 7, 1945
[Le Havre]

Dear mother, daddy and Butch,

It's all over now, so says the BBC and, therefore, this is a sort of paen of Victory and rejoicing. We've been awaiting the official declaration for at least four days and if it weren't for the radio, we would not know the difference—no whistles, no bells, no parade. I just gave our waitress a glass of benedictine and the rest of us are sitting around, drinking a toast to the future. It's a sober armistice and this time, we are fully aware of the responsibilities of the victor. Perhaps it won't be too long before we'll all be together again—not too long in terms of years, a long time in terms of months.

We really had our celebration last night—Frank & I, Maggie and Douglas. And still celebrating, I had to go to work at 0200—ow, Thank God, those long lines of troops aren't marked for combat, but for each living face, there are two or three to haunt me. If only the Pacific war lets up, the ETO will be a happy place!

More later—I have to eat dinner and here comes Frank, my dinner guest for the evening. He's leaving for 8 days tomorrow, thus delaying our projected Paris trip—

Enclosed is a Nazi home guard patch for Butch—it came all the way from Germany with a RAMP who gave it to me. The snapshots will make Mr. Wood happy—London on a sunny day last winter. Do you recognize any of it? Don't misplace them!

Love to all of you!
Elizabeth

[p.s.] Daddy, do you know a Mr. Brigham—a salesman with BALL-BAND in Upstate New York? His daughter [Betty Brigham] is here with us—in fact—she came over with me in July. We just discovered our BALL-BAND link up.

In her diary later the same day Liz reported the sounds of celebration, muted by realistic understanding of larger meanings. She and Frank had an evening together before his scheduled departure for Germany.

Diary, May 7, 1945
[Le Havre]

We first heard of the Armistice this afternoon over the B.B.C.—the Germans accepted unconditional surrender terms at 2:40 this morning in Reims. Now it is past midnight and the ships in the harbor are blowing their whistles and in between, much small arms firing, even in our front yard—but it took all that time for the news to penetrate. It sounds rather like a peace-time fourth of July. Underneath nobody is really excessively affected by what we all have been expecting. This is the first night since I arrived in Le Havre that everybody has been in bed by midnight and Margaret and I had a cup of coffee against the background of whistles and firing.

Frank leaves tomorrow for an eight day convoy trip into Germany. He came up to dinner, slightly delayed by a flat tire en route. Then he had an 8:30 meeting and dashed into the night mounted on his rusty jeep.

Le Havre put on a grand victory parade. Approximately 10,000 U.S. soldiers and sailors marched in a line six kilometers long through streets festooned with Allied flags. Citizens clapped and waved as the marchers passed.[1] Liz and several colleagues joined in, bringing up the rear in their jeep. The work continued, including serving 400 gallons of coffee to liberated prisoners.

Diary, May 9, 1945
[Le Havre]

Normandy Base Section celebrated the advent of peace with a parade, through the main street of Le Havre. We saw it from a jeep, six of us, joining. The populace in their "vive L'Amerique!" and waving frantically to the men we knew. The city had a festive air—British, French and American flags—the hammer and sickle of Russia—all were hanging from windows and people lined the curb, applauding and shouting. It's the first time I've seen any evidence of enthusiasm. The day was hot and sultry and as a result, the parade was not up to West Point standards. While we were standing on the hood of the jeep, a very drunken Frenchman chose the driver's seat as his resting place—and only a tire "descendé" [flat] kept the jeep from being covered with children, women, men and transient animals, not including G.I.s and sailors. When the army had passed us, we followed, much applauded by the French. Helen, bolstered by V-E day calvados and scotch, returned the applause graciously, waving a paper tricolor on the back of which was the sage advice to shop in Le Havre stores.

The maids celebrated too. They sang loudly all afternoon—their specialty was "It's a long Road to Teep-er-ar-reay." The lunch dishes weren't cleared until 4:00 and our beds must have been made by remote control.

Today at the airport, we used more than 400 gals. of coffee—the sky was black with C-47s and the line of RAMPS stretched back like some odd snake, punctuated by German helmets, fatigue hats and other miscellaneous headgear. The men look pretty good—they're mostly air corps. Last night, working late there, the sky was illuminated with red, green and yellow flares.

Le Havre celebrated the end of the European war with a parade. Liz described it to her parents in a letter of May 10, 1945: "Little tricolors, American flags, Russian and British blossomed out of windows and on lamp posts and the populace lined up obligingly for a parade. We saw it from a jeep and afterwards, got quite a reception from the crowd." *Courtesy Mary Haynsworth Mathews.*

A letter home provided details of the victory celebrations and the chaos of Chateau Hysteria.

May 10, 1945
[Le Havre]

Dear mother and daddy,

John's picture arrived yesterday, unwrinkled and unruffled. Naturally, I am most proud and impressed. So are Lillian and Yvonne, our moron femmes de chambre. They almost swooned in admiration, although they think his hair is too short. Lillian and Yvonne go for flowing locks in a big way. This morning, I'm O.D. The schedule is out of the way, the telephone has stopped ringing and perhaps I can get off an uninterrupted letter . . . Perhaps.

Our town finally reacted to peace. Little tricolors, American flags, Russian and British blossomed out of windows and on lamp posts and the populace lined up obligingly for a parade. We saw it from a jeep and afterwards, got quite a reception from the crowd. Little schoolgirls with flowers in their hair shrieked "Vive L'Amerique" and we shrieked, "Viva La France" and shook hands enthusiastically with everybody and anybody. The night was loud with boat whistles and small arms fire—flares illuminated the sky. Somebody chose our front yard in which to empty the magazine of his carbine.

Did I say that this was going to be an uninterrupted letter? The planes are already coming in, so I must corale our forces and leave. To give you some idea of the amount of work we have at that one place alone, we served over 400 gallons of coffee yesterday afternoon from 1:00 to 5:30. As a whole, they are looking better than the first groups we had, but their better is not good[. . . .]

And now I must leave—you can imagine under what handicaps every sentence was written. The telephone started ringing as soon as I said it wasn't and about ten people and ten problems have wandered in on review. This is a horrible house for letter writing—too many people, too many conversations, too many languages. The person who christened it "Chateau Hysteria" was most perceptive.

So love to you all and I'll try again soon—

Elizabeth

Liz's most intense wartime romance was with Lt. Frank Policastro. Their ups and downs caused her to write him on May 11, 1945, that "I wish I could love you in a sort of calm, disinterested way." Policastro was in charge of a unit of Ducks, amphibian trucks that moved cargo and men from ships anchored at Le Havre. *Courtesy Rose Policastro.*

Liz wrote Frank Policastro fifteen minutes after he left for Germany, a departure expected several days earlier but delayed for unknown reasons until May 11. This is the only known letter from her to Frank. She signed her full first name, not the "Liz" used by her friends. Her words leave little doubt that she was head-over-heals in love, not in the "calm, disinterested way" she wished nor in the more restrained way she had written her parents about Frank.

209

[May 11, 1945]
[Le Havre]
Friday night
9:35

Darling,

You've been gone for about fifteen minutes—scooting away in a very smooth jeep of doubtful origins—and I'm sitting on my sack with the windows open, while outside F.B. (alias Snooks) yelps at what I hope is an imaginary rat. After last night, I don't count too heavily on that imagination stuff. That <u>was</u> a rat we saw promenading so casually on the wall, wasn't it?

Perhaps this letter will bring a sackful of mail in your direction, all full of good news and amusing little items. Anyway, darling, consider this as a small gesture of my love for you. Here I am, proping my glazed eyelids up with sheer will power while 20 minutes away by jeep (25 minutes by clubmobile) you are, I hope, preparing for at least twelve hours of uninterrupted slumber. This is it! What other test of my devotion could you ask?

By the way, Lt. Policastro, what is it about you that grows and grows on a person, until that person suddenly discovers that without you, time is an unfilled and empty void? Qu'est que ce? [What is it?] What will I do the day that Red Cross, or deployment, or cruel circumstance tears me from you? I know it's coming, but I'd just as soon not face it. And I wish I could love you in a sort of calm, disinterested way—but I guess that wouldn't be a very stable sort of love, would it?

Marie just left for the "General Ernst"—she's so excited that I have my doubts about how she'll navigate the gang plank. And Maggie and Haynsworth are discussing Marlene Dietrich. Net conclusion: she is older. You see what fine intelligent conversations we have on the second floor, especially when I'm trying to take the place of three weeks of mailess mail call.

My eyes just shut. They did it automatically.

But even in the misty land between sleep and being awake, I still have the strength to say—in a somewhat cracked voice, I admit—that I love you very much. I think I must even love that temper of yours!

Hey! I sort of like this one sided conversation! I can go on in my own sweet way, with no obstruction, no back talk, no remarks. But whatever I said, it would all boil down to the same thing said in a million different ways, my darling.

Your—
Elizabeth

Liz finally had a 48-hour leave, but she failed in an attempt to repeat her trip up the Seine on the *President Warfield*. She then hitched an airplane ride to Reims, location of Supreme Headquarters, Allied Expeditionary Forces [SHAEF]. She visited the cathedral and had a jeep sightseeing tour that included nearby World War I battlefields. The trip home was a bumpy ride, hitched in a transport plane filled with RAMPs recently liberated from Stalag Luft 1 in Barth, Germany, which had held over 7,000 American prisoners of war.[2]

Diary, May 13, 1945
[Le Havre]

Margaret and I had planned to spend our 48 hours going up the Sienne on the "President Warfield." It was due to leave the pontoon pier at noon and accordingly, we packed our musette bags and presented ourselves. But the pier was deserted except for three tugboats, on one of which we had coffee. By the time one of the boys had taken me around the basin in a row boat, the "Warfield" was sighted down in area I and when we boarded her, it was to discover that her trip was delayed. We had a turkey dinner in the wardroom and returned to 10 Rue Chef de Caux.

Then Mary Haynsworth came in from Weisbaden, Germany with a pilot in tow. He offered to take me to Reims. I accepted. The day was lovely, white clouds high above and an infinitely neat countryside below. We followed the Sienne to Rouen, which from the air looks not nearly as damaged as Le Havre. Then we gained altitude, passed Beavais and after two hours, landed at the main Reims airport. The land here was pockmarked with shell holes and the hangers were bombed and burnt. But the airstrip, corregated, was good and while Roy fueled up his L5, someone found me a ride in a General's car, to Reims. Reims looked festive after Le Havre. There were many little cafés, and music, and French families promenading with G.I.'s in tow. I had dinner at the transient officer's mess and listened to an Air Force lieutenant (drunk) try to get a date with a French SHAEF telephone operator. Her tactics were brilliant and she eluded him gracefully. My billet was on the third floor of the Oise Base Section Officers mess—a square little room overlooking a series of roofs and nothing else. Two Public Relations men from SHAEF, one a Lt. from the 30th Division, the other a captain, invited me for a jeep ride, they were "bored stiff" and produced the usual about Reims being a good G.I. town, but bad for officers, the girls were too religious, the cafés crowded . . .

So along with the two officers and two G.I.s, all from public relations, we toured Reims. The cathedral was breathtaking in the twilight. "If you look carefully" said the lieutenant, "You'll see that the gargoyles have the faces of John D., Nelson and Winthrop Rockerfeller." It is even more soaring than King's Chapel at Cambridge and Chester Cathedral and far more intricate—and yet, with all this, extremely compact and solid.

We took a long white road out of Reims and through World War I battlefields, now a wilderness of brambles and rusted barbed wire, then through Verzy and other little towns, sheltered in the curves of low lying hills. The countryside was rich and well-tended, the grape vines green, the soil well turned. It was late when we came back to Reims, to a stolen apple pie in the bleak room of the Captain.

This morning, I woke up at eight and went directly to the SHAEF motor pool across the street. They in turn, referred me to the Oise Base Section motor pool and a weapon's carrier took me out to the Air Field. There, I was stranded—no C-47's for Le Havre and the next field was a good 25 kil. from there. A tech. sgt. with a piper cub furnished me a ride to an airfield where they were loading RAMPS—it was about a 20 minute ride by plane over that patch quilt country, covered with the snake-like markings of old trenches and fortifications. We landed nicely and a command car took me to the flying control tower where a confused lieutenant and a sgt. were handling the job of landing C-47 after C-47 and directing even more into the air. I finally was directed down to the end of the runway to C-47 593, called Boopsy, waiting to be loaded. 29 ex-prisoners made their appearance, I made the 30th. They were all air corps and hadn't been in a plane since various disasters had met them over a year ago. When we saw the Sienne, one of the boys said, "I baled out near here fourteen months ago." The ride was bumpy and I would have been happier in a smaller and less over-loaded plane. They had the usual souvenirs, including snapshots that they had looted from German homes (smiling boys in gaudy uniforms, smiling girls kissing smiling boys, family groups, snapshots of the Christmas present table). The boy next to me, a gunner on a liberator, got sick and we landed at Le Havre at noon.

Again, Liz imagines coming home, a subject on the minds of many Americans overseas in 1945. Some, like Gretchen Schuyler, could joke that she feared she might sit "crossing my legs as though still in trousers . . . throwing butts and ashes on the floor." Others, more serious, predicted that "we shall return a strange lot who will need every ounce of understanding you are capable of giving us."[3]

This letter home showed Liz's new enthusiasm for airplane travel, and particularly for the small L-5 Sentinel. She had learned how easy it was for a young American woman to hitch a plane ride. With victory, the military censor was no longer looking over her shoulder, so she could reveal her location and note a few of the many details of the last year.

May 14, 1945
Le Havre

Dear mother and daddy,

Your letter of April 26, remailed May 1st, arrived today—pretty good time for a change. Summer must be almost upon the Patch—it was about a year ago that I left it. Could it have been that long ago? Sounds as if Mother had embarked on a re-forestation project and by the time I get home, the yard will be something out of "Better House and Garden."

Elizabeth has taken to the air in a big way and after flying, other

213

means of transportation seem dull, indeed. My first ride was in a Piper Cub over Le Havre, the harbor and the sorry ruins. My second, yesterday, was to Reims, along the Sienne and cross country[. . . .] This morning, by various and sundry means, I got a C-47 back to Le Havre, along with about thirty released prisoners. We were pretty high up and crowded, so I couldn't see much—anyway—I was too busy listening to a thousand little tales of prison life and looking at souvenirs. The piper cub is more to my liking, soaring low on the Sienne, climbing over the neatly wooded hills and looking down on the toy villages and the scars of two wars. Around Reims, the trenches of World War I are still in evidence, not bothered a bit by a newer and more fluid war.

People are really going home (and to the Pacific). So far, Red Cross hasn't said anything about what will happen to us, but I daresay we'll be kept in the ETO for many a month. There are the occupation troops to take care of, and if we remain here, we'll soon have enough to keep a regiment busy. The RAMPS alone keep us busy now—all eleven of us.

The "Stars & Stripes" says that we can not only give our location, but also our means of transportation across the ocean blue—in my case, the "Queen Elizabeth" in five days from New York to Scotland, with no enemy action, although we twisted enough to elude the entire German navy. So you see, what with the boat train from Paddington to Dieppe, I've had luxury accommodations all the way. After Washington, we spent a week at the St. George in Brooklyn and you can imagine how tempted I was to call everybody, but it definitely was not being done. Otherwise, you no doubt have a pretty good idea of my various bases in England, so I won't have to go into that.

John's picture arrived and it's scrumptious. This is just in case you didn't get my last letter.

Mail service is or should be better by now. So don't forget to write. For some reason or other, I'm having a hard time writing these days—too much excitement and speculation in the air. My love to everybody—
Elizabeth

VE Day brought new challenges of morale. All GIs counted and re-counted the points they had accumulated for length of service, time over-

seas, number of dependents, and combat awards. Total points determined how soon they would leave Europe and whether or not they
would continue on toward combat in the Pacific War. Waiting and uncertainty caused severe strain. A writer for the French newspaper *Le
Monde* described Le Havre as "the port of bitter men." A concerned Red
Cross official reported to Washington headquarters in early July that "extreme drunkenness & foul language are much more prevalent than before
VE Day." Across Western Europe Red Cross workers noted increases in
drinking and brawling and a general restlessness. In the weeks and
months after V-E Day some American soldiers evolved from liberators to
conquerors and anything but their country's best ambassadors.[4]

The future of Red Cross personnel was even less clear than that of
GIs. Many Red Cross women were as eager as the men to go home.
Priscilla Alden wrote from London headquarters a month before the
Germans surrendered: "The girls can think of nothing except going as
soon as the last gun is fired. You couldn't pay them to leave now, but they
are all tired and homesick." The end of war did not mean an immediate
trip home. As late as July an official told the newsletter *Overseas Woman*
that "there will be no one-way tickets for ETO Red Cross workers for a
long time to come."[5]

Facing such uncertainty, morale became a serious issue. A Red Cross
field administrator reported to the head of the European operation on
June 4 that "Most of our people are tired. They feel they have done their
job. VE blues are in their blood. We need fresh, enthusiastic workers—
men and women who are not in a rut and who do not know what can and
what cannot be done." A month later another Red Cross administrator
confessed that there were "a number of people here whom we feel are not
only failing to carry their burden with the Department but are actually of
negative value." One Clubmobiler, Hattie Engelhardt, lamented that
summer, "I have asked for a release, which will not be granted, so I watch
Clubmobiling, which was once the best thing going for the ARC, die a
slow, agonizing death." Stuck at a desk job at Paris headquarters in early
1946, Jane McKee spent months trying to resign because she was "just
marking time in the ARC." Morale was a special challenge because of
everyone's high expectations of the women. As Mary Metcalfe recalled,
"just because we were Red Cross girls, everyone expected that we'd never

feel downhearted. We were always supposed to be bright and cheerful, not gloomy." Back in the States the Red Cross struggled to convince qualified women to join.[6]

American Red Cross leaders were very aware of sagging morale. They sometimes responded with bureaucratic pig-headedness. A piece in the July 7 issue of the organization's European newsletter *Over Here* admonished against the growing laxness in obeying Red Cross uniform regulations. Too many women were seen wearing colored blouses, hair longer than the regulation shoulder length, and without their Red Cross hat. A more sympathetic editorial in the same newsletter advised, "While you're building GI morale don't forget our own." Most important, the Red Cross began more liberal leaves policies that allowed personnel to travel to Switzerland and other vacation spots. In May, headquarters created a new administrative position with responsibility for the morale and welfare of its female workers.[7]

Liz had enjoyed only a few days off duty since her trip to the southwest of England in early February. Her letters and diary in early summer suggested touches of the V-E blues that were sweeping through Europe, but her humor and tendency to make the best of things remained. In this letter she reported that Frank had returned from Germany and a goat had moved into Chateau Hysteria. The photograph referred to, of a tall Liz in "teddy bear suit" standing next to the short MP from Brooklyn, was taken by Mary Haynsworth, likely on the trip to Fécamp described in Liz's diary on April 21.[8]

May 18, 1945
[Le Havre]

Dear mother and daddy,

Chateau Hysteria is its usual hysterical self this afternoon. The two moron chamber maids and two little men in very loud plaid business suits are having a most intense and incomprehensible conversation in the hall, the phone is ringing, the ladies are leaving for the afternoon shift, the BBC is bellowing chamber music—and the goat is bleating. (Do goats bleat?) Ah yes, the goat. It is very, very young and female and

A short "snowdrop" and a tall Liz in Normandy in April 1945. Liz sent the snapshot to her parents with the comment "you can see what I mean when I refer to our teddy bear suits. The M. P. is from Brooklyn, the background is the hills of Fécamp." *Courtesy Charles Richardson, Jr.*

sounds like a doll that cries mama. Margaret and I acquired it yesterday from some G.I.'s who in their turn had acquired it in the mists of a cognac binge. It goes by any number of names—"Tout Suite," "Rotation," "Old Goat," but I call her Lillian after one of the above mentioned chamber maids. They look alike. Lillian is now being fed via bottle and all household work has stopped while the entire French staff gathers about in wonder and admiration.

Frank has returned from an eight day trip into Germany. He says that the devastation is frightening, that ghost city after ghost city marks the progress of the war. Four of our crew leaves for the forward region at the end of the week—I'm not going again, but I daresay I won't be able to put it off much longer.

The enclosed handkerchief, Mother, is from Antwerp. One of the G.I.s sent me two—I gave one to Frank for his mother, the other is for you. As for the snapshots, you can see what I mean when I refer to our teddy bear suits. The M. P. is from Brooklyn, the background is the hills of Fécamp.

The other has not quite such a pastoral background. Once upon a time, the "Normandy" used to dock there and the "Paris." The latter is docked there now, as you can see, only it's on its side and its sailing days are over.

Everything is in such a state of flux, no body knows which end is up or where they're going next and all we talk about are points, who's going to the CBI [China-Burma-India], who's going home and what-will-the-Red-Cross-do-with-us. Every G.I. has spent the last few days counting and recounting their accumulated points and the first question in a conversation is "How are you coming on points?" Food has taken a back seat.

We got a wonderful liquor ration this month—one cognac, one champagne, one scotch, 1/2 bottle cointrau (an apéritif) and 1/2 bottle of gin. The usual method is to take one of the above to the club and by the time everybody has had a drink, c'est finié. Therefore, there is no danger of your daughter becoming an alcoholic.

On this cheery note, I must stop. Pul-leese write as often as possible and love to you all—

Elizabeth

This diary entry reflected the general unease in the weeks following V-E Day and the challenges created by so many men eager to leave Europe behind. Demand for ship transport was stretched far beyond available supply. Harbor congestion and bottlenecks caused growing frustrations. Restless men lived in a "sea of mud." One Red Cross worker at

Camp Lucky Strike, Edith Steiger, wrote that "there just isn't any bottom to the mud when it rains." RAMPs had first priority, but even they had to wait. By mid-May the Red Cross estimated there were 47,000 RAMPs jammed into Lucky Strike and assigned the camp "A.1. priority" as it rushed more workers to the site.[9]

At home the American Red Cross depended on the voluntary contributions and the goodwill of millions of Americans. Thus the organization naturally engaged in public relations work to show itself in the best light. Some of that image-making was happening at Lucky Strike, or so Liz thought, and she wanted no part of it.

Diary, May 27, 1945
[Le Havre]

This is a time of great unrest and general vagueness. Nobody knows what will happen or why or for that matter how. The port is preparing for the debarkations to come and trying to get the RAMPs home, while as yet, no great amount of ships have come in. Meanwhile, thousands upon thousands of RAMPs wait at Lucky Strike, Twenty Grand—even at the airport and the 15th Repl. Depot. The 1st Army is due to come through here as soon as the RAMPs are disposed of. And the Red Cross is concentrating at least 50 personnel at Lucky Strike—club, home service, clubmobile and what have you.

Headquarters phoned Tuesday and ordered three of us to Lucky Strike. Accordingly, myself and Peggy Evans and the Bedford drove up—Lucky Strike was a sea of mud and long queues of men waiting for chow, for processing, for clothing, for anything.[10] We were billeted in a largish farm house where a huge Girl Scoutish sort of woman, greeted us with a speech about co-ordinating Red Cross and then went back to preparing some sort of stew over a burner. We spent the night in a tent and the next morning, I went down to the motor pool and got a ride back to Le Havre in a truck driven by one of the 467 ATC's [illegible word].

From then until now we have had a steady deluge of people, supposedly headed for Lucky Strike—but they have a tendency to stop here and go no further. Red Cross is making a great play on this Lucky

Strike business, obviously for political reasons and I want no part of it. We also have two girls from seventh army—old veterans who have come up from Italy—who have us glassy-eyed with their tales.

Later

I've just come back from the quai d'Escale [the primary troopship berth] where we took care of 900 U.K. leave troops. At first, there was the usual confusion about where—the station was empty except for four open trucks and we finally landed at the pier at least an hour before the troops showed up. It's now almost five o'clock and I must take a bath and get ready for dinner. The day is gray—everybody is dissatisfied and restless. Mary Haynsworth and I just ate a can of fried oysters she got in a package. So I could blame it on indigestion . . . Frank has been back from Germany for almost two weeks—he went as far as Nurmburg and says that the destruction we have in Normandy is nothing to that in the Saar Valley and on into Germany. Now, his unit expects shipment at any moment to Marsailles and the CBI, so we have little time left.

In a matter-of-fact sort of way, Liz told her parents more about Frank, her "nice habit" and "steady diet," who she now admitted is the reason she didn't want to leave Le Havre. Liz commented again on her unwillingness to waste time doing the kind of busy work at Camp Lucky Strike that would only help the Red Cross score political points at home. Her decision not to follow orders was unusual and suggests her interest in meaningful work and disgust with public relations showiness.[11]

Le Havre
May 28, 1945

Dear mother and daddy,

Two letters arrived from you today. . . .

I was sent up to one of the big RAMP camps last week on temporary duty. Red Cross apparently was making much big show and after wading through about 50 extra R. C. personnel, I decided that there was more work in Le Havre, and took off. Chateau Hysteria has been like a hotel all week and we have about three Old Veterans who sit about the dinner table discussing their combat experiences and are most anxious to rejoin their various units in Germany. I'm used to the men going over every minute on the line, but when my fellow-females do it, I feel as if I were in some sort of [Salvador] Dali dream.

But I am anxious to get into Germany and the only thing that is holding me back is Frank, who will be leaving soon—and not for home. We live on rumors and if rumors were food, we'd be <u>very</u> fat. If I haven't told you about him, he's a 1st. Lieut. of the ATC (which means Ducks), landed in France on D-Day and has been here ever since. We have good times together and after three months, he's a nice habit. I met him the second night I was in Le Havre and except for two weeks when he was in Marsailles and one when he went to Germany, he's been my steady diet. So much for that . . .

The weather has been horrible—much drooling rain, chilly and all this adds to our common mood of uncertainty. Everybody wants to get home. Here's the jeep—more later.

Just spent the afternoon calling for the laundry, dry cleaning and other sundry necessities—PX rations and all the rest. Write—what is Marion Campbell in? Club? Hospital? Home Service? Civilian Relief? Where is she?

Love
Elizabeth

Liz wrote a newsy letter to Sue Stevens, her brother John's fiancé, perhaps now wife, congratulating her on graduating from college. Liz showed some of her wit as she listed the pets at Chateau Hysteria and commented on middle-aged GIs with enough points to go home.

Le Havre, France
May 31, 1945

Dear Sue,

This is wildest imagination, but I do hope that this arrives before your graduation. In my day, people graduated in mid June, but things have changed since then and you are no doubt by now an Educated

Woman. And I am so far behind on news that you might even be married! At least, you know that my thoughts and well-wishes are with you both.

Your nice letter arrived yesterday, along with some tidbits of news dated mid-December, so it was doubly appreciated for its modernity. And I'm still in Le Havre and if the Gods are kind, I'd like to stay for some time before Germany. Our work with the ex-POW's is almost over and then begins redistribution or embarkations or call it any name you desire. It's still standing on the docks at 3 AM, usually in rain. (It always rains for a night operation). Everybody seems to be headed westward except ourselves and at this point, it looks as if I wouldn't be leaving the continent Europa for at least a year.

June 3

You can see that letter-writing is most extra, extra curriculum. It's now Sunday morning, the sun is out and I have just returned from a morning's work with 600 point men, all over 42, bound for home (eventually). They refered to themselves as the Lost Battalion, left over from the World War I army of occupation and if I looked at one picture of a large and mature family, I looked at sixty. The other inmates of Chateau Hysteria are coming in from their labors—no! no! One has a puppy—she got it off a ship. Its name is Thomas Johnson (she says) and it increases our livestock population. We now are supporting one female goat (black and white—age four weeks), one adolescent spaniel, one very young puppy and now, T. Johnson. We don't count the rats in the basement as livestock.

I wrote Johnny and told him that I had met a friend of yours from Akron, Danny O'Neill, who used to play tennis with you. When I saw him he was fresh from a German POW camp and therefore innocent of any insignia, but by now, he must be home and getting fat. So I don't know whether he was air corps or infantry or Mess Kit Washing Battalion.

But I do know one thing—if I'm ever going to get this letter off, it will have to be NOW. Do keep on writing and tell your husband-to-be that I am pining for news of him.

Love,
Elizabeth

In a V-Mail Liz thanked Aunt Gertrude Richardson for buying her a pair of shoes, a rationed item at home and for Liz a greatly anticipated diversion from GI boots.

Le Havre
May 31, 1945

Dear Aunt G.,

Your letter about the shoes arrived and I am filled with anticipation—they sound trés jolie and I'm only sorry that you had to give up a shoe [ration] stamp in order to get them. Right now I'd take any old footgear, just so it isn't G.I. The rains of Angleterre [England] did something to my antique civilian gear. And the cobbles of France finished them. . . .

At the present, I'm quite satisfied with Le Havre and the hot and cold running water. The ETO has made me more comfort-loving than ever. We are really working, mostly with ex-POW's, all of whom are recovering nicely—in fact—they are three times as exuberant as ordinary G.I.'s. Thanks again for buying the shoes—

Love,
Elizabeth

To Winifred Wood Liz wrote of recent events at Chateau Hysteria, her trip to Reims, work with RAMPs, and her observation on the larger world, "one hell of a world."

Le Havre, France
June 4, 1945

Dear W.W.,

Hot dawg! Zee mail eet is koming inn right smartly! [. . .]

V.E. day has changed things—instead of incoming troops, they're outgoing and so far, they've mostly been Kriegies—ex-POW's to you. For 24 horrible hours, I was on temporary duty at a camp [Lucky Strike] about 50 miles from here where they are brought for processing.

223

Picture Milwaukee as a tent city and you have a good idea of the outward aspect of their home away from home. Then add 10 feet of mud interlayed with layers of dust and you have it! In spite of my dread of a Red Cross court martial, I went AWOL back to Le Havre where we at least have coherent work amidst the ruins. Now, our Kriegies are homeward bound and we are being deluged with point men and divisions enroute for the C.B.I. via 30 days in the states. It's a funny feeling to see them get on that ship, knowing that if you walked up the gang plank, you'd be seeing the Battery in ten days.

Yesterday, two of us were working with what we thought looked like a most mature bunch of G.I.'s. They turned out to be all over 42, most of them with three years overseas behind them. One little man with a 21 year old son in the navy showed me a V-mail he had just received. "Dear Bill," it read, "I hate to tell you this, but your house just burned down . . ."

The RAMPS started coming through in mid-April and I've heard enough horror stories to keep Eric Von Stroheim [a film actor known for playing villains] in business for years to come. But they're true stories and to me, the German mind is no longer an enigma. A few weeks ago, I rode up to Reims in a piper cub and back in a C-47 filled with some of the boys from Stalag 1 in Barth. Thanks to the Germans releasing to them Red Cross packages before they left to make room for the Russians, they were only semi-starved—nothing like the boys who first came through. As for the Russians, Attila had nothing on them. So Prof. Richardson's net conclusions are:

It's one hell of a world.

As for Reims, it's a charming city, very French in spite of SHAEF. The cathedral is gorgeous and just to see one city without any ruins was a pleasure. I love flying, especially in a L5. We'd sweep down along the Sienne, then up over the Normandy hills and woods and finally high above an incredibly neat Champagne country with its dim scars of another and milder war. I've never felt so far removed from earthly trappings.

The personnel has changed completely at Chateau Hysteria. Not only do we have seven new girls (the rest have left for Germany), but we also have a young goat named Lillian, a black and white cocker named

Cammy and a curb-stone setter named Thomas Johnson. The latter sounds from Dixie, but it's named after a Liberty ship—no remarks. Two of our new girls are from the Army and they sit around swapping combat stories—"And then the 88's let loose. We were cut off with only a doughnut machine between us and the goons. I grabbed a BAR etc. etc. etc. etc." In comparison, my ten gray hairs, acquired during several close communions with the Almighty and V2 (also V1) are nothing, Lord, nothing.

I've heard nary a word from Clarey. My brother is about to step on a westbound boat as a 2nd Lieutenant, but he wants to get married first. And there you have my version of homefront news.

My current luv life of the DUKW's (amphibious truck companies) is about to shove off—our farewell parties are beginning to interfere with my doughnut doling. And so, W.W., on this weary note I'll end these ramblings, chiding you to keep up the letters—I need 'em! Remember me to your mother, to Esco, to "that party," and to any other interested party. Don't work too hard and say hello to the green bus for me.

This letter home contained a photograph of Liz and fellow worker Mary Haynsworth serving doughnuts, coffee, and smiles. It was one of the few letters not written on Red Cross stationery.

Le Havre, France
June 4, 1945

Dear mother and daddy,

Regardez the fancy stationery. One of our rapidly moving personnel left it amidst the flotsam and jetsam when she pulled out for Paris and we vultures promptly divided the spoils, snarling over the extra envelopes. "There's one thing I'd just as soon not look at," Maggie said, "and that's a map of the world." But it gives a nice civilian touch to things.

Poor beat-up Le Havre is settling down once more and the army appears to know in a vague sort of way what it's doing[. . . .] I see in

225

Liz Richardson (left) and Mary Haynsworth with smiling GIs in front of the Clubmobile in Normandy. Liz's caption to this photograph when she sent it home on June 4, 1945, reads: "The enclosed masterpiece shows Miss Normandy Base Section (on the left) and Miss Oise Base Section (on the right) snapped informally during their working hours. Miss Oise Base Section is Mary Haynsworth of Greenville, South Carolina, suh. That blur in Miss N.B.S's left hand is a doughnut. And it's just as well that it wasn't photogenic." *Courtesy Mary Haynsworth Mathews.*

today's "Stars & Stripes" that Mrs. Sloan Colt from the fastness of Tuxedo, N. Y. has advised us that we'll be here in the ETO for at least another year.[12] So don't shake the moth balls out of my woolies yet. One of our new girls was just carted away in an ambulance with a critical case of TB—she had been up with the 14th Armoured Division all winter and was sent back while things were getting settled. Now, she's going home as soon as possible.

Le Havre is getting tidied up—[German] PWs are piling rubble and a group of little Frenchmen have been working for two months on the road below our house. And if the way those Frenchmen work is any indication, France should be built up by 2199. On the day after V-E day, the owner of this house (who hasn't been in it since the day the Germans ordered him out) appeared, thinking in his straight-forth

Gaelic way, that since la guerre finie, we were finie too. I think the reason the natives cheered us so lustily at the V-E day parade was because they thought we were marching straight for the boat.

The enclosed masterpiece shows Miss Normandy Base Section (on the left) and Miss Oise Base Section (on the right) snapped informally during their working hours. Miss Oise Base Section is Mary Haynsworth of Greenville, South Carolina, suh. That blur in Miss N.B.S's left hand is a doughnut. And it's just as well that it wasn't photogenic[. . . .]

This is my day off and do I love it! Tonight, Frank, myself and Frank's fellow beach officer, Mac, are going off to have a French meal in some undiscovered spot in the direction of Fécamp. It's undiscovered, allright, and I daresay we'll be wandering for hours, mealess and unfed. I'm going to take along a box of K ration just in case. This morning, Maggie and I stayed in the sack until the moron girls started mopping under the bed[. . . .]

Awk! I just realized that June 9th is an anniversary! Congratulations, Maw and Paw and many more. Mebbe next year I'll be there to shake yo' hand in person.

Love—beaucoup to both of you,
Elizabeth

Liz remembered in her diary the D-Day anniversary. She provided detail on the camps and units around Le Havre and the ongoing back up of men waiting for ships. By this time there were far more men leaving Le Havre than arriving: 204,261 troops embarked in June compared to the 50,690 who disembarked there. And there was time to enjoy excellent French food and drink with Frank Policastro. Unlike many Americans, Liz jumped enthusiastically into French cuisine. She did not comment on any plan to celebrate her twenty-seventh birthday the next day.[13]

Like many Americans, Liz noticed black GIs strolling with white French women. The Le Havre newspaper noted color too. In reporting traffic accidents, bar fights, and other incidents involving GIs the local paper commonly identified those who were black as "soldats noirs." Confrontations between African American and white GIs sometimes led to violence. The U.S. military continued its policy of segregation and of assigning most black GIs to low-level work in support units. The American Red Cross remained responsive to white racial prejudices and military policy and continued its practice of encouraging black GIs to go to "Negro-staffed" clubs, such as the Potomac in Paris, and, after it opened in Le Havre in mid-summer 1945, the Massillon.[14]

Diary, June 7, 1945
[Le Havre]

A year ago yesterday was D-Day—a year ago today Frank landed at Omaha Beach and I was in Washington living at the Emery Hotel on G Street. Today, the coast of France is covered with torn and rusted wreckage and grass is growing over the pill boxes. And Germany is a conquered nation, conquered at an unbelievable cost.

Divisions already have arrived at the various staging areas around Le Havre for redeployment. The 97th is at Old Gold, another scattered tent city past Balbec near the town of Yuerbelle. Maggie, Bette Brigham and myself went up Tuesday and stayed with the divisional artillery all day. As far as combat goes, they haven't had much—they arrived in the latter part of January in time for the finish of the Battle of the Bulge and went from there across Germany with Patten as far as Pilsen in Czechoslvakia. Now, after a short time in the states, they'll ship to the Pacific. But that's a lot of territory to cover in four months. The 89th is also at Old Gold and another is at the erst-while 15th Repl. Depot. And there are still about 30,000 RAMPS at Lucky Strike and "critical point" there, mostly from the 1st and 5th divisions. The harbor area is filled with ships, but they can't seem to get in enough to take care of all the men—even the ex-PWs have only 5th priority now.

We had a 1000 point men boarding a liberty ship the other night at 1:00 A.M. Most of them were drunk and their concern over catching the boat was almost childish. They were sure that with the usual doughfoot luck, it would sail away without them. It was 3:30 before the last one got on board.

Monday night, Frank, John Mellen, his captain, and Mac and Morris Green plus myself went out to a little restaurant on the Sienne

road to Douville. It was hidden and badly advertised—a very bad dirt
road brought us to the door and John's French brought us our dinner—
soup, omelette, rabbit, lettuce salad, red wine and champagne. The food
was nicely prepared, the wine and champagne excellent and we ate well.
Last night, Frank and I returned only to find La Roserie closed—so we
stopped at another place, not as clean but we had a good omelette,
French fries, and strawberries with heavy cream and sugar. Two very
happy G.I.s who ply a converted duck up and down the Sienne and who
had known Frank in Marsailles stopped in and a large French family
had dejeuner at the next table, washing the food down with much cidre
and vin rouge. The little boy—about three years old—had his too. No
wonder the French have such a capacity.

The country around this section is lovely—cream limestone cliffs,
rich green fields down to the Sienne and the channel. Below the cliffs
are little shacks, rather like West Virginia. And along the road, the
French girls stroll with the local G.I.s who are very black.

Liz wrote Clarissa Hanson, now Mrs. Watson, after she saw one of
Chris's old boyfriends on the Le Havre docks. With this close friend
from college, she could complain a bit about her mother ("St. Henrietta"), register doubt about brother John's marriage, and gossip about
mutual friends.

Le Havre, France
June 12, 1945

Dear Silent One,

Perhaps I would have gone on forever, patiently waiting news from
the new Mrs. Watson, except for a chance meeting yesterday on the
docks (where I spend most of my waking hours). There I was, passing
out donuts to troops returning from leave in the U.K., when a voice
said, "Hey, Red Cross, what's your name?" And I turned around to see
Murph—a bigger, bonnier Murph—but undoubtably the same Lyman.
I dropped the doughnuts and carted him away to our billets and later on
in the afternoon, took him to the U.K. Leave Center up the road about

40 k. We covered the last thirty-six months completely, aided by Murph's English gin[. . . .]

Enough of that—[Margaret] Flood is in Germany some place. She should be coming home soon, but Murph lost track of her after his wedding—except for a Christmas card.

What with my non-writing friends and St. Henrietta's continuous lectures on international relations, my mail is nothing to smack my lips over. No news from 1718, although W. Wood comes though occasionally with a masterpiece. And Schuster's still sends me the overseas Sentinel. It looks good in our wastepaper basket.

Brother John is now a shavetail [second lieutenant] and a husband—he married the girl—on what, I don't know. The family are both pleased and surprized, but more surprized than pleased.

Meanwhile, I'm turning into a doughnut and if I see less than 15,000 men at a time, I feel lonesome. CLAREY! WRITE! Surely your new life as a gay-young matron leaves some time for a scratchy old v-mail to Aunty[. . . .]

Languishingly yours,
Liz

Liz made a quick trip to Paris to attend a wedding and see the sights. She had a cognac with Betty Goit, who had been with her on the *Kansas City* in England. In order to get back to Le Havre, she forged a travel document.

Diary, June 20, 1945
[Le Havre]

This afternoon and tonight, I'm O.D., exhausted by two days in Paris. Morris Green drove up Monday morning in the jeep and I went along—a beautiful day and the road along the Sienne was at its best. Morris, being a prospective groom, misplaced his pass and we were delayed in starting, but we were in Paris by 2:30. Morris's bride-to-be, a WAC 1st lieut., has charge of a Signal Corps motor pool and after getting our billets behind the opera in the American Express building, I

left them to themselves. The next person I saw was Betty Goit and her
paratrooper from the 101st. She had flown from London to
Bergeistgarten last week and they were married, with a honeymoon in
some Nazi ex-bigwig's chateau. We had a drink in a sidewalk café, the
sun beating down on our tepid glasses of cognac.

I stayed at the Normandy, in a room shared with two others, one
just a week over from the States. Owing to rather extensive festivities of
the night before, I retired early and the next morning strolled towards
the Place de la Concorde—several good galleries filled with [illegible]
art—mostly oils. After headquarters, another RC er and I walked
passed Schraiparelli's [designer Elsa Schiaparelli's boutique] (a G.I.
sitting on the steps, a plaster sphinx in the window with the head of
Marie Antoinette and a hat like a pot) and Coty's and the Royal Air
Force buses. On the Champs Elysee, we took a wobbly carriage back to
the Red Cross mess and from there, I took a Red Cross taxi to the
American Cathedral where Morris and Emmy were being married. The
ceremony was simple and lovely; Mac and I sat in the front row and
beamed approvingly. The reception was held in the WAC officer's
billet—a hotel—with enough champagne and scotch to make Mac the
belle of the Ball. After dinner, I checked out of the Normandy and went
via tube-metro-subway-what have you to Gare St. Lazare [train station]
and then to the RTO [Railway Traffic Officer]. No travel orders, so I
tramped back to headquarters and forged some on a French
typewriter. . . .

A typewritten V-Mail message to Aunt Gertrude and Uncle John
Richardson acknowledged joy in news of her brother's marriage to Sue
and in receiving the shoes Aunt Gertrude sent from a Chicago department store. Liz reported that young brother Butch was worried that she
would never marry and become the much lamented "old maid." In referring to her single status to friends as "aunty" and "aunt Liz" the prospect of
an unmarried future likely concerned her, though less so since Frank
Policastro showed up. Another impediment had recently disappeared
when Red Cross headquarters announced in late May that the "status of
personnel . . . will not be affected because of the presence of a spouse."[15]

Le Havre, France
June 26, 1945

Dear Aunt G. and Uncle J.,

Spot the typewriter! Civilization at last hits Le Havre! We are also getting a [illegible] ration, two bottles a week and all these things together are at least giving us the outward veneer of normal people. So I now have a new sister and little Johnny is a married man—much married and in the most Emily Post manner. How I wish that I'd been there to keen and lament in the background. Butch is taking care of my interests, though. In his last letter, he practically ordered me to take unto myself a husband, painting a drab picture of my future life as the Richardson old maid keeping house for that crusty but lovable old bachelor, C. M. Jr. . . . [T]he mail just arrived—with a much battered package from Carson's containing the shoes unbattered. They're just what I ordered and quite wearable, so I owe you a paen of thanks, Aunt G. I'll have mother send you the money, if she hasn't done so already (and I hope she has). I would have picked the same kind myself, considering all things and the Wehrmacht gray outfit that goes with 'em. That was awfully nice of you and if you had heard my little screams of joy as I feverishly tore at the wrappings, you'd know how much I appreciate your trouble. Le Havre is a pretty busy place at this stage of the game what with deployment and stuff. We know the docks by heart.

Love to you both!

A normally faithful correspondent, Liz apologized for delay in writing home.

Le Havre
June 29, 1945

Dear mother and daddy,

Sorry that I haven't been writing as regularly as I should have been, but we have been working and things have so mounted up that letter writing wasn't on the schedule for a couple of weeks. However, it won't happen again. As it is, I'm writing this just before going out again and I just had lunch after being on the beach since seven this morning (without breakfast). The men are loaded on the liberty ships and ships of a similar category from pontoon piers built by the Sea Bees and the few remaining usable French piers. But the bigger ships have to be loaded by LST from the beach and it's a bit drafty in the morning. They came in from the big staging areas in trucks looking like so many Tillys going to market, but all of them are uniformly happy to be leaving these shores.

John and Sue's wedding sounds wonderful and I'm only sorry that I wasn't there to lurk in the background[. . . .]

Talking about weddings, I went to one in Paris. An officer in Frank's Company married a WAC Lieut. and I drove up with the groom and attended the ceremony in the American Cathedral and the reception afterwards. . . . And I came back to Le Havre in a troop train filled with men bound for UK leaves. The train commander put me in a compartment labeled "female," which had the same effect as putting honey in a bear trap. As a result, by the time we pulled out of St. Lazare, the compartment was infested by the more agile and I spent the night listening to assorted tales rather than sleeping. This is not due to my fatal beauty that drives men mad—I'm just a victim of circumstances and non-fraternization.

Margaret has gone on her leave to Marsailles. Her love of the moment is leaving the ETO and not in the right direction and pauvre [poor] Frank will be following shortly, I daresay, although they are hoping that they will be deployed through the states. We have disposed of Lillian after she literally ate the magazines we had scrounged from one of the ships. Our newest animal is a horrid little white spitz belonging to a chaplain who has since gone home. She barks early in the morning, tears up the front yard after the PWs have raked it and refuses to be house broken. Her name is Snooks and I won't tell you what most people call her. We also have a number of rats that run up and down our garden wall and last night, Mary Haynsworth was kept awake by a mouse. She finally had to open her door and let it out[. . . .]

Must go to work now. For Pete's sake, WRITE[. . . .]

Love,
Elizabeth

Liz's last extant diary entry focused on the Le Havre dock work and the units moving through, including one they had known in Barrow-in-Furness and another they had worked with at Biddulph. There are men she remembered by name. The long days of hard work were numbing. And there was a territorial squabble with the military.

Diary, July 3, 1945
[Le Havre]

The weeks in Le Havre have a sameness that gives time a certain dateless quality. The weather too is deceiving. It's rather like May at home, even cold at times and never really hot. All day, the troops are being loaded in the transports—97th division, 95th, 87th and now 4th division. The 97th, 95th and 104th are at home by now—half the 4th must be in mid-ocean. Danny and I were at Quai de l'Eurz at six this morning and fed an infantry regiment and ordinance, then this afternoon we fed another on another troopship. The men have on their new battle jackets, their ribbons, their regimental badges. Their "B" bags bulge with German equipment, swords—and K ration. And down the pier, a negro port band plays, the music drowned in the clatter from a French crane and the voice of the loading officer calling out name after name.

Last week, standing in the rain at Phoenix Pier, I recognized the 101st Cav. Recon.—the same men we had been with in Barrow last December. But Bob Shaeffer and Lt. Paquet were dead and they had many casualties. Now they are going home for thirty days and then the Pacific. Today in Area I where they load the LST's for the bigger ships like the "West Point," we coffeed and donuted hdq. company of the 87th Division. I last saw them in Biddulph in early December. Since that time, they have been across Germany into Austria and Czechoslavakia and now they've being redeployed. Joe Chesterman was in the first truck that drove up—I'd seen him in Paris two weeks before.

The channel is very blue and there's dust rising in white clouds. The port engineers have moved in next store [door] and tapped our water tank. When I came in yesterday afternoon, a colonel, Capt. Curly Carpenter, a sqt. from troop movement, plus five of us, were in the midst of a battle of words. Who had the right to tap the water tank? Who had authority over our billet? Etc. etc? The colonel departed and the decision of the battle rests upon the amount of hot water we get for the next few days.

The frustrations of being "boss" at Chateau Hysteria continued, including the new Red Cross recruits who the veteran Liz saw as "spoiled brats." Friends were leaving or preparing to leave, including Frank and his hot temper. Lillian the goat returned.

Le Havre
July 8, 1945

Dear mother and daddy,

Your wayward daughter speaking—and with difficulty. I dated this letter at least two hours ago, but what with at least 10 separate and individual problems coming up at spaced intervals, I don't seem to be getting very far. The water tank has gone off in the donut kitchen. Betty Brigham took off on an unauthorized flight to Noville, the newer arrivals don't like their dormitory, somebody insulted M. Voltaire [Velter], our French donut authority (who is worth exactly one beat-up franc note), the officers next door have tapped our water tank and, therefore, no hot water for us. (The age of chivalry is past), and the jeep's battery is caput—etc. etc. etc. And my hair is getting grayer and I've lost my girlish laughter.

Our new recruits are a bunch of spoiled brats. While we swooned over hot water and mattresses and somebody to cook doughnuts for us, they growl during their spare time and object to working in the rain. Meanwhile, troops are still pouring out of this port and will be for some time to come, as you probably know if you have any conception of the size of this deployment job.

Still later.

You see how my letter writing time is rather cramped. I've just been out—alone—with our Navy carry all and its usual load. My driving is quite presentable now. I double clutch and all the rest, with no casualties so far. I think that Betty (Brigham) and I might get the loan of a jeep for our leaves coming up and we intend to make a tour through France to the Swiss border. The Swiss are pretty strict about visas and such, but perhaps by that time, the borders will be open. After that, I'd like to transfer to the 7th Army around Heidelburg—but that remains to be done. Frank's days here are very numbered, but we are having a good time (between scraps and disagreements). He has a temper that would put Vesuvius to shame. However, most of the old group have gone—and not where they'd like to—and we are the old timers around these parts. I can't say I like the idea of being boss—much rather be a PFC in the doughnut racket. Margaret has just returned from her leave—in Marsailles—where she waved goodbye to one of her friends. She says that it's a mad house, hot, dirty, everybody in a foul mood. Of course, here in Le Havre, there isn't much of a morale problem for the troops coming through. They're afraid of only one thing—that they'll miss their boat—and that boat is something they've been looking forward to for a long time.

Butch's V-Mail is the only mail I've had from Dragoon Trail for over three weeks. . . .

Lillian just strolled into the barnyard. She is quite adolescent with small horns and she eats everything, preferably current magazines. Helen, our French housekeeper, is quite attached to her and when we threatened to banish Lillian, she said she'd take her out into the country. But alas, Lillian ate all the flowers and the very young vegetables—and she also drank quantities of milk. So she is back and is at present nibbling on a blanket. Our front yard has been landscaped by a group of gentlemen from Germany (not because they wanted to landscape it). We have a driveway lined with whitewashed bricks, a heart-shaped flower bed ("I wonder what they think we're here for," somebody wondered dreamily the other day) and much shrubbery around the front of the house. What Lillian doesn't destroy, other PW's do, when they deliver coal with such energy that they scatter it every place but in the coal bin. (Lillian is now eating the deck chair) Awk! She just took off with the envelope to this opus!

Mother, please get me about 1/2 doz. pair stockings, net if possible, nothing drab and as sheer as possible, Size 10 1/2 long, and

I think that lady at Wyman's will see that you get the kind I like. Thanking you.

If it's stationery you need, I can send you some of this liberated stuff. WRITE!

> Love to all,
> ELIZABETH

Chris Hanson Watson finally wrote, prompting a quick reply, filled with news. Liz continued her stance against marriage while in Europe and suggested some doubt whether Frank Policastro really was the guy to marry.

> Le Havre, France
> July 14, 1945
> BASTILLE DAY

Dear Clarey,

It's so nice to be getting mail from the new Mrs. Watson that I have just grabbed the typewriter from one of the kiddies (she was busy forging travel orders to the U. K. anyway, a not very honest occupation) and I'm settling back for a long talk. There's so much to ask you, but I've learned long ago that asking questions via the mails is a most frustrating affair, so I'll hold back in the mad hope that your next will be all inclusive. Yes, I finally got all the pictures. . the master piece from Atlanta of you and your most charming husband the snapshots from the Azores[. . . .]

Damm it, I'm getting to know every troop ship that sails the ocean blu. Of a night, sitting on the balcony of the local DKW club, I can distinguish the "Wakefield" from the "Marine Wolf" even when they're five miles out and I know that such and such a ship takes 6000 troops and therefore 18,000 doughnuts and an equally nauseous amount of coffee. At the rate that deployment is going, we should be finished with this bulk business by next winter and by then, I hope to be far away from the dock area. Most of the beaten up old timers in the R.C. are trying to get home, and I say trying, because at present, we have a backlog of more than 300 personnel in Paris, awaiting transportation (the hypen is missing in this machine). They must be recruiting like mad back home, because we have a steady stream of fresh newcomers, all terribly young and naive. Unfortunately, they will learn very easily. Most of them are being sent to Germany, to take care of the occupation troops and although from all reports it's a beautiful and clean country, non fraternazation does present a problem. France is beautiful, too, of course . . . This region around the mouth of the Sienne is Cezanne country. You know those wonderful colors . . . siennas and intense blues and red tile roofs. But sometimes, the smell from the gutters dulls my aesthetic senses, thus proving, of course, that I'm not a real artist. They say that the Italians are worse, but I find it hard to believe. Paris is pretty modern. Toilets that flush and elevators that run, offset only a little by transportation by the smelliest Metro in the world or little landeaus drawn by very tired horses with roses in their manes. Every time I see one of the local nags with varnished hooves (hoofs hoves, what have you), a tuft of pink flowers above his harness and more roses entwined in a plaited mane, I think of you and also that other horse that we used to see somewhere between N. Farwell and Third Street. That one, I remember, had a lace coat.

Ernst [Kuenstner] is being sent home, whether on deployment or permanently, I don't know. He urges me to do same, but I have forgotten what he looks like and the charm of an accent has worn off. Andy [Anderson] . . . haven't thought of him in months. We parted permanently in Washington. The paratrooper [Larry Pickard] has been missing since the Ardennes. And for the last four and a half months, the current affair has been with some one in the ATC (Amphibious Truck Company to you). I can't figure out whether it's a habit or not, but I am very fond of him and perhaps if his immediate destination were not the CBI, we'd do something about it. I still don't believe in getting married over here, although plenty of people are doing it, but I'd just as soon start some thing as permanent as marriage with a little more definite future on the horizon. He is a Catholic, but not a very good one and anyway, that doesn't make much difference, to me. Also Italian American (the day that I become infatuated with a Chinese American is the day I stop), but that doesn't make much difference either. Perhaps it's just as well that fate has so arranged things that we can't go home together and/or get married over here. St. Henrietta would have a fit. He has a temper, too, which I, also, find very interesting[. . . .]

I'll write again soon and you do same—love to you both, Clarey—
Liz

Liz expressed discontent to her parents for not writing more frequently. The work of serving men "with horrible appetite for doughnuts" was slowed by a shortage of ships, giving a period of needed rest that included a trip to the beach. This letter reached C. M. Richardson's office in Mishawaka, Indiana, on July 30, and was then forwarded to her parents' vacation spot at the Sylvan Beach Hotel, Whitehall, Michigan.

Le Havre, France
July 18, 1945

Dear mother and daddy,

I should really be writing to Butch . . . he seems to be my only steady family correspondent. But innate loyalty or perhaps it's habit, keeps me going. I suppose it's only natural that when one has been away from home for over a year, writing becomes one of those things. I find it hard to write myself. Thanks for that one letter I got last month, though. Yes, I'm mad and yes, I feel neglected. So there. And don't give me that line about the mails being slow. They'll never be better than they are now, scowl, scowl.

Now that I've gotten that off my chest, we can go on to lighter things. It's taken me all morning, what with sundry interruptions, to get to lighter things, but notice that I have persisted[. . . .] Everybody is coming in from their morning runs and bedlam is breaking loose. Odette is scrubbing the floor, the telephone is ringing, Nancy Fiske who is here waiting transportation to the states, has had her barracks bag lifted from the transient billet. She keeps remembering valuables there were in it, with little gasps and gurgles. And if Odette doesn't stop scrubbing with her little brush she'll reach China (along with a lot of other people).

We have had about three days rest from the docks . . . they've run out of ships, only temporarily I'm afraid. But we have a brand new "cigarette" camp, which is rapidly filling up with thousands of men, all with horrible appetite for doughnuts. What with the men, and the wind from the channel, the air is so full of dust that if somebody accidently dropped a seed in my hair, it would sprout. [. . .]

We fired our two chambermaids. And I wrote them a recommendation in English and High School French. I rather miss them especially their accounts of their amatory adventures of the previous night. They were quite fond of the See Bees, but as a whole, they didn't think much of the Americans as lovers and Romeos. The ladies of Le Havre are also intrigued with the duskier G.I.s, which sometimes makes things interesting.

Bastille day was quiet enough. A big carnival flourished on one of the main drags, and somebody let off with a few flares, and the officers down the street had an alcoholic song session, but it will take a few years for the French to recall how they used to celebrate it, at least here. Paris, of course, is different[. . . .]

Chow time and I am hungry. This O. D.ing wears me out. For that matter, I'm so busy being an executive these days, that I don't have too much time for little things like doughnut doling. How I wish the R. C. could dream up something else beside the Doughnut! Repulsive, greasy things that they are!

Tell Butch that I'll write him very shortly. Is he going to camp this summer? How are the melons? Love to everybody, especially Freckles.

Elizabeth

A Sunday letter home dropped the sudden news (but not until the third paragraph) that Liz and Frank had decided to break up. Liz reported the decision in her calm, matter-of-fact manner, though surely she was more deeply upset than she let on to her parents. And perhaps this was only a lovers' quarrel that would have soon healed. After the surprising third paragraph she put the letter down and returned to finish it the next day, Monday.

Her letter reported also on another doughnut run, a quick trip to

Paris, this time on a B-24, and a short air hop across the mouth of the Seine to the elegant resort of Deauville. By this time, she knew and loved airplanes. Liz was breaking military and Red Cross rules by hitching plane rides without authorization, but the practice was widespread and easy, particularly so for American women with a smile, who, as one Red Cross official slyly noted, "were in greater demand as social companions for military pilots."[16]

Liz planned another trip to Paris Wednesday to say goodbye to Pvt. Bernie Levine.

Le Havre
July 22, 1945

Dear mother and daddy,

Sunday morning—my day off—the sun is flirting with the clouds—and in five minutes, deenair weel be raidee. Time, therefore, to write to you. Not that I've had any mail, Auntie said viciously . . .

Deenair is fineeshed. I have half an hour before the L5 [plane] from across the Sienne comes to pick me up for swimming. Yesterday, I went up to Paris in a B-24—40 minutes—far above the winding river, over Versailles with its amazing pattern of gardens, above the maze of Paris with the Eiffel Tower dominating and then landing at Ville de Coublet. After our Colonel collected his daughter, USO dancer and very lush, we flew back in the same time. The B-24 is a wonderful plane, four engined and a Liberator tail. I stood at the waist gunner window and went up front via the catwalk over the bomb bay. It rides smoothly and with terrific power—an L5 is bumpy and dull compared to it (naturally).

Frank and I have decided, after much discussion last night, that we had better go our separate ways. There comes a stage in all relationships when one thing or another has to be settled and I do not want to be married over here, especially with the immediate prospect of Frank leaving, nor do I think our marriage would be a success for very long even under normal circumstances. I hate to have it end like this after six months of good companionship, but both of us know that it's the best way, even though it's hard to do at the present.

One day later.

I've just come in from a run to Balbec—a little town on the road to Rouen about 29 Km. from Le Havre. There's a huge PW cage there, plus a box factory, manned by G.I.'s and run by PW's. The box factory is making much furniture for our local R.C. Clubs, plus wooden donut racks for us, so we pay them a call with coffee and those things. I drove the weapon's carrier, with Susie and an MP who is off during the day as escort. The countryside is not at all dry but still as green and mellow as it was in May and June. But there's a big deployment camp [Philip Morris] between Le Havre and Balbec which produces acres of dust. We have 5 girls there—their coffee is made by the Krauts, all of whom work most willingly and energetically.

I started this letter yesterday just before leaving for Douville, on the other side of the Sienne. A group of liaison pilots there are most obliging in flying us back and forth. It's a sort of double resort—Douville and Trouville and Trouville has a big waterfront casino, now occupied by the army and a wonderful saltwater swimming pool on the beach. After landing at the airport (where the pilots live in a still camouflaged air terminal still labeled "Kanteen" in German Letters), we all went swimming—terrific. And then we sat on the beach along the faded awning cabanas, and the boys admired the French bathing suits (or rather, the lack of them) and then we jeeped back to the airport, hopped into an L5 and flew across the muddy mouth of the Sienne, across the toy piers and the gaping center of the city, buzzed our house on the side of the hill and landed at the Le Havre airport, which lies on high cliffs overlooking the channel.

I'm going to Paris again on Wednesday. Do you remember Bernie [Levine] from Barrow-in-Furness? He's in Paris awaiting shipment home. Something is wrong with his knee and so I'm meeting him at 2:30 at the Hotel Normandy for a farewell get-together. I can't believe it, but it's been almost seven months since we said goodbye to them on a snowy night in Barrow. They were going to France and once more, we were packing up the Clubmobile and our footlockers.

Interval while I take Betty Brigham in a jeep down to the "Gen. Brooks" for dinner. Last time that ship was in, the entire staff of officers invaded Chateau Hysteria with three cases of beer and proceeded to drink it all themselves. They also broke some furniture and scattered sawdust over our side lawn. We are planning to retire to the hills until the Gen. Brooks is outward bound. Oh, load her quickly, please, 16th Port! Got another Xmas package yesterday.

Love to you all,
ELIZABETH

In her last letter home Elizabeth Richardson wrote about wedding and birthday gifts as she prepared to leave for Paris the next day.

Le Havre
July 24, 1945

Dear mother,

This is a postscript of my letter of yesterday. Enclosed is a money order which I wish you'd use in purchasing a wedding present for John and Sue. You know what they have and what they haven't. I'd prefer that it was something more or less lasting . . . Love to get them a good watercolor over here, but the mail problem eliminates that. If I see something that I like in Paris tomorrow, I'll get it anyway, but meanwhile, please try to get them something nice . . . sterling, linen, or what have you just to let them know that I haven't gone AWOL. Then you can save whatever is left over for Butch's birthday a month from now, say $10 or $15.

Sorry that I have to ask you to do all these things, but prices are so out of this world over here and though you might not think so, it's much easier to get stuff at home. Perhaps Aunt G. could select something in Chicago.

Love,
Elizabeth

[9]

One Plane Crash

When Elizabeth Richardson decided to go to Paris she hitched a plane ride, as she had done several times before. The two-seater airplane she climbed into on the morning of July 25, 1945, was an L-5 Sentinel, a versatile work horse of the military sometimes known as the "Flying Jeep" because of its toughness and reliability. "I love flying, especially in an L5," she had written a friend several weeks earlier. Above the ground, the war's destruction was more muted and the colors of the French countryside she so loved more like an artist's palette.[1]

Liz jumped into the L-5 with Sergeant William R. Miller of the Ninth Air Force. Miller had logged almost 500 hours flying the plane and was "an excellent pilot," a buddy later recalled. They took off from Le Havre at 8:00 AM in good weather but within an hour, near Rouen, encountered heavy ground fog "with visibility lowering to 400 feet." The U.S. Army Air Force's official form "Report of Aircraft Accident" provided the raw details. Attempting "to let down in order to orient himself," Miller "struck trees on top of a hill and crashed to the ground. The plane immediately caught fire and was completely destroyed. Both pilot and passenger were instantly killed." It was one fatal accident among many and two deaths among the 55 million or so of World War II. The official report was silent about the meaning of the lives lost and the loved ones left behind.[2]

Liz's death was not unusual even for the Red Cross. Seventy-two American Red Cross personnel died overseas during World War II, 15 of them in plane accidents. Two of Liz's European female colleagues had died in separate plane crashes that May of 1945. The organization's newsletter *Over Here* carried a notice of the July 25 accident. It presented the simple facts, with no sentiment. Still, the death of a twenty-seven-year-old Clubmobile girl was not part of the expected cost of war.[3]

Letters poured into the Richardson home in Mishawaka, Indiana. Those who knew Liz well struggled in their letters of sympathy to capture what she meant and to dampen their own sorrows. Evident too is their kindness in trying to provide information and solace to the family. Close friends coordinated their letter writing. Mary Haynsworth was delegated to describe the plane accident. More than 50 years later Mary told an interviewer that "the loss of Elizabeth was dreadful," the worst tragedy she experienced during her two years in wartime Europe.[4]

AMERICAN RED CROSS

July 31st
Le Havre

Dear Mr. & Mrs. Richardson:

I know that you are anxious to know all the details of the accident, so to the best of my ability I will give you the exact facts.

Last Tuesday Liz was called to Paris for a conference at HQ the next day. She wanted to arrange air transportation to save time. We got in touch with the airport here and found that a pilot of the 173rd Liaison Squadron was scheduled to return to his base in Paris the next morning, leaving at 8:00 in an L-5 plane. He had no passenger scheduled and agreed to take Liz. The weather was good here so they took off as scheduled around 8:00 A. M. Just outside of Rouen, they encountered heavy fog in a small valley, and in trying to get below the fog, they hit a tree and the plane crashed. Without question they were both killed instantly. The plane burst into flames and both bodies were badly burned. An American Driver from the 179th General Hospital in Rouen rushed to the scene and reported the accident to the hospital. From then on the hospital took charge of everything.

We were notified here in the afternoon. We were all so stunned we scarcely knew what to do. Mrs. [Eleanor] Gray, the head of the

A R C at the hospital, took charge of the funeral arrangements. She is a lovely person and was so kind and helpful. She arranged for the service to be in the Red Cross Hall at the hospital on Saturday afternoon at 3:00 and the burial to be Sunday afternoon at the military cemetery at St. Andre not far from Paris.

Saturday morning a truck left here for Rouen loaded with flowers. They were sent by all kinds of people here who loved Liz—GI's, Officers, French Staff, as well as ourselves. I will not go into detail about the service as Bette Brigham is writing you all about it. We had a Sergeant take a few pictures after the service to send to you.

The pilot was a sergeant William Miller. I don't know his family's address. We did not know him. His funeral was conducted by his own squadron in Paris.

Liz and Marge and Bette and I had been trying for several weeks to effect our transfer to the 7th Army in Heidelberg. Liz had gotten the operation here running smoothly and we felt we were ready to move. One of the reasons she was going to Paris Wednesday, was to talk over our Transfer with H Q.

Now the three of us want more than ever to leave, so H Q has arranged the transfer, and we leave tomorrow morning.

We have packed all of Liz's things in her foot locker and dufflebag. There is a note to you inside the foot-locker, explaining a few items. We are taking them to Paris tomorrow and they will be shipped by H Q to you.[5]

I know that I have given you the facts quite bluntly, but I feel certain that it is better to know exactly what happened as one's imagination can always make things even worse.

We miss Liz now, but I know that we shall miss her even more as time goes on. For now we are thinking of her all the time, talking about her, and quoting her, and remembering all the funny and wonderful things she has said and done, so that it is almost as if she were still here in the next room.[6]

I, myself, have been with Liz for only four months, but that's a long time over here where things change so rapidly. I shall always remember her as one of the finest and most delightful people I've ever known.

Please call on us for anything we can do over here. I hope we can come to see you when we get back to the States before very long.

> With deepest sympathy,
> Mary Haynsworth

The service at Rouen took place in a hospital auditorium that Margaret Flood later recalled was "jammed" with Red Cross friends and with "GI's from all over [who] had hitched rides."[7] Bette Brigham wrote Liz's parents about the Rouen service and the burial at the American Military Cemetery at St. Andre, 50 miles west of Paris. At the cemetery, with Chaplain Edwin Hale in front, the mourners lined up by twos behind the flag-draped coffin on that sunny summer day. They walked quietly past long straight rows of freshly made wooden crosses to the burial site. The standard military service was exceptional only in that the deceased and all but one of the mourners who had known her were female.

The cemetery at St. Andre had been opened in August 1944 and would eventually be the temporary burial ground for 2,066 Americans who had helped drive the Nazis from France.

> Le Havre, France
> July 31, 1945

Dear Mr. and Mrs. Richardson:

I hardly know where to begin—but Mary has told you that I would go into detail about the services, so I'll start there.

Mary and I went to Rouen early Saturday with Mr. Bertram Clarke, the Regional Director, who was very fond of Liz and who had been very helpful to us since the accident. We arrived to find Mrs. Eleanor Gray had arranged things beautifully. The flowers were there, so we arranged them as best we could—they were many and beautiful—tho' neither number or beauty could ever show how much was thought of Liz by all who knew here. I am enclosing all the cards that came with the flowers and I've noted on the back what they were and I'll also add the address to which you could write, if you want to. Don't feel you must, because we have thanked them either verbally or by note. But I want to include any bit of information you might want.

I am also enclosing pictures taken after the service, so that you can see just how it all looked. There are still some not yet developed. I'll send them on as soon as I get them.

The coffin, given by Red Cross Headquarters, was chosen by Mrs. Gray—they are made in Rouen and are French style, but it was simple and plain, as we knew Liz would want—a light wood with a plain cross on top. They are shaped differently from ours, as you can see. There was no steel available for a plate, so Mrs. Gray had one made from an American gun shell—of fine brass—so that after the war you might perhaps want to come over and take that home. That, too, was plain—printed with Elizabeth Ann Richardson and the date of her birth and death. As it was a military funeral, the casket was flag-draped.

The service itself was fairly short and quite nice—four of Frank's [Policastro] friends, who knew Liz well, acted as pallbearers. They were Capt. John Mellon, Lt. Wm. Sharp, Lt. Allen Larson, Lt. Donald Brooks[. . . .]

The Army Chaplain was Capt. Edwin E. Hale[. . . .] He planned the service—there was music as the congregation entered, and then two nurses from the hospital sang, as a duet, "The River of Life"—it was a sweet song.

I'm afraid I've forgotten the Scripture he used, but there was a long prayer and a short talk in which he did quite well considering he knew Liz not at all—but those of us who knew her didn't need his words. I'm sure each of us at that time thought of the gal we knew and loved, than whom there is none better. I've never known anyone whom all loved as much. I came overseas with Liz last July and have been with her here at Le Havre since April—and it's been like losing a life-long friend—in fact, she isn't lost—it seems as if she's just away. I'm sure none of us have realized she's gone. We've been so busy doing what we could and also getting ready to leave for Germany—it's all very unreal to us now—

But I'll get on with the service—

There were many there—Of course all of us from her unit, and Frank, plus our G. I. Drivers, and Jean, the Frenchman at the doughnut kitchen and four of our maids here at "Chateau Hysteria" who asked to go. Also Isabel Brickly from the Club in the forest and Marie Braven from the Normandie Club in town.

Then from Paris—Nancy Nicholas, Nancy Brown and Polly Haskins—all old Le Havre girls came down—Nancy N. and Polly are coming back to Le Havre this week to take over the unit. Also Margaret Flood, who went to Milwaukee-Downer with Liz. Then, too,—Mr. Don Momand, the Deputy Commissioner from Paris and Camilla Goss, head of Clubmobile. I'm sure there were some others, too, but they were just faces to me.

We arranged for the burial to be the next afternoon, Sunday. Mr. Clark gave us his comfortable staff car for the trip. Maggie, Frank, Ruth Bedford, who just arrived from leave in England on Saturday night, Mary and myself—and the two Nancy's plus two friends of us, who took some colored pictures at the cemetery. They'll be sent to you as soon as they're developed.

We set out at 10 A. M. and had lunch at the hospital. Mary and I picked out four of the best floral pieces and took them with us— two gladiolas and the large Red Cross and a white spray which was new for Sunday. We followed the ambulance—oh, yes, the two Nancy's and Polly came, too—it was about a 2 hr. ride from Rouen—south—to St. Andre del'Euve, near Evreux. It's a fairly new little cemetery—but beautiful in its simplicity on a small hillside with about 5,000 neat white crosses. The grass hasn't come up yet, but there are plots of lovely red geranium between the blocks of graves and in the center the American Flag at half-mast—and the whole cemetery surrounded by a neat white fence. Liz was the first American girl buried there—along in a line with others who had given their all—and surely for no better reason than did Liz—no one ever did more for people in all ways than she did.

Chaplain Hale again conducted a very short service at the grave with the usual burial scripture and a prayer. Afterwards they folded up the flag from the casket and gave it to us and we have packed it in Liz' footlocker. It's a lovely flag.

And so we came back to Le Havre to start all over again. Maggie, Mary and I leave tomorrow morning for Paris and Germany. Liz was to have been with us—and she will be every minute of the

Interment service for Elizabeth Richardson, July 29, 1945, at the American Military Cemetery at St. Andre, France. Bette Brigham wrote her parents on July 31 that "Liz was the first American girl buried there—along in a line with others who had given their all—and surely for no better reason than did Liz." Chaplain Edwin E. Hale leads the GIs carrying the coffin. Margaret Morrison sent the photograph to Liz's parents with this identification of the mourners:

a. Frank [Policastro] and I [Margaret Morrison]
b. Ruth Bedford (nearest), Bette Brigham (dark glasses)
c. Mary Haynsworth (nearest), Nancy Brown
d. Polly Haskins (nearest), Nancy Nicholas.

Courtesy Charles Richardson, Jr.

way. I hope all of us can keep a little of the spirit of Liz with us always—it was a wonderful one.

We are determined not to be sad—Liz wouldn't want it, I know. We keep thinking of her wonderfully quick and humorous way of seeing a situation—It has helped us through this time and I know it will continue to help us, as I indeed know it will her family.

Our thoughts have been so much with you and John and Butch—she spoke so much of her family—we feel as if we know you—and it is for you we are sad. Liz had a good life, living each moment for its best—and she was so happy to be flying to Paris—

so I know she had no regrets—and it came quickly. So we try not to grieve for her too much.

Perhaps my father will come by to see you—Tell him I am well and happy and excited over our transfer to Germany. He's to be in Mishawaka for a meeting soon. He's with the Sales Department—has a N. Y. territory—C. A. Brigham. And when we all get home, I hope I can meet you folks.

I do hope I have covered all this satisfactorily—please write and ask anything I may have forgotten to note. We three want to do all we can to help you.

Please know how much we think of you and want to help.

Sincerely,

Bette Brigham

Margaret Morrison had served in England and France with Liz and knew her best. She wrote the shortest letter but captured her well.

AMERICAN RED CROSS

Paris

August 2, 1945

Dear Mr. & Mrs. Richardson—

I am the Maggie who has been with Elizabeth for the past year. Because of that fact, it would be much easier for me to talk with you than try and write anything very coherent.

Mary Haynesworth and Bette Brigham have written you all the things you would want to know. They have been wonderful.

However, I would like to make an attempt to tell you of the terrific zest Liz had for her work—how thrilled she was at new things we saw—how her sense of humor was the keynote to our daily living, even when we were past tiredness. You know all these qualities, but it's like having something lovely in your home—you are happy when other people recognize it as being lovely.

Please forgive me for rather stupidly trying to convey to you that I loved Liz very much.

My thoughts and deepest sympathy are with you all.

Sincerely,

Margaret Morrison

One of the most touching testimonies came from a French civilian, I. M. Velter, who as the doughnut kitchen supervisor in Le Havre reported to Liz. He wrote in his best English on July 26 to Red Cross executive Bertrand Clarke.

> Will you please accept at the name of all my staff, and my personal name, our sincere condolences, for misery who strike us by the loss of our very regretted Miss Elizabeth RICHARDSON, our dear friend.
>
> We have been all of us overthrowed by this atrocious news.
>
> Myself, I have seen her on Tuesday, so young and happy at the idea of this trip, and that I can't yet realize this very sad end.
>
> I remain, Sir,
> Your respectfully,
> I. M. Velter

[10]

The Long Memory

Charles and Henrietta Richardson were vacationing at a lakeside resort in Michigan when news of their daughter's death reached them. Fifteen-year-old "Butch" (Charley) was at Boy Scout Camp when the family minister arrived to tell him the sad news. Marine brother John was somewhere in the Pacific. None ever got over the sadness. Henrietta Richardson was most obviously affected. Charley recalled "hearing her crying after I'd gone to bed." He was convinced that grief contributed to his mother's early death at age sixty-five. Charley never forgot his big sister. He saved her letters and her diary, her watercolors, the family photos, and scrapbooks, the stamps and birthday cards she had sent him. And the Nazi souvenir helmet. Into the twenty-first century the brother she called "Butch" spoke of her as the big sister he continued to admire and love.[1]

Frank Policastro was devastated at the loss of the woman he loved. He wrote Liz's parents several times, describing their time together, his deep affection for her, and the grave at St. Andre. In late October 1945, he lamented to the Richardsons, "I've been so lonesome, I don't half know what to do."[2] Perhaps Frank and Liz had reconciled after they had agreed, a few days before her death, to part. Frank eventually returned to his hometown of Hammanton, New Jersey, and re-joined the family wholesale petroleum business. He married in 1948 and had three children. The World War II veteran died in 1991. His widow, Rose, recalled him mentioning a Red Cross girlfriend in the war but she knew no details.[3]

Liz's friends stayed in touch with each other and with her family. Several eventually came to visit at The Patch in Mishawaka. More than a half century later, Chris Hanson Watson, Betty Twining Blue, Ann Bumby Fallon, Anne Bodle Schuknecht, and Mary Haynsworth Mathews would say with heartfelt conviction, as Mary did in 2003, "I'll never forget her." To Chris she was still "a genius. A special mind—special wit—a special and much missed person." As her brother Charley observed in 2003, "How many people have a life that ends at twenty-seven that 55 years later are still remembered?"[4]

Milwaukee Downer College hosted an exhibition of Liz's watercolors in May 1946, and friends and family established an art prize in her name. She was the school's only war casualty. The Downer alumni magazine claimed in 1946 that "as surely as men gave their lives for their country, so did she." At Mishawaka High School a plaque lists the names of the 78 graduates who died in World War II. Liz's name is among them.[5]

At the end of war the American Graves Registration Service began the task of moving thousands of bodies from numerous temporary burial grounds to a few large, permanent cemeteries. American families were given a choice of having the remains of loved ones returned for burial in the United States or selecting final interment in one of the new cemeteries in Europe. The choice was troubling for many parents and spouses; some wanted loved ones near to home in a more personal memorialization; others wanted them near where they had died and alongside those they had fought with, thereby marking to the world the national as well as personal meaning of their sacrifice. Charles and Henrietta Richardson thought that since their daughter so loved England she would have preferred burial there, but the authorities offered only a new cemetery in France, which the family eventually approved. In July 1948, their daughter's body was moved from St. Andre to St. Laurent, the Normandy American Cemetery. The new site overlooked Omaha Beach, one of the D-Day invasion beaches, and was completed in 1956. Today it contains a semi-circular memorial, reflecting pool, chapel, and 9,387 graves. Marking each grave is a Star of David or Latin cross of white marble set in green grass and standing perfectly aligned. Row upon row of war dead.[6]

Each marker at Normandy represents one simple statement of per-

Elizabeth Richardson's remains were transferred in July 1948 to the Normandy American Cemetery. Overlooking Omaha Beach and the English Channel, the cemetery's white marble markers denote the graves of 9,387 American World War II military dead. *Courtesy American Battle Monuments Commission.*

sonal and national sacrifice. Few of the million or so Americans who visit each year leave the Normandy Cemetery without tears. Many doubtless sense the order, serenity, and peace the cemetery so carefully evokes. This sacred soil, so lovingly maintained, tends to obscure the horrors of the most brutal war in history, one some Americans today call a "good war."

Most who visit Normandy wander quietly among the marble grave markers. Some come seeking a special one among the many. A few have traveled there to stand at Grave 5 in Row 21, Plot A. Liz's Milwaukee roommate, Betty Twining, journeyed there in September 1951. Her friend's death was still a raw memory, as raw as the site of the unfinished cemetery. Damaged landing boats lay off shore. Temporary wooden crosses marked graves. Twine was told that a white marble cross would be placed at Liz's grave later that fall. She wanted to take photographs but because the cemetery was still "under construction" that was prohibited. The visit, Twine wrote Liz's parents, left her "pretty much an emotional wreck." More than 50 years later she vividly remembered that day at Normandy: "I just had to go," she said, but it was "a terrible day for me. All I could think was that Liz was gone." Twine remained close to the family, visiting often in Mishawaka, where they sat and "talked endlessly about Liz." She named her daughter for her best friend. Twine and Charley, once the "horrible little brother Butch," became good friends and stayed in touch into the new century. Twine joined the Richardsons on a trip to Chicago to visit with Margaret Morrison, Liz's closest Red Cross colleague. Two women who had never met gathered to talk about their lost friend. Margaret kept in her scrapbook several special photographs, including one the family gave her of Liz leaving The Patch for the train to Washington in May 1944, and another of her flag-draped coffin in Rouen.[7]

Aunt Lily Kimbel was among others who visited the Normandy grave. She signed the registration book on December 10, 1949, and came back a second time. After Henrietta died, Charles Richardson, Sr., married Lily, Henrietta's cousin, and together they visited the cemetery. Another early visitor was a friend from South Bend traveling in Normandy in 1952; she picked wild daisies from the grave and sent them back to Mishawaka, where they became part of the family's collection. Brother Charley visited twice, once soon after he graduated from Stanford Law School and again near the end of the century.[8]

The body of Elizabeth Richardson rests today among thousands of American men who died in Europe. Most visitors to the Normandy site likely think only of the men buried there and, more generally, of the masculine qualities of war—of the paratroopers from Liz's beloved 82nd who jumped into the night, of the bravery on Omaha Beach just below the cemetery, or further away at the Battle of the Bulge or across the world at Iwo Jima and Okinawa. War remembrances are most often about men in combat and center on sailors, airmen, paratroopers, GIs. Such deeply embedded images of men at war are reinforced at Normandy by the remnants on the nearby landing beaches and by the carvings, maps, and inscriptions at the cemetery. On the memorial chapel wall, for example, one inscription reads: "This chapel has been erected by the United States of America in grateful memory of her sons who gave

Elizabeth A. Richardson's marble marker at the Normandy American Cemetery. *Courtesy American Battle Monuments Commission.*

their lives in the landings on the Normandy beaches and in the liberation of Northern France."[9]

Occasionally, someone has remembered the women of World War II. General Dwight Eisenhower specifically cited "the Red Cross girl" when he addressed Congress in June 1945:

> The Red Cross, with its clubs for recreation, its coffee and doughnuts in the forward areas, its readiness to meet the needs of the well and help minister to the wounded—even more important, the devotion and warm-hearted sympathy of the Red Cross girl! The Red Cross has often seemed to be the friendly hand of this nation, reaching across the sea to sustain its fighting men.[10]

Another exception to the predominantly masculine messages of World War II came when Nancy Reagan, wife of the President, visited the Normandy Cemetery on a cold, rainy June 6th in 1982. Mrs. Reagan placed flowers on Elizabeth Richardson's grave. A photograph in

First Lady Nancy Reagan placed flowers on Liz's grave at the Normandy American Cemetery on June 6, 1982. *Courtesy Ronald Reagan Library.*

Testimony to the long memory of war, in May 2007, six women who served with the American Red Cross in World War II placed flowers on Elizabeth Richardson's grave. Left to right: Marge Gully, Mary O'Driscoll, Christine Sleeper, Ginny Hannum, Mary Lou Chapman, Jane Cazort. *Courtesy Barbara Bruegger.*

newspapers around the world gave Liz a moment in the spotlight. Yet there remained a tendency to think of men and war even in reporting this event. The *New York Times*'s caption for the photograph of the First Lady laying the flowers stated incorrectly that "Miss Richardson, an American Red Cross worker, was killed during the Normandy invasion." The *Washington Post* ran its photograph as an insert above one of Robert Capa's iconic photographs of the D-Day landings. Perhaps the reporters didn't know or were not interested in the life and death of a woman who never charged onto a landing beach but "only" slung doughnuts and coffee for the boys.[11]

An outpouring of memories, books, films, and public programs began in the early 1990s to accompany the 50-year anniversaries. Times had changed in the decades since the 1940s, and now there was more room for women. Rosie the Riveter became a key feature of home-front celebrations. Some attention moved to women in uniform, which included the dedication in 1997 of The Women In Military Service For America Memorial at Arlington National Cemetery. New historical scholarship on women and gender broadened definitions of war and modified the war stories and the "guy talk" that often dominated those stories.[12]

Red Cross Clubmobile women knew even before they returned home that forgetting the war would never be possible.[13] They kept their stories alive, if often quietly. They saved their letters, made scrapbooks, and wrote down or otherwise recorded their memories.[14] A few published their accounts. They formed the Clubmobile Association and produced a newsletter, *The Sinker, Jr.*, with reports of marriages and births, jobs and travels, and reminders of a war growing more distant.

Beginning in 1946 Clubmobile women gathered for annual reunions in New York City, Washington, D.C., and elsewhere. Most elaborate was the special reunion they organized in London in 1962. Sixty Clubmobile women, described by the *London Telegraph* as "now middle-aged," gathered with their families for a banquet at the Savoy Hotel. The menu listed the last course as "Le Souffle Surprise My Lady"—a surprise revealed when waiters entered the dining room carrying silver trays piled high with American doughnuts. Some of the "girls," now designated "ladies," purposefully had not eaten a doughnut since 1945. Nor had many seen London since the war. The city was nearly "unrecognizable without the barrage balloons" and with its bright lights and choices of "food—tons of it!" The women walked around Grosvenor Square to lament that their old headquarters at No. 12 was gone and to notice that "there was not a uniform in sight."[15]

Like aged military veterans, Clubmobile women continued to exchange newsletters, phone calls, and email into the twenty-first century. Children and grandchildren accompanied the declining number of elderly women to reunions. "We do have fun," Eloise Reilly recalled in 2005, though each time, many thought, this might be the last gathering.[16]

In recent years living history re-enactors in the United States and in England have dressed in Clubmobile uniforms to portray these women alongside World War II airplanes or at 1940s-era dances where they serve coffee and doughnuts to men in vintage military uniforms. World War II buffs in France rebuilt an old Clubmobile and demonstrated its functions. Model manufacturers offered collectors replicas of Clubmobiles and Red Cross volunteers.[17]

Elizabeth Richardson's most public memorial appeared at the new visitor center that opened at the Normandy American Cemetery in June 2007. The center's Sacrifice Gallery features brief stories of several Americans buried in the nearby cemetery. One is Elizabeth Richardson. A few sentences and a large photograph of Liz carrying a Red Cross coffee urn in northern England hint at her role. The image and words doubtless linger with some who exit the center to walk among the markers and contemplate men and women at war.[18]

The American Red Cross Clubmobile women knew in their heart how important their job was. They knew, as Mary Metcalfe Rexford wrote, that "few women have had a more meaningful or gratifying wartime experience." For Red Cross Clubmobile Captain Elizabeth A. Richardson slinging doughnuts for the boys offered "more satisfaction in the doing than anything Auntie has ever done."[19]

Appendix: Wartime Writing

Liz Richardson wrote on Red Cross stationery with a fountain pen, sometimes a pencil, and occasionally she used a typewriter. Often she told her correspondent exactly what she was doing at the moment, as in this to her brother John on November 1, 1944: "I'm sitting on top of the fireplace, writing on my lap and waiting for a Special Service Lieut. who is dying to have somebody laugh at his shaggy dog stories. And I'm the lucky girl, so I must go now and climb into my laughing clothes."[1]

Diaries and letters from World War II are among the best way for us to know a time so different from our own. They have an immediacy that offers a sense of being there, of knowing someone from an earlier time, of feeling close to that person, and gaining insights as to what happened and what it meant.[2]

Reading primary sources sometimes takes more patience than watching a film or reading a historical narrative, which the creator has carefully packaged for tidy presentation. Letters and diaries contain repetitions, fragments, and interrupted stories. They are created in the present time of the writer who cannot know the future the way the later historian does. That uncertainty runs through Elizabeth Richardson's writings and gives them power and poignancy. So does her conviction that she was living in the midst of momentous events. She wrote not only to share with her correspondents back home but as a way to think about and make sense of the turmoil around her and, later, to remember.

It's not hard to imagine Liz's return to America after the war, perhaps to her old job in retail advertising, perhaps living as mother and wife in America of the 1950s and 1960s, perhaps even combining career and family, but certainly never forgetting. Likely she would have attended the Red Cross Clubmobile reunions to laugh and reminisce, but more important, on an occasional evening, she would sit and read through her old letters and diary entries, pondering, shedding a few tears, and understanding more fully in the distance of time what she had seen and done. As with others of her generation, she would likely have mostly held these thoughts in her heart so that those of the next generation could never fully comprehend. Today, her words written so long ago and those of other veterans allow us to glimpse this war in a way more "real" and more compelling than any other source.

Notes

Preface

1. Unless otherwise noted, Richardson family correspondence and documents are from the collection of Charles Richardson, Jr. I have reproduced Liz's diary and letters as she wrote them. She claimed to be a poor speller, and there are some misspelled words and place names, but her spelling and grammatical usage are generally good. Errors have usually not been corrected. People, places, and references, including French words, are identified only when helpful to understanding a larger issue. Liz sometimes placed only the date at the top of her letters; sometimes she added "England," but not a more specific location because of war censorship. I have omitted a few of the extant 92 letters and also portions of letters that were repetitive or of slight consequence. My deletions are indicated by ellipses enclosed in brackets in order to distinguish them from the three or more dots that Elizabeth sometimes inserted in her writing.

2. ER to Henrietta and Charles Richardson, Sr., May 28, 1945, December 1, 1944; Max Hastings, *Armageddon: The Battle for Germany 1944–1945* (New York, 2004), 141.

3. For an introduction to the complexities and ambiguities of this war, see Michael Bess, *Choices under Fire: Moral Dimensions of World War II* (New York, 2006), esp. 9–17.

4. ER to John Richardson, December 27, 1944; ER to Henrietta and Charles Richardson, Sr., July 18, 1945, ER diary, January 10, 1945.

5. ER to Betty Twining, April 22, 1945.

6. ER to Henrietta and Charles Richardson, Sr., August 18, 1944; ER to Winifred Wood, April 19, 1945.

7. Just where women fit in war and war stories remains a contested issue. Historian Leisa Meyer has written about the tendency of military history to function as a "thundering Greek chorus that so often conflates 'war' with 'combat' and constructs both as predominantly 'masculine' endeavors. Women's and men's 'war stories' in this context are slotted into gendered categories defined by the iconic dichotomies of 'homefront/battlefront,' 'warrior'/'nurturer/mother,' 'protector'/'protected' and the differential value assigned to each." The interesting question, Meyer adds, is "what happens when these fictive binaries are blurred. . . ." Leisa Meyer, "Women in War Stories," *Journal of Women's History* 14 (2002): 162. Liz Richardson's war story is one that blurs the categories.

8. ER to Winifred Wood, April 19, 1945.

9. ER to Betty Twining, September 4, 1944.

1. Growing Up, Leaving Home, and Preparing for War

1. Charles M. Richardson, Jr., interview with author, June 11, 2003.

2. Anne Bodle Schuknecht, interview with author, November 15, 2003; Richardson, interview with author.

3. Schuknecht, interview with author; Schuknecht to Nancy Reagan, folder "Richardson, Elizabeth" WHORM: Alpha File, Ronald Reagan Presidential Library, Simi Valley, Calif.; Richardson, interview with author; *Miskodeed 1936* [Mishawaka High School yearbook], pp. 17, 67.

4. Elizabeth Ann Richardson, transcript, Milwaukee-Downer College, 1936–1940 (Lawrence University Archives, Appleton, Wisc.); *Milwaukee Journal*, November 23, 1939; Betty Twining Blue, interviews with author, November 14, 2003, June 9, 2005; Ann Bumby Fallon, interview with author, June 26, 2003; Ann Bumby Fallon to author (2003), in author's possession. An overview of Liz's Downer years with some documents and art work is on the Lawrence University site: http://www.lawrence.edu/library/archives/richardson/index.htm. For background on the university, see Lynne H. Kleinman, "The Milwaukee-Downer Woman" (Appleton, Wisc., 1997), at http://www.lawrence.edu/news/pubs/mdwoman/index.shtml. Milwaukee-Downer merged with Lawrence University in Appleton, Wisconsin, in 1964. The old campus buildings became part of the University of Wisconsin–Milwaukee.

5. Blue, interviews with author; Fallon, interview with author, June 26, 2003; Fallon to author (2003); *Students' Handbook* (College Government Association of Milwaukee-Downer College, 1940), 36.

6. Blue, interviews with author; Fallon, interview with author. The words "girl" and "girls" were commonly used in the 1930s and 1940s and are sometimes used in this book to described adults who today would be referred to as women.

7. Blue, interviews with author; Fallon, interview with author.

8. Fallon to author (2003); Blue, interview with author, November 14, 2003. Liz also referred to "St. Henrietta" in writing to her brother John and on one occasion imagined their mother entertaining guests and "flapping in the breeze like an old sheet." ER to John Richardson, November 26, 1942, July 15, 1943.

9. *The Kodak* [Milwaukee-Downer], October 1936, pp. 4–5, October 1939, p. 8, March 1940, p. 14; ER, diary, passim.

10. ER to parents, November 2, 1939; *Hawthorn Leaves* [Milwaukee-Downer], April 1940, p. 2; ER, diary, September 19, 1939, May 19, 1940; Blue, interviews with author; Fallon to author (2003).

11. ER, diary, June 20, 29, July 12, August 24, 1940; Blue, interview with author, November 14, 2003; ER to Twining, March 10, 1941.

12. *Keeping in Touch* [Schuster's], September 1945; ER to Lillian Kimbel, January 1, 1942.

13. Blue, interviews with author, November 14, 2003, June 9, 2005; Clarissa (Chris) Hanson Watson, interview with author, May 29, 2003; ER to John Richardson, November 26, 1942; John Gurda, *The Making of Milwaukee* (Milwaukee, 1999), 306–317.

14. ER to John Richardson, September 20, November 26, 1942; ER to parents, n.d.; Blue, interview with author, November 14, 2003; ER to Charles and Henrietta Richardson, July 1, 1944.

15. Gurda, *The Making of Milwaukee*, 306–317.
16. ER to Lillian Kimbel, January 1, 1942; ER to parents, n.d.; Watson, interview with author; *Saturday Evening Post*, September 26, 1942.
17. ER to parents, n.d.; Watson, interview with author; Meghan K. Winchell, "'To Make the Boys Feel at Home': USO Senior Hostesses and Gendered Citizenship," *Frontiers: A Journal of Women's Studies* 25, no. 1 (2004): 190–211.
18. Watson, interview with author; Richardson, interview with author.
19. Interview with Kathryn Kirkpatrick Huehl, June 14, 2006; Leisa D. Meyer, *Creating GI Jane: Sexuality and Power in the Women's Army Corps during World War II* (New York, 1996), 2–10, 25–28; Susan M. Hartmann, *The Home Front and Beyond: American Women in the 1940s* (Boston, 1982), 31–48. Some women in military uniform did serve overseas and even close to the front lines. The women's military units struggled for respectability, however, and had been hard hit by a slander campaign. Mattie E. Treadwell, *The Women's Army Corps* (Washington, D.C., 1954), 191–218; D'Ann Campbell, *Women at War with America: Private Lives in a Patriotic Era* (Cambridge, Mass., 1984), 19–46; M. Michaela Hampf, "'Dykes' or 'Whores': Sexuality and the Women's Army Corps in the United States during World War II," *Women's Studies International Forum* 27 (2004): 13–30; Cecilia Hock, "Creation of the WAC Image and Perception of Army Women, 1942–1944," *Minerva* (March 1995), 40–55; Ann Elizabeth Pfau, "Miss Yourlovin: Women in the Culture of American World War II Soldiers" (Ph.D. dissertation, Rutgers University, 2001), 53–91. For an overview of women in war service, see Emily Yellin, *Our Mothers' War: American Women at Home and at the Front During World War II* (New York, 2004).
20. Foster Rhea Dulles, *The American Red Cross: A History* (New York, 1950), 353; Studs Terkel, *"The Good War": An Oral History of World War Two* (New York, 1984), 566; F. A. Winfrey to Chapter Chairmen, October 29, 1941, Box 1346, Records of the American Red Cross, 1935–1946, Record Group 200, National Archives at College Park, Md. (hereafter cited as RG 200, NACP); S. D. Hoslett, "The History of the American Red Cross: Vol. XVIII; Red Cross Personnel Administration in World War II," 31, typescript, 1950, Hazel Braugh Records Center and Archives, American Red Cross, Lorton, Va. (hereafter cited as Braugh Records Center); "The History of the American Red Cross: Vol. VI; National Headquarters in World War II," 28–35, typescript, 1950, Braugh Records Center; Robert Keith Murray, "The History of the American Red Cross: Vol. XXX; A Study of American Public Opinion on the American National Red Cross from Newspapers and Periodicals, 1881–1948," 149–154, typescript, 1950, Braugh Records Center. For a very negative view of the American Red Cross that evidences little understanding of the role of female volunteers, see Gwendolyn C. Shealy, *A Critical History of the American Red Cross, 1882–1945: The End of Noble Humanitarianism* (Lewiston, N.Y., 2003), 81–103.
21. Michael E. Stevens and Ellen D. Goldlust, eds., *Women Remember the War, 1941–1945* (Madison, 1993), 71; Hoslett, "Red Cross Personnel Administration," 49, 61–66.
22. Dulles, *The American Red Cross*, 158; Helen Keating Neal, "Why Not Join Them?" *Independent Woman* 23 (April 1944): 119; "Life Visits Red Cross Girls in England," *Life* 16 (February 28, 1944): 111; B. J. Olewiler, *A Woman in a Man's War* (n.p., 2003), 23; *Washington Times Herald*, December 14, 1943. For contrasts with World War I service, see Susan Zeiger, *In Uncle Sam's Service: Women Workers with the American Expe-*

ditionary Force, 1917–1919 (Ithaca, 1999), 51–76. For Red Cross women in Vietnam, see Ron Steinman, *Women in Vietnam* (New York, 2000), 23–25, 197–219.

23. Elizabeth Ann Richardson, "Employee Service Record," American Red Cross Headquarters Personnel Office, Washington, D.C. The photograph is in the Charles Richardson, Jr., Collection and also in the Margaret Morrison Scrapbook in possession of her son, Kevin Cornyn.

24. *Baltimore & Ohio Railroad System Time Tables* (April 30, 1944); ER to Charles and Henrietta Richardson, May 14, 1944.

25. ER to Charles and Henrietta Richardson, May 14, 25, 1944; ER to John Richardson, June 1, 1944; Scott Hart, *Washington at War: 1941–1945* (Englewood Cliffs, N.J., 1970), 40, 203; David Brinkley, *Washington Goes to War* (New York, 1988), 76, 227–282; Paul K. Williams, *Washington, D.C.: The World War II Years* (Charleston, S.C., 2004), 7–9, 16, 41, 62–65, 95.

26. *Washington Star*, August, 20, 1944; ER to Charles and Henrietta Richardson, May 19, 1944; Rosemary Norwalk, *Dearest Ones: A True World War II Love Story* (New York, 1999), 15; Kathleen Havens Gezzi, ed., *Journey Between Mountains: The Letters and Journal of Mary Hall Baroudi* (Bloomington, Ind., 2006), 15.

27. Harry D. Cross, "University of Mercy," *The Courier* (American Red Cross) (January 1944), 5; Kenny Lucas, "Campus Reveille, 1941–1945," *American Magazine of American University* 52 (Summer 2001): 16–17, 28–29; Contracts of Lease, American Red Cross and American University, May 24, 1943, February 26, 1944, Box 2, History Files, American University Archives, Washington, D.C.

28. Hoslett, "Red Cross Personnel Administration," 79–83, 102–103, 213–215; American Red Cross, "Uniform and Uniform Regulations, Services to Armed Forces" mimeographed, March 1944, Box 1408, RG 200, NACP; Barbara Pathe, interview with Brien R. Williams, August 5, 1999, Oral History Collection, Braugh Records Center.

29. *Los Angeles Times*, August 20, 1944; Cross, "University of Mercy," 5.

30. ER to Charles and Henrietta Richardson, May 19, 1944. See also Kathryn Kirkpatrick Huehl, interview with author, June 2, 2003.

31. ER to Charles and Henrietta Richardson, May 25, 1944.

32. ER to Charles and Henrietta Richardson, May 31, June 10, 1944. See also Hoslett, "Red Cross Personnel Administration," 83; Marjorie Lee Morgan, ed., *The Clubmobile: The ARC in the Storm* (St. Petersburg, Fla., 1982), 36–39.

33. ER to Charles and Henrietta Richardson, June 19, June 25, 1944; Elizabeth Ann Richardson, "Employee Service Record," American Red Cross Headquarters Personnel Office, Washington, D.C.

34. ER to Charles and Henrietta Richardson, June 19, 25, July 1, 1944; ER, diary, January 10, 1945; John A. Prosser, Order No. 347, American Red Cross Headquarters, July 5, 1945 (Charles Richardson, Jr., Collection); Hart, *Washington at War*, 37, 178.

35. ER to Charles and Henrietta Richardson, July 6, 1945.

36. ER to Charles and Henrietta Richardson, "at sea," n.d.; ER, diary, January 10, 1945; Pathe, interview with Williams; Norwalk, *Dearest Ones*, 27, 28.

37. ER to Charles and Henrietta Richardson, "at sea," n.d.; ER, diary, January 10, 1945; Eloise Reilly to author, March 6, 2003, January 29, 2006; Norwalk, *Dearest Ones*, 30–32; David Reynolds, *Rich Relations: The American Occupation of Britain, 1942–1945* (London, 1995), 242–243; W. Somerset Maugham, *The Great Exotic Novels and Short Stories of Somerset Maugham* (New York, 2001), 3–42.

38. ER to Charles and Henrietta Richardson, "at sea," n.d.; ER, diary, January 10, 1945; Alister Satchell, *Running the Gauntlet: How Three Giant Liners Carried a Million Men to War, 1942–1945* (Annapolis, 2001), 74; Norwalk, *Dearest Ones*, 33–34.

2. The Yanks in England

1. Maureen Waller, *London 1945: Life in the Debris of War* (London, 2004), 1–12. For a glimpse of the large Red Cross role in preparation for D-Day, see Judy Barrett Litoff and David C. Smith, *We're in This War, Too: World War II Letters from American Women in Uniform* (New York, 1994), 155–156.

2. Joanna Mack and Steve Humphries, *London at War: The Making of Modern London, 1939–1945* (London, 1985), 128–143; Waller, *London 1945*, 20–33; Robert Bremner, et al., "The History of the American National Red Cross: Vol. XIII; American Red Cross Service in the War Against the European Axis," 377, typescript, 1950, Hazel Braugh Records Center and Archives, American Red Cross, Lorton, Va. (hereafter cited as Braugh Records Center).

3. Charlotte Colburn to family, August 4, 1944, http://www.clubmobile.org/L098August4_44_2.html; *Los Angeles Times*, September 3, 1944; *ARC London Light* (newsletter), July 8, 1944; Mollie Panter-Downes, *London War Notes, 1939–1945* (New York, 1971), 334.

4. "Bailing out the British" was the way American GI William A. Madison explained his time in England in 1944 to his son.

5. ER to John Richardson, December 13, 1944.

6. David Reynolds, *Rich Relations: The American Occupation of Britain, 1942–1945* (London, 1995), 107–126, 393; John Costello, *Virtue under Fire: How World War II Changed Our Social and Sexual Attitudes* (Boston, 1985), 229–243; James Tobin, *Ernie Pyle's War: America's Eyewitness to World War II* (New York, 1997), 162; Ministry of Information, *Meet the U.S. Army* (London, 1943), 17, 20, 23–24.

7. Ministry of Information, *Meet the U.S. Army*, 17, 20, 23–24; Anthony Aldgate and Jeffrey Richards, *Britain Can Take It: The British Cinema in the Second World War* (Edinburgh, 1994), 277–298.

8. *Over There: Instructions for American Servicemen in Britain, 1942* (reprint, Bodleian Library, University of Oxford, 1994), 2, 4, 10, 15. For doubts about the effectiveness of such "directed understanding," see the 1943 dispatch from London by John Steinbeck in *Once There Was a War* (New York, 1958), 80–83.

9. *The Sinker*, November 24, 1944.

10. Reynolds, *Rich Relations*, 252–261, 421–422; Samuel A. Stouffer et al., *The American Soldier: Adjustment during Army Life* (Princeton, 1949), I, 59, 246; Kathryn Kirkpatrick Huehl, interview with author, June 2, 2003; US Army Special Services Forces, "What the Soldier Thinks of Recreation and Entertainment Facilities in ETO," mimeograph, February 8, 1943, Box 4111, Records of the American Red Cross, 1935–1946, Record Group 200, National Archives at College Park, Md. (hereafter cited as RG 200, NACP). One of Liz's colleagues wrote home in early 1945: "Oh—I'm glad I'm an American! I'm broad minded and I continue to like England—which is more than most Americans do, but it keeps reminding me of a wormy apple. It needs a good reorganization and house cleaning and sunshine and vitamins." Margee Main to family, January 29, 1945.

11. Dwight D. Eisenhower, *Crusade in Europe* (Garden City, N.Y., 1952), 238;

George Korson, *At His Side: The Story of the American Red Cross Overseas in World War II* (New York, 1945), 260–262; *New York Times*, February 23, 1943, March 7, 1943, February 27, March 1, 16, 1944; Reynolds, *Rich Relations*, 154–163; Foster Rhea Dulles, *The American Red Cross* (New York, 1950), 367–368, 424–430.

12. "Red Cross Fun," *Life* 14 (February 8, 1943): 185–193; Richard Lee Strout, "Red Cross Club in England," *Christian Science Monitor*, October 14, 1944; *ARC London Light* (newsletter), July 8, 1944; Toni Frissell, "I Went to England for the Red Cross," *Vogue* (February 1, 1943): 47–48; Allan M. Brandt, *No Magic Bullet: A Social History of Venereal Disease in the United States since 1880* (New York, 1985), 163–165; Larry B. McAfee to L. M. Mitchell, February 20, 1943, Box 4111, RG 200, NACP. The Red Cross surrendered to the military the role it had played in World War I in providing hospitals, ambulances, and nurses. Most nurses overseas in World War II were military, not Red Cross nurses.

13. U.S. Army, Special Services Forces, "What the Soldier Thinks about the Red Cross in ETO," February 17, 1943, Box 4111, RG 200, NACP; Korson, *At His Side*, 264–267; Marjorie Lee Morgan, ed., *The Clubmobile: The ARC in the Storm* (St. Petersburg, Fla., 1982), viii; *The Sinker*, October 26, 1944, pp. 1, 4; *Chicago Tribune*, August 24, 1944.

14. Postcard in author's personal collection.

15. Ann Elizabeth Pfau, "*Miss Yourlovin*: Women in the Culture of American World War II Soldiers" (Ph.D. dissertation, Rutgers University, 2001), 9–52; Jane Mersky Leder, *Thanks for the Memories: Love, Sex, and World War II* (Westport, Conn., 2006), 115–132; Peter Schrijvers, *The Crash of Ruin: American Combat Soldiers in Europe during World War II* (New York, 1998), 178–190. Barbara G. Friedman, *From the Battlefront to the Bridal Suite: Media Coverage of British War Brides 1942–1946* (Columbia, Mo., 2007).

16. B. J. Olewiler, *A Woman in a Man's War* (n.p., 2003), 76; Clubmobile Houston Report, March 4, 1944, Jane McKee Jack Papers, 95-M124, American Red Cross Clubmobile Service Collection, Schlesinger Library, Radcliffe Institute, Harvard University.

17. "Summary Suggestions," typescript, January 1944, Box 1408, RG 200, NACP; Eleanor Stevenson and Pete Martin, *I Knew Your Soldier* (Washington, D.C., 1945), 57, 79–82, 91; Mary Haynsworth Mathews, interviews with author, March 28, June 28, 2003; Huehl, interview with author.

18. Max Hastings, *Armageddon: The Battle for Germany 1944–1945* (New York, 2004), 312–313.

19. "Doughnut Girl in England," *Ladies Home Journal* 60 (April 1943): 12; *Los Angeles Time*, August 20, 1944; *Washington Star*, August 20, 1944; Avon advertisement, 1944, author's collection.

20. Margaret Randolph Higonnet et al., eds., *Behind the Lines: Gender and the Two World Wars* (New Haven, 1987), 1–12.

21. Reynolds, *Rich Relations*, 61–70; Schrijvers, *The Crash of Ruin*, 178–179; Paul Fussell, *Wartime: Understanding and Behavior in the Second World War* (New York, 1989), 79–114; "Red Cross Fun," 88; Oscar Whitelaw Rexford, ed., *Battlestars & Doughnuts: World War II Clubmobile Experiences of Mary Metcalfe Rexford* (St. Louis, 1989), 3; Leisa D. Meyer, *Creating GI Jane: Sexuality and Power in the Women's Army Corps during World War II* (New York, 1996), 9, 148–178; Barbara Pathe, interview with author, October 31, 2005; Stevenson and Martin, *I Knew Your Soldier*, 60–61, 91–92; Eva Christensen, "Doughnut Girl: The Diary of a Red Cross Girl in England," *Ladies Home Journal* 61

(September 1944): 4. Wearing lipstick in wartime raises interesting questions of gender, sex, and women's place. For possibilities that lipstick was a sign of female agency (which it likely was for Clubmobile women), see Page Dougherty Delano, "Making Up for War: Sexuality and Citizenship in Wartime Culture," *Feminist Studies* 26 (Spring 2000): 33–69.

22. Mary Haynsworth Mathews, interview with author, March 28, 2003; *The Sinker*, May 12, 1944, p. 2; Olewiler, *A Woman in a Man's War*, 33; *Harper's Bazaar*, March 1945.

23. S. D. Hoslett, "The History of the American Red Cross: Vol. XVIII; Red Cross Personnel Administration in World War II," 64, typescript, 1950, Braugh Records Center.

24. Gretchen Schuyler to parents, June 1, 1943; to father, May 15, 1944; both, Gretchen Schuyler Papers, 2005-M150, American Red Cross Clubmobile Service Collection, Schlesinger Library.

25. Margaret Gearhart to parents, October, 29, 1944, Margaret Gearhart Brodie Papers, 96-M25, American Red Cross Clubmobile Service Collection, Schlesinger Library.

26. The large degree to which Red Cross doughnuts, coffee, and young American women were part of GI culture is glimpsed in an amusing letter that the mother of Clubmobiler Jane Anne McKee Jack wrote her at the end of the war. The elder McKee was a Red Cross volunteer who greeted GIs as they disembarked from transport ships anchored in the Hudson River. Mrs. McKee and her fellow Red Cross canteen volunteers were a generation or two older than the Clubmobile women. They arrived at the docks on this July day with two trucks filled with half pints of milk packed in ice to serve the highly spirited GIs, only seven days removed from Europe and perhaps doughnuts served at Le Havre by Liz Richardson.

> They wanted to know where the girls were. I said, "It is Grandma's time to meet you, that's why we are here." Such a shout of laughter and calls went over the boat. They didn't care what we said just so we talked back to them. "Got coffee for us?" "No, <u>milk</u>!" "Want schnapps, want cognac, want calvados."
>
> "What are you all? German, French? We are expecting American boys. We have <u>MILK</u>." Then the roar that went up, "We like milk, we want milk, but can't we have a doughnut? We haven't had one for 7 days."
>
> "No doughnuts for you now, the army is giving you a steak dinner in a little while. We must not spoil your appetites." "You couldn't spoil our appetites lady." And so, on and on.

Mrs. N. T. McKee to Jane Anne McKee Jack, July 22, 1945, Jack Papers.

3. V-1 ROCKETS, THE *KANSAS CITY*, AND THE 82ND AIRBORNE

1. The address of the apartment they shared in Milwaukee.

2. John Bodle was a brother of Mishawaka friend Anne Bodle. Laurence Rolston was Liz's cousin. Both were in military service.

3. *The Sinker*, August 4, October 26, 1944, p. 4; Althea M. Bush, "American Red Cross Clubmobile Operations in Great Britain and Western Europe, April 1942–July

1946," 27, typescript, September 1, 1947, Box 67, Monograph Collection, Hazel Braugh Records Center and Archives, American Red Cross, Lorton, Va. [hereafter cited as Braugh Records Center]; S. Keene Mitchell, Jr., to Harvey D. Gibson, January 8, 1945, Box 1493, Records of the American Red Cross, 1935–1946, Record Group 200, National Archives at College Park, Md. (hereafter cited as RG 200, NACP).

4. Wearing a Red Cross skirt overseas was an unusual event for Liz and many others. Gretchen Schuyler went eight months wearing only trousers. Gretchen Schuyler to Katie _____, March 1, 1944, Gretchen Schuyler Papers, 2005-M150, American Red Cross Clubmobile Service Collection, Schlesinger Library, Radcliffe Institute, Harvard University.

5. Rosemary Norwalk, *Dearest Ones: A True World War II Love Story* (New York, 1999), 45; Marjorie Lee Morgan, ed., *The Clubmobile: The ARC in the Storm* (St. Petersburg, Fla., 1982), 21; B. J. Olewiler, *A Woman in a Man's War* (n.p., 2003), 43; ER letters of September 12, 1944, November 1, 1944, January 28, 1945.

6. The Red Cross Clubmobile home was opened that February at 103 Park Street. It had central heat and hot water—amenities that veteran Clubmobilers returning to London later would more fully appreciate. *The Sinker*, February 17, 1944.

7. Officials warned American women against putting lipstick kisses on V-Mail, since the lipstick might blur the writing and make it illegible on reproduction. *New York Times*, July 31, 1942.

8. Nigel Fountain, ed., *The Battle of Britain and the Blitz* (London, 2002), 125. In classic understatement, the chief of the British Imperial Staff, Field Marshal Alan Brooke, wrote in his diary on August 3, 1944: "Buzz bombs very noisy last night, hope they behave better tonight!" Alex Danchev and Daniel Todman, eds., *War Diaries 1939–1945* (Berkeley, 2001), 577.

9. Ben Beazley, *Wartime Leicester* (Stroud, England, 2004), 51–69, 106–122, 134; Terence C. Cartwright, *Birds Eye Wartime Leicestershire, 1939–1945* (Leicester, UK, 2002).

10. These two military publications were widely read by American soldiers in Great Britain. A survey in early 1943 showed that nine of ten GIs read both and that what they most liked to read were the stories from home. U.S. Army Special Services Forces, "Soldier Opinion of *Stars and Stripes* and *Yank*," mimeograph, February 13, 1943, Box 4111, RG 200, NACP. *Yank* and *Stars and Stripes* were important reading for Clubmobilers as well for, as one recalled, they "would often tell us what was on the conversational menu for the day." Olewiler, *A Woman in a Man's War*, 148.

11. The *Kansas City* was a 10T10 Regal single-decker bus, manufactured in 1938 and loaned by London Transport to the American Red Cross in June 1943. http://www.countrybus.org.uk/T-regal/T8a.htm.

12. Deryk Wills, *Put on Your Boots and Parachutes! Personal Stories of the Veterans of the United States 82nd Airborne Division* (Leicester, 1992), 39–41, 116–123; Phil Nordyke, *All American All the Way: The Combat History of the 82nd Airborne Division in World War II* (St. Paul, Minn., 2005), 181–407; T. Moffatt Burris, *Strike and Hold: A Memoir of the 82d Airborne in World War II* (Washington, D.C., 2000), 96; James Megellas, *All the Way to Berlin: A Paratrooper at War in Europe* (New York, 2003), 82; John D. McKenzie, *On Time On Target: The World War II Memoir of a Paratrooper in the 82d Airborne* (Novato, Calif., 2000), 37–48.

13. Norwalk, *Dearest Ones*, 55.

14. *The Sinker*, October 13, 1944.

15. Morgan, *The Clubmobile*, 26–27; Eleanor Stevenson and Pete Martin, *I Knew Your Soldier* (Washington, D.C., 1945), 55–56; "Summary Suggestions," typescript, January 1944, RG 200, NACP; "Instructions and Suggestions to Clubmobile Operators," typescript, October 7, 1944, Box 1408, RG 200, NACP; John Conway, "Purchasing and Procurement Department," typescript, n.d., 67–77, Box 67, Braugh Records Center; "Serial Numbers of Doughnut Machines on Loan from Doughnut Corporation of America to American Red Cross," November 15, 1945, Box 1400, RG 200, NACP; George C. Smith to Richard F. Allen, July 22, 1944, Box 1400, RG 200, NACP.

16. Barbara Pathe, interview with author, October 31, 2005; Scrapbook, Patricia Maddox Collins Papers, 95-M107, American Red Cross Clubmobile Service Collection, Schlesinger Library.

17. Kathleen Havens Gezzi, ed., *Journey Between Mountains: The Letters and Journal of Mary Hall Baroudi* (Bloomington, Ind., 2006), 68; Barbara Pathe, interview with Brien R. Williams, August 5, 1999, Oral History Collection, Braugh Records Center; Pathe, interview with author, October 31, 2005.

18. Karon S. Bailey, "Harriett Engelhardt: A Job Worth Having," *Alabama Heritage* 57 (Summer 2000): 30; "Summary Suggestions," typescript, January 1944, RG 200, NACP.

19. Gretchen Schuyler to Edy Schuyler, May 26, 1943, Gretchen Schuyler Papers, 2005-M150, American Red Cross Clubmobile Service Collection, Schlesinger Library; Margee Main to parents, December 22, 1944.

20. *The Sinker*, January 19, 1945.

21. Stephen Coote, *John Keats: A Life* (London, 1995), 42–43.

22. Helen Hokinson's cartoons in *The New Yorker* satirized society matrons and their fashion.

23. Wills, *Put on Your Boots and Parachutes!*, 42–43; Olewiler, *A Woman in a Man's War*, 75; John Costello, *Virtue under Fire: How World War II Changed Our Social and Sexual Attitudes* (Boston, 1985), 121–132; David Reynolds, *Rich Relations: The American Occupation of Britain, 1942–1945* (London, 1995), 263–264.

24. Norwalk, *Dearest Ones*, 119; Jeanne Carswell et al., eds., *Ours to Defend: Leicestershire People Remember World War II* (Leicester, 1989), 59–60.

25. Jean B. Sleath memoir, http://www.wartimeleicestershire.com/pages/mem oir_files/40.htm.

26. U.S. Army Special Services Forces, "Interests of Soldier in Talks and Their Reading Preferences in ETO," mimeograph, February 16, 1943, Box 4111, RG 200, NACP; James L. Baughman, "Who Reads *Life*?" in Erika Doss, *Looking at Life Magazine* (Washington, D.C., 2001), 41, 43–44.

27. The Red Cross was less likely to object to non-regulation clothing if it was red. Oscar Whitelaw Rexford, ed., *Battlestars & Doughnuts: World War II Clubmobile Experiences of Mary Metcalfe Rexford* (St. Louis, 1989), 9.

28. *The Sinker*, January 19, 1945, p. 3.

29. McKenzie, *On Time On Target*, 46.

30. Foster Rhea Dulles, *The American Red Cross* (New York, 1950), 376–377; Norwalk, *Dearest Ones*, 14, 98, 116; Olewiler, *A Woman in a Man's War*, 68–72; Edith Steiger Phillips, *My World War II Diary* (New York, 1973), 176; Michael E. Stevens and Ellen D. Goldlust, eds., *Women Remember the War, 1941–1945* (Madison, Wisc., 1993), 71–74; Rexford, ed., *Battlestars & Doughnuts*, 12, 80; Robert Keith Murray, "The History of the American Red Cross: Vol. XXX; A Study of American Public Opinion on the Ameri-

can National Red Cross from Newspapers and Periodicals, 1881–1948," 141–144, type-script, 1950, Braugh Records Center.

The complicated issue of dating officers was one that Red Cross headquarters struggled over throughout the war. Some female employees developed such strong offi-cer support that they could ignore Red Cross supervision, or so their superiors feared. The issue not only affected work in the field but also caused significant public relations challenges. One official lamented that the whole dating matter was "a very delicate sub-ject and there is very little that we can do about it." After the war some women returned home with a reluctance to talk about their service because of the scurrilous rumors. Bar-bara Pathe, interview with author, October 31, 2005; Hoslett, "Red Cross Personnel Ad-ministration in World War II," 208–209. For the military's struggles with these issues, see Leisa D. Meyer, *Creating GI Jane: Sexuality and Power in the Women's Army Corps during World War II* (New York, 1996), 128–139.

31. _____ Bucknell to The Chairman, May 15, 1944, cablegram, Box 1406, RG 200, NACP; Norwalk, *Dearest Ones*, 191; Phillips, *My World War II Diary*, 196–197; Gerald F. Linderman, *The World Within War: America's Combat Experience in World War II* (New York, 1997), 190, 317–318; George H. Roeder, Jr., *The Censored War: American Vi-sual Experience During World War Two* (New Haven, 1993), 48.

32. Like many, Liz was thinking about the Allied advance toward Paris. A week later the Germans were gone. Six months later Liz would see the city that had been spared war's destruction.

4. WAR COMES CLOSER

1. Biffy is slang for toilet.

2. This estate might have been Papillon Hall, where the 319th Glider Artillery Regiment was billeted. Deryk Wills, *Put on Your Boots and Parachutes! Personal Stories of the Veterans of the United States 82nd Airborne Division* (Leicester, 1992), 59–60; Wills to au-thor, January 26, 2005.

3. Chris Way, *Glenn Miller in Britain Then and Now* (London, n.d.), 65.

4. Siegfried Sassoon is best remembered as a poet of the grimness of World War I. His *Memoirs of a Fox-Hunting Man* (London, 1928) was a mostly autobiographi-cal account of his youth and his experiences in the trenches. "The intimate mental his-tory of any man who went to the War," Sassoon wrote, "would make unheroic reading" (291).

5. Raphael Sabatini wrote novels of romance and adventure in the early twenti-eth century.

6. The classic account of Market Garden is Cornelius Ryan's *A Bridge Too Far* (New York, 1974). See also Phil Nordyke, *All American All the Way: The Combat History of the 82nd Airborne Division in World War II* (St. Paul, Minn., 2005), 414–431; James Megellas, *All the Way to Berlin: A Paratrooper at War in Europe* (New York, 2003), 90–93. Prior to their departure the 82nd presented an American flag to St. Denis Church, Evington; it stands there today. In the years since, many veterans of the unit have re-turned to Leicestershire for reunions.

7. Gretchen Schuyler to parents, June 1, 1943, to father, May 15, 1944, Gretchen Schuyler Papers, 2005-M150, American Red Cross Clubmobile Service Collection, Schlesinger Library, Radcliffe Institute, Harvard University.

8. Max Hastings, *Armageddon: The Battle for Germany 1944–1945* (New York, 2004), 15.

9. Being so close to men in the days just before they went off to battle was among the most intense emotional experiences for Red Cross workers. Gysella Simon wrote home on June 8, 1944, just after she had worked with men off to the Normandy invasion beaches: "There were times when I could scarcely see for the tears in my eyes. It wasn't easy, but I did my best to hold back my feelings—a hard thing to do at a time like that." Judy Barrett Litoff and David C. Smith, *We're in This War, Too: World War II Letters from American Women in Uniform* (New York, 1994), 156.

10. A 1943 Hollywood musical comedy, with lots of headline stars.

11. The article appeared in *The Sinker*, September 15, 1944, and is reprinted above.

12. Liz was off by a day. Friday was September 15. The 82nd left on Sunday, September 17.

13. Perhaps Liz appreciated too the ambiguities of the film. See Michael O'Shaughnessy, "'What wouldn't I give to grow old in a place like that': A Canterbury Tale," in Pat Kirkham and David Thomas, eds., *War Culture: Social Change and Changing Experience in World War Two Britain* (London, 1995), 41–47.

14. Althea M. Bush, "American Red Cross Clubmobile Operations in Great Britain and Western Europe, April 1942–July 1946," typescript, September 1, 1947, Box 67, Monograph Collection, Hazel Braugh Records Center and Archives, American Red Cross, Lorton, Va.

15. This is Lt. James Megellas. A photograph of him is at http://www.ww2-airborne.us/units/504/504_trp.html. For his memoir, see Megellas, *All the Way to Berlin*.

16. "Instructions and Suggestions to Clubmobile Operators," typescript, October 7, 1944, Box 1408, Records of the American Red Cross, 1935–1946, Record Group 200, National Archives at College Park, Md. (hereafter cited as RG 200, NACP); S. Keene Mitchell, Jr., to Harvey D. Gibson, January 8, 1945, Box 1493, RG 200, NACP. Red Cross attention to detail included instructions that doughnuts in trays were to be lined up precisely before serving. Barbara Pathe, interview with author, October 31, 2005.

17. The promotion to captain, the Red Cross Commissioner later wrote, came "as a result of her ability and excellent services." It was not made formal until December 1, 1944. Frederick A. Carroll to Charles and Henrietta Richardson, July 27, 1945.

18. *The Sinker*, November 24, 1944, p. 2.

19. Coal supplies in Leicester that winter reached an all-time low and produced severe rationing and long queues of citizens. Ben Beazley, *Wartime Leicester* (Stroud, England, 2004), 120.

20. John Barbirolli, of Hallé Orchestra, was one of the world's most distinguished conductors and had recently left the New York Philharmonic to return to his native England. Liz in fact did go to the concert, as stated in her letter of November 5.

21. Margaret Morrison's son recalled that his mother never liked confined spaces, which she told him reminded her of taking shelter under pianos during the buzz bomb attacks in London. Kevin Cornyn, interview with author, September 2, 2005.

22. Lt. Edward W. Kennedy and Sergeant William H. White died in Holland when they stepped on German mines while on night patrol on October 30, 1944. T.

Moffatt Burris, *Strike and Hold: A Memoir of the 82d Airborne in World War II* (Washington, D.C., 2000), 158–159, 206.

5. INTO THE ENGLISH PROVINCES

1. Derek J. Wheelhouse, comp., *Biddulph* (Chalford, UK, 1997).

2. "How Green Was My Valley" was a 1941 Academy Award–winning film set in a Welsh mining town. It was based on a bestselling book of the same title by Richard Llewellyn.

3. "Hellzapoppin" was a 1941 Hollywood film remarkable for its madcap and zany scenes.

4. William F. Ross and Charles F. Romanus, *United States Army in World War II, The Technical Services: The Quartermaster Corps: Operations in the War Against Germany* (Washington, D.C., 1965), 130.

5. For the 87th, see http://www.87thinfantrydivision.com/History/345th/Offi cial/index.html. A half year after Liz's death, her parents received a long, sweet letter from Mrs. T. C. Murphy in Biddulph, who had only recently learned of the tragedy. She fondly recalled Liz and the two pair of silk stockings. Mrs. T. C. Murphy to Charles and Henrietta Richardson, January 12, 1946.

6. This is Biddulph Old Hall, which still stands.

7. June Thistlethwaite, *Cumbria: The War Years* (Kendal, UK, 1997), 148. For very interesting insight into the war's effect on Barrow, see Richard Broad and Suzie Fleming, eds., *Nella Last's War: A Mother's Diary 1939–1945* (Bristol, UK, 1981). See also B. Trescatheric and D. J. Hughes, *Barrow at War* (Chorley, UK, 1979).

8. S. Keene Mitchell, Jr., to Harvey D. Gibson, January 8, 1945, Box 1493, Records of the American Red Cross, 1935–1946, Record Group 200, National Archives at College Park, Md. (hereafter cited as RG 200, NACP).

9. American Red Cross, "Uniform and Uniform Regulations, Services to Armed Forces," 10, mimeograph (March 1944), Box 1408, RG 200, NACP.

10. S. D. Hoslett, "The History of the American Red Cross: Vol. XVIII; Red Cross Personnel Administration in World War II," 203 (typescript, 1950), Hazel Braugh Records Center and Archives, American Red Cross, Lorton, Va. (hereafter cited as Braugh Records Center). Some Red Cross officials concluded that their selection process produced better female than male personnel. Ibid., 66. So did at least one Clubmobiler. Gretchen Schuyler to Katie _____, June 20, 1944, Gretchen Schuyler Papers, 2005-M150, American Red Cross Clubmobile Service Collection, Schlesinger Library, Radcliffe Institute, Harvard University.

11. This letter is marked as arriving in Indiana on January 5, 1945.

12. Liz refers to Furness Abbey, founded in 1123 and today under the care of English Heritage.

13. Marjorie "Margee" Main to parents, December 22, 1944.

14. Margee Main wrote similarly about Christmas homesickness: "It's kind of hard. But I wouldn't be anywhere else for anything." Main to parents, December 22, 1944.

15. Barbara Pathe, interview with author, October 31, 2005.

16. Main to family, December 29, 1944.

17. Will Durant, *The Story of Philosophy: The Lives and Opinions of the Greater Philosophers* (New York, 1926); Joan Shelley Rubin, *The Making of Middlebrow Culture* (Chapel Hill, N.C., 1992), 231–254.

18. *Dragon Seed* was a 1944 Hollywood movie depicting heroic Chinese resistance to the Japanese invaders. Critics tended to agree with Liz's negative opinion of the film. Clayton R. Koppes and Gregory D. Black, *Hollywood Goes to War: How Politics, Profits, and Propaganda Shaped World War II Movies* (Berkeley, 1987), 240–242.

19. Main to family, January 17, 1945.

20. Main to family, January 29, 1945.

21. Liz drew doodles of the group during that bridge game, with the slogan "Keep alive in 45." Main to family, January 29, 1945.

22. Bob Hope's bestselling *I Never Left Home* (1944) included stories of his entertainment shows for Americans overseas. The *Kansas City* crew read the book aloud and, Margee wrote, "enjoyed it immensely—specially the part about N.Y. and England, since we'd had many of those experiences, too." Main to family, January 29, 1945.

6. From the Gray Midlands to Sunny Cornwall

1. Margee Main wrote that the meal tasted like "library paste." Main to family, February 5, 1945. The chain of government-run British Restaurants offered nutritional food at reasonable prices for hard-pressed British citizens. Over 2,000 existed by mid-1943. British Information Services, *The Production and Distribution of Food in Great Britain* (New York, 1943), 19.

2. Main to family, February 5, 1945. See also Ben Shephard, *A War of Nerves: Soldiers and Psychiatrists in the Twentieth Century* (Cambridge, Mass., 2001), passim.

3. *The Sinker*, March 16, 1944, p. 4.

4. Margee Main wrote, "Amputations and burns and things like that are sort of a shock to see, but after a while you are just seeing the fellows getting cheered up and that makes you feel so thankful. . . . At any rate, if the men can stand to go out and get wounded, I guess I should have enough nerve to feed them coffee and doughnuts." Main to family, February 5, 1945.

5. The military censor cut out words here, very likely "Barrow-in-Furness." Liz seldom made this kind of mistake.

6. Graham Smith, *When Jim Crow Met John Bull: Black American Soldiers in World War II Britain* (New York, 1987); David Reynolds, *Rich Relations: The American Occupation of Britain, 1942–1945* (London, 1995), 216–237; Ministry of Information, *Meet the U.S. Army* (London, 1943), 14; Walter White, *A Rising Wind* (Garden City, N.Y., 1945); George H. Roeder, Jr., *The Censored War: American Visual Experience During World War Two* (New Haven, 1993), 56–57; Rosemary Norwalk, *Dearest Ones: A True World War II Love Story* (New York, 1999), 69–70; Deryk Wills, *Put on Your Boots and Parachutes! Personal Stories of the Veterans of the United States 82nd Airborne Division* (Leicester, 1992), 41–42; Barbara Brooks Tomblin, *G.I. Nightingales: The Army Nurse Corps in World War II* (Lexington, Ky., 1996), 123–124, 197; Graham A. Cosmas and Albert E. Cowdrey, *United States Army in World War II: Medical Service in the European Theater of Operations* (Washington, D.C., 1992), 123.

7. Richard F. Allen to Harvey D. Gibson, September 11, 1944, Box 1406, Records of the American Red Cross, 1935–1946, Record Group 200, National Archives at College Park, Md. (hereafter cited as RG 200, NACP); Kathryn Richardson Tyler, "The History of the American Red Cross: Vol. XXXII; American Red Cross Negro Personnel in World War II, 1942–1946," 3, 59–61, typescript, 1950, Hazel Braugh Records Center and Archives, American Red Cross, Lorton, Va. (hereafter cited

as Braugh Records Center); Clubmobile Houston Report, March 2, 1944, Jane McKee Jack Papers, 95-M124, American Red Cross Clubmobile Service Collection, Schlesinger Library, Radcliffe Institute, Harvard University; Postcard, Nancy Chase Papers, 95-M109, American Red Cross Clubmobile Service Collection, Schlesinger Library; Althea M. Bush, "American Red Cross Clubmobile Operations in Great Britain and Western Europe, April 1942–July 1946," typescript, 23, 52–53, September 1, 1947, Box 67, Monograph Collection, Braugh Records Center; Leisa D. Meyer, *Creating GI Jane: Sexuality and Power in the Women's Army Corps during World War II* (New York, 1996), 95–96. Segregation began with separate hotels for black recruits in the Red Cross training program in Washington. Lois I. Laster, interview with Brien R. Williams, February 23, 2000, Oral History Collection, Braugh Records Center.

8. Bush, "American Red Cross Clubmobile Operations in Great Britain and Western Europe," 30.

9. Walter White to Norman Davis, December 16, 1942, Box 1416, RG 200, NACP; Harvey Gibson to Norman H. Davis, November 27, 1943, Box 1406, RG 200, NACP; Robert Bondy to Mr. Allen, July 2, 1945, Box 1406, RG 200, NACP; *Pittsburgh Courier*, November 25, 1944; Kathryn R. Tyler to Louis Hackermann, April 1, 1947, and Jesse O. Thomas, "Commentary for monograph by Mrs. K. R. Tyler on ARC Red Cross Negro Personnel in World War II," n.d., both in Box 2, Monograph Collection, Braugh Records Center.

10. Margee Main wrote that "Most of the men are just back from the front lines where they've had only K-rations for months, and so the food is just heavenly. Steak, chicken, pork chops, wonderful vegetables, lots of everything—but still no milk." Main to family, February 5, 1945.

11. Mollie Panter-Downes, *London War Notes, 1939–1945* (New York, 1971), 358.

12. "Since You Went Away" (1944) was a sentimental melodrama, with several war-time goodbyes, wounded GIs in a veterans' hospital, and other scenes that doubtless constituted miseries too close to Liz's real life experiences. Clayton R. Koppes and Gregory D. Black, *Hollywood Goes to War: How Politics, Profits, and Propaganda Shaped World War II Movies* (Berkeley, 1987), 154–161; Thomas Doherty, *Projections of War: Hollywood, American Culture, and World War II* (New York, 1991), 169–173.

13. Margee Main wrote that "the whole day was so unexpected that it seemed like a dream." Main to family, February 11, 1945.

14. For another Clubmobiler's report on a similar trip to Cornwall a week later, see Norwalk, *Dearest Ones*, 128–132.

15. http://www.countrybus.org.uk/T-regal/T8a.htm.

16. Along with millions of other Americans, Liz had listened to Edward R. Murrow's CBS radio reports from London during the Battle of Britain.

17. Liz's pay increased from $150 to $175 a month on March 1, 1945. Elizabeth Ann Richardson, "Employees Service Record," American Red Cross Headquarters Personnel Office, Washington, D.C.

7. Across the Channel and into France

1. See Max Hastings, *Armageddon: The Battle for Germany 1944–1945* (New York, 2004).

2. Many others agreed with Liz's favorable review of "None But the Lonely

Heart," a 1944 Hollywood film that earned several Academy Award nominations and featured Cary Grant.

3. Kathryn Kirkpatrick Huehl, interview with author, June 2, 2003; James Tobin, *Ernie Pyle's War: America's Eyewitness to World War II* (New York, 1997), 201.

4. Ian Ousby, *Occupation: The Ordeal of France 1940–1944* (New York, 1997), 115–139, 159–161. For a fictional account by a writer who escaped Paris in 1940 but not the Holocaust, see Irène Némirovsky, *Suite Française* (New York, 2006).

5. United States War Department, *Pocket Guide to Paris and the Cities of Northern France* (Washington, D.C., 1944), 1; *Chicago Tribune*, March 18, 1945; David Pryce-Jones, *Paris in the Third Reich: A History of the German Occupation, 1940–1944* (New York, 1981), 94–111; Harvey Levenstein, *We'll Always Have Paris: American Tourists in France since 1903* (Chicago, 2004), 73–93.

6. Antony Beevor and Artemis Cooper, *Paris after the Liberation, 1944–1949* (London, 1994), 250.

7. "Ranging" was the Red Cross term for welcoming American troops arriving at the docks with coffee and doughnuts. B. J. Olewiler, *A Woman in a Man's War* (n.p., 2003), 95.

8. Levenstein, *We'll Always Have Paris*, 83.

9. Liz was right: Herman Göring did commandeer the Royal Suite at the Ritz Hotel. Levenstein, *We'll Always Have Paris*, 73.

10. Liz wrote "froid," French for cold, but she probably meant "chaud," that is, hot.

11. Jean Legoy, *Le Havre 1939–1945: Les Havrais dans la Guerre* (Le Havre, n.d.), 41–59.

12. "History of the U. S. Navy in Le Havre, France," typescript, [1946?], FCH415.5, City of Le Havre Archives, Le Havre, France; Legoy, *Le Havre 1939–1945*, 41–59; Joseph Bykofsky and Harold Larson, *United States Army in World War II: The Technical Services; The Transportation Corps; Operation Overseas* (Washington, D.C., 1957), 312, 316–318; Roland G. Ruppenthal, *United States Army in World War II: The European Theater of Operations: Logistical Support of the Armies. Volume II: September 1944–May 1945* (Washington, D.C., 1959), 96–102; quote from Peter Schrijvers, *The Crash of Ruin: American Combat Soldiers in Europe during World War II* (New York, 1998), 199. A good introduction to the postwar reconstruction of the city is Hugh Clout, "The Reconstruction of Upper Normandy: A Tale of Two Cities," *Planning Perspective* 14 (1999): 183–187. Le Havre was declared a World Heritage City in 2005. "Amongst many reconstructed cities, Le Havre is exceptional for its unity and integrity." http://whc.un esco.org/en/list/1181.

13. Legoy, *Le Havre 1939–1945*; Monica Stirling, "The French Look So Healthy," *Atlantic* 175 (May 1945): 56.

14. Pierre Aubery, *Les Américains au Havre* (Paris, 1948), 77, 14, 85; Valérie Moulin, Daniel Baccara, and Jean-Michel Harel, *Le Havre, 16th Port of Embarkation, 15 Septembre 1944–21 Octobre 1946* (Le Havre, 1996), 50–59; Joe Weston, "GIs in Le Havre: Americans in France Are Envoys of Ill Will," *Life* 19 (December 10, 1945): 19–20. Broader contexts are found in Alice Kaplan, *The Interpreter* (New York, 2005), 27; Elizabeth Coquart, *La France Des G.I's.: Histoire d'un Amour Déçu* (Paris, 2003), 137–161; and Armand Frémont, *La Mémoire D'Un Port: Le Havre* (Paris, 1997).

15. One Red Cross worker stationed outside Le Havre had heard that "the people in Le Havre hate Americans," and that "French men and women actually spit on Amer-

icans. . . . The people say the Americans deliberately bombed them." Liz did not report such extreme feelings. Edith Steiger Phillips, *My World War II Diary* (New York, 1973), 270. For larger contexts, see Hilary Footitt, *War and Liberation in France: Living with the Liberators* (New York, 2004), 147–174.

16. Althea M. Bush, "ETO Club Department," typescript, n.d., 184, Box 67, Monograph Collection, Hazel Braugh Records Center and Archives, American Red Cross, Lorton, Va. (hereafter cited as Braugh Records Center); Robert Bremner et al., "The History of the American National Red Cross: Vol. XIII; American Red Cross Service in the War Against the European Axis," 507–508, typescript, 1950, Braugh Records Center; Althea M. Bush, "American Red Cross Clubmobile Operations in Great Britain and Western Europe, April 1942–July 1946," 93–94, typescript, September 1, 1947, Box 67, Monograph Collection, Braugh Records Center.

17. Report of P. Aubrey in Moulin, Baccarat, and Harrell, *Le Havre, 16th Port*, 54–55; Nancy Nicholas, "Dock Service—Le Havre," in Marjorie Lee Morgan, ed., *The Clubmobile: The ARC in the Storm* (St. Petersburg, Fla., 1982), 169; Jean-Claude Marquis, Valerie Herson, Jean-Louis Jordanian, *Les Camps Cigarette: Les Americans en Haute Normandy à la Liberation* (Rouen, 1994); Foster Rhea Dulles, *The American Red Cross: A History* (New York, 1950), 462–463; *Newsweek* 25 (June 4, 1945): 48; *New York Times*, July 30, 1945; Levenstein, *We'll Always Have Paris*, 84–87.

18. Mary Haynsworth Mathews, interview with author, March 28, 2003.

19. This is probably Allene Cushing of Buffalo, N.Y.

20. Olewiler, *A Woman in a Man's War*, 64; Gretchen Schuyler to Edy Schuyler, May 26, 1943, Gretchen Schuyler Papers, 2005-M150, American Red Cross Clubmobile Service Collection, Schlesinger Library, Radcliffe Institute, Harvard University.

21. Sylvie Bardot to author, July 1, 2003; Mathews, interviews with author, March 28, June 28, 2003.

22. Nicholas, "Dock Service—Le Havre," 169.

23. Interview with Rose Policastro, January 25, 2005; Bykofsky and Larson, *United States Army in World War II: Operation Overseas*, 190, 317; Chester Wardlow, *United States Army in World War II, The Technical Services: The Transportation Corps: Movements, Training, and Supply* (Washington, D.C., 1956), 442–449.

24. Frank Policastro to Henrietta Richardson, October 20, 1945.

25. Frank Policastro to Henrietta Richardson, August 26, 1945.

26. *Dictionary of American Naval Fighting Ships* at http://www.history.navy.mil/danfs/p11/president_warfield.htm.

27. The Red Cross director of personnel requested that each Elizabeth Richardson ask her correspondents to use her middle name rather than only initial and a more specific address. L. W. Neatherlin to Schubert E. Smith, June 15, 1945 (Charles Richardson Collection).

28. Margaret Gearhart to parents, October 29, 1944, Margaret Gearhart Brodie Papers, 96-M25, American Red Cross Clubmobile Service Collection, Schlesinger Library; *ARC London Light* (newsletter), n.d.

29. Nicholas, "Dock Service—Le Havre," 169.

30. William F. Ross and Charles F. Romanus, *United States Army in World War II, The Technical Services: The Quartermaster Corps: Operations in the War Against Germany* (Washington, D.C., 1965), 541–542.

31. Arieh J. Kochavi, *Confronting Captivity: Britain and the United States and Their*

POWS in Nazi Germany (Chapel Hill, N.C., 2005), 1; Phillips, *My World War II Diary*, 266; _____ Bahn, "Camp Lucky Strike," typescript, n.d., 15–16, Box 1018, Records of the American Red Cross, 1935–1946, Record Group 200, National Archives at College Park, Md.; *Newsweek* 25 (June 4, 1945): 48; William L. Cupp, *A Wartime Journey: Bail-Out over Belgium, World War II* (n.p., 2002), 395–397; Robert D. Reeves, "Peoria to Munich: A Prisoner of War," http://www.lp-net.com/pow/default.htm; Dwight D. Eisenhower, *Crusade in Europe* (Garden City, N.Y., 1952), 420–422; Paul A. Porter, "General Ike and Hair," Paul Porter Memoir, Box 5, Harry C. Butcher Papers, Dwight D. Eisenhower Presidential Library, Abilene, Kans.; Harry Spiller, ed., *Prisoners of Nazis: Accounts of American POWs in World War II* (Jefferson, N.C., 1998), 76.

32. Kurt Vonnegut, Jr., to Kurt Vonnegut, Sr., May 29, 1945, in *Traces of Indiana and Midwestern History* 3 (Fall 1991): 45.

33. *Newsweek*, September 17, 1945; Margaret Morrison Scrapbooks, in possession of Kevin Cornyn; Bush, "American Red Cross Clubmobile Operations in Great Britain and Western Europe," 67; Nicholas, "Dock Service—Le Havre," 169. Kurt Vonnegut later drew on his memories as a prisoner in Dresden in *Slaughterhouse-Five; Or, The Children's Crusade, a Duty-Dance with Death* (New York, 1969). The Nazis generally treated American and British prisoners better than Russian, Polish, and certainly Jewish prisoners. Nonetheless, many Americans suffered greatly in German prisons.

34. Mathews, interviews with author, March 28, June 28, 2003.

35. Moulin, Baccara, and Harel, *Le Havre, 16th Port*, 54; Clout, "The Reconstruction of Upper Normandy," 187–188.

8. V-E Day and V-E Blues

1. Valérie Moulin, Daniel Baccara, and Jean-Michel Harel, *Le Havre, 16th Port of Embarkation, 15 Septembre 1944–21 Octobre 1946* (Le Havre, 1996), 52.

2. Arieh J. Kochavi, *Confronting Captivity: Britain and the United States and Their POWS in Nazi Germany* (Chapel Hill, N.C., 2005), 86–97. See also John A. Vietor, *Time Out: American Airmen at Stalag Luft 1* (New York, 1951), 188–191.

3. Gretchen Schuyler to Katie _____, January 14, 1945, Gretchen Schuyler Papers, 2005-M150, American Red Cross Clubmobile Service Collection, Schlesinger Library Radcliffe Institute, Harvard University; Judy Barrett Litoff and David C. Smith, *We're in This War, Too: World War II Letters from American Women in Uniform* (New York, 1994), 258.

4. Samuel A. Stouffer et al., *The American Soldier: Adjustment during Army Life* (Princeton, 1949), II, 546–595; *New York Times*, May 20, 1945; *Stars and Stripes*, May 11, 1945; Harvey Levenstein, *We'll Always Have Paris: American Tourists in France since 1903* (Chicago, 2004), 85; Joe Weston, "GIs in Le Havre: Americans in France Are Envoys of Ill Will," *Life* 19 (December 10, 1945): 19–20; Kathleen Havens Gezzi, ed., *Journey Between Mountains: The Letters and Journal of Mary Hall Baroudi* (Bloomington, Ind., 2006), 146; Robert A. Hull to Frederick A. Carroll, July 4, 1945, Box 1493, Records of the American Red Cross, 1935–1946, Record Group 200, National Archives at College Park, Md. (hereafter cited as RG 200, NACP); Robert Bremner et al., "The History of the American National Red Cross: Vol. XIII; American Red Cross Service in the War Against the European Axis," 509, typescript, 1950, Hazel Braugh Records Center and Archives, American Red Cross, Lorton, Va. (hereafter cited as Braugh Records Center); *New York Times*, November 8, 12, 1945.

5. Priscilla Alden to N. T. McKee, April 7, 1945, Jane McKee Jack Papers, 95-M124, American Red Cross Clubmobile Service Collection, Schlesinger Library; *Overseas Woman* I (July 1945): 29.

6. Bremner et al., "The History of the American National Red Cross," 469, 467 (June 4 quote); Hull to Carroll, July 4, 1945, Box 1493, RG 200, NACP; Richard F. Allen to Carroll, June 2, 1945, Box 1406, RG 200, NACP; Karon S. Bailey, "Harriett Engelhardt: A Job Worth Having," *Alabama Heritage* 57 (Summer 2000): 34 (Engelhardt never made it home: she died in a jeep accident that fall.); Jane McKee to parents, January 2, 1946, Jack Papers; Alden to Mrs. N. T. McKee, March 24, 1946, Jack Papers; Oscar Whitelaw Rexford, ed., *Battlestars & Doughnuts: World War II Clubmobile Experiences of Mary Metcalfe Rexford* (St. Louis, 1989), 70. Morale continued to worsen as reported from Paris by a long-time Red Cross administrator in spring 1946: "Here at Headquarters, where we see so much going on that is against Red Cross ideals, and hear so much griping, we often go down to the depths ourselves. . . ." Alden to Mrs. McKee, March 24, 1946, Jack Papers.

7. *Over Here*, June 1, July 7, August 11, 1945; Richard F. Allen to Carroll, May 31, 1944, Box 1406, RG 200, NACP.

8. Mary Haynsworth Mathews to author, April 11, 2003.

9. Chester Wardlow, *United States Army in World War II, The Technical Services: The Transportation Corps: Movements, Training, and Supply* (Washington, D.C., 1956), 182–190; Joseph Bykofsky and Harold Larson, *United States Army in World War II: The Technical Services; The Transportation Corps; Operation Overseas* (Washington, D.C., 1957), 362–363; *Chicago Tribune*, August 3, 1945; Edith Steiger Phillips, *My World War II Diary* (New York, 1973), 266; _____ Bahn, "Camp Lucky Strike," typescript, n.d., 18–19, Box 1018, RG 200, NACP.

10. It was about this time that Sgt. William A. Madison was standing in those long lines at Camp Lucky Strike. The hot shower he had there was one of the few memories of his World War II experience that he shared with his son.

11. A Red Cross official at Lucky Strike reported six Clubmobile women arriving there on May 24. Liz's name was not on the list. Bahn, "Camp Lucky Strike," 18–19.

12. Mrs. S. Sloan Colt was American Red Cross deputy commissioner for Great Britain and Western Europe. At a June 1 press conference she urged American women between 25 and 45 to volunteer for Red Cross duty as they were "badly needed" to serve occupation troops in Europe. *New York Times*, June 2, 1945. In a Chicago speech she reminded Americans, "The Red Cross women are 'spending their hearts'." *Chicago Tribune*, June 5, 1945.

13. "History of the U. S. Navy in Le Havre, France," 12, typescript, [1946?], FCH415.5, City of Le Havre Archives, Le Havre, France; Pierre Aubery, *Les Américains au Havre* (Paris, 1948), 117–118.

14. Moulin, Baccara, and Harel, *Le Havre, 16th Port*, 51, 52, 54, 58. In early August 1945, the local newspaper reported gunfire between MPs and black soldiers on the rue de la République. Ibid., 58. Kathryn Richardson Tyler, "The History of the American Red Cross: Vol. XXXII; American Red Cross Negro Personnel in World War II, 1942–1946," 41–56, typescript, 1950, Braugh Records Center; Althea M. Bush, "ETO Club Department," 186, typescript, n.d., Box 67, Monograph Collection, Braugh Records Center; Studs Terkel, *"The Good War": An Oral History of World War Two* (New

York, 1984), 369–370. For additional context, see Alice Kaplan, *The Interpreter* (New York, 2005).

15. Frederick A. Carroll to All ARC Personnel, May 23, 1945, Box 1406, RG 200, NACP.

16. S. D. Hoslett, "The History of the American Red Cross: Vol. XVIII; Red Cross Personnel Administration in World War II," 207, typescript, 1950, Braugh Records Center.

9. One Plane Crash

1. ER to Winifred Wood, June 4, 1945.

2. U.S. Army Air Forces, Report of Aircraft Accident, L-5B, No. 44-16903, July 25, 1945, Headquarters Air Force Historical Research Agency, Maxwell AFB, AL; Frank J. Malinak to author, July 12, 2003. For plane specifications, see http://www.nationalmuseum.af.mil/factsheets/factsheet.asp?id=519.

3. Henry A. Wann to Janice Punch, February 4, 1946, Box 2, Monograph Collection, Hazel Braugh Records Center and Archives, American Red Cross, Lorton, Va. (hereafter cited as Braugh Records Center); Marshall Smelser to Louis Hackman, April 4, 1946, Box 2, Monograph Collection, Braugh Records Center; *Over Here*, May 1, 15, August 11, 1945. Of the approximately 400,000 American deaths in World War II, about 100,000 were from non-combat causes, including accidents, illness, and suicide. Michael Sledge, *Soldier Dead: How We Recover, Identify, Bury, and Honor Our Military Fallen* (New York, 2005), 65.

4. Mary Haynsworth Mathews, interview with Eric Elliott, November 9, 1999, Women Veterans Historical Collection, University of North Carolina at Greensboro. http://library.uncg.edu/depts/archives/veterans/Mathewstrans.html.

5. A thief broke into the footlocker and removed jewelry, clothing, and other items. Frank Policastro to Charles Richardson, Sr., September 30, 1945.

6. Mary Haynsworth Mathews laughed when in 2003 she told the story of how Liz got dressed in her Red Cross uniform in the morning. In front of her mirror in Chateau Hysteria, she would ask, "Mirror, mirror, on the wall, who's the prettiest girl of all?" and then shout "Elizabeth Richardson!" Her friends loved the playfulness of this "funny gal." Mary Haynsworth Mathews, interview with author, March 28, 2003.

7. Daisy Tucker, "Nancy Reagan Honors Memory of Milwaukee-Downer Grad," *Lawrence Alumni Magazine*, 1982.

10. The Long Memory

1. Charles M. Richardson, Jr., interview with author, June 11, 2003.

2. Frank Policastro to Charles and Henrietta Richardson, September 16, 30, October 20, 1945.

3. Rose Policastro, interview with author, January 25, 2005.

4. Mary Haynsworth Mathews, interview with author, March 28, 2003; Chris Hanson Watson to author (June 2003); Charles Richardson, Jr., interview with author, June 11, 2003.

5. *The Sinker, Jr.* (ARC Clubmobile Association), December 1946; *Hawthorne Leaves*, January 1946; David Eisen, ed., *A Mishawaka Mosaic* (Elkhart, Ind., 1983), 31.

6. Disinterment Directive, St. Andre, EA Richardson, ARC 42741 T44A (Charles Richardson, Jr., Collection); American Battle Monuments Commission, *Normandy American Cemetery and Memorial* (n.p., n.d.), 6–7, 28–92; interview with Charles Richardson, Jr., June 11, 2003; Edward Steere and Thayer M. Boardman, *Final Disposition of World War II Dead, 1945–51* (Washington, D.C., 1957), 279, 307–308, 325–327; Michael Sledge, *Soldier Dead: How We Recover, Identify, Bury, and Honor Our Military Fallen* (New York, 2005), 140–151. Approximately 170,000 of 280,000 recovered remains were returned to the United States at the request of family members. Boardman, *Final Disposition*, 151. Red Cross worker Eleanor Stevenson, who got to know GIs well, wrote in 1945: "I think if it were left up to the dead soldier himself, he would want all that remains of him to stay with those others who died with him, as long as they stay there." Eleanor Stevenson and Pete Martin, *I Knew Your Soldier* (Washington, D.C., 1945), 235.

7. Betty Twining Blue to Charles and Henrietta Richardson, September 22, 1951; Betty Twining Blue, interviews with author, November 12, 2003, June 9, 2005.

8. Blue to Charles and Henrietta Richardson, September 22, 1951; Charles Richardson, Jr., interview with author, June 11, 2003; Marge Sandoz to Charles and Henrietta Richardson, October 24, 1952. Other visitors included Le Havre Red Cross colleague Mary Hankins, who visited the cemetery in 1948 and again in 1972 and Milwaukee Downer classmate Mary Wiersig, who went there in 1984. Mary Hankins to Nancy Reagan, August 8, 1982, and Mary Wiersig to Nancy Reagan, July 9, 1985, folder "Richardson, Elizabeth" WHORM: Alpha File, Ronald Reagan Presidential Library, Simi Valley, Calif.

9. American Battle Monuments Commission, *Normandy American Cemetery and Memorial*, 6–7, 15–16, 28–92; Christina S. Jarvis, *The Male Body at War: American Masculinity during World War II* (DeKalb, Ill., 2004), 162–163.

10. *New York Times*, June 18, 1945.

11. *New York Times*, June 7, 1982; *Washington Post*, June 7, 1982. The Associated Press wire story correctly noted that Liz "died in a plane crash after the invasion." *Augusta Chronicle*, June 7, 1983. The American Red Cross put the photograph on the cover of its magazine, *The Good Neighbor* X (Summer 1982). Newspaper coverage produced letters to Nancy Reagan with warm memories of Liz from college classmates Betty Blue and Mary Wiersig, Le Havre Red Cross colleague Mary Hankins, and high school best friend Anne Schuknecht. Betty Blue to Nancy Reagan, September 6, 1982; Mary Wiersig to Reagan, July 9, 1982; Mary Hankins to Reagan, August 8, 1982; Anne Schuknecht to Reagan, n.d. (1982), all in folder "Richardson, Elizabeth" WHORM: Alpha File, Reagan Library.

12. Marianna Torgovnick, *The War Complex: World War II in Our Time* (Chicago, 2005), 2–3.

13. See, for example, Judy Barrett Litoff and David C. Smith, *We're in This War, Too: World War II Letters from American Women in Uniform* (New York, 1994), 258.

14. The Schlesinger Library at Harvard University began in 1995 a project to collect and preserve these sources. The Library invited several Clubmobile veterans to tour its collections of women's history and then served them coffee and doughnuts, which, one of them wrote, "really won our hearts." Barbara Kratz to Anne Engelhart, September 23, 1996, Barbara Bray Kratz Papers, 96-M127, American Red Cross Clubmobile Service Collection, Schlesinger Library, Radcliffe Institute, Harvard University.

15. Interview with Kathryn Kirkpatrick Huehl, June 14, 2006; *London Daily Telegraph*, July 31, 1962; *The Sinker, Jr.*, April 1962, December 1962, 1967.

16. Eloise Reilly to author, December 14, 2005, March 6, 2006.

17. For concern that the women would be forgotten, see Margaret Fleming to Bernadine Healy, December 12, 2000, Veterans History Project, Library of Congress, at: http://lcweb2.loc.gov/cocoon/vhp/story/loc.natlib.afc2001001.01768/pageturner?ID=pm0001001&page=26&submit.x=14&submit.y=9.

18. http://www.abmc.gov/nvc/index.php.

19. Oscar Whitelaw Rexford, ed., *Battlestars & Doughnuts: World War II Clubmobile Experiences of Mary Metcalfe Rexford* (St. Louis, 1989), 135; ER to Betty Twining, September 4, 1944.

Appendix

1. ER to John Richardson, November 1, 1944.

2. See Steven Stowe, "Making Sense of Letters and Diaries," *History Matters: The U.S. Survey Course on the Web*, http://historymatters.gmu.edu/mse/letters/, July 2002.

Note on Sources

Primary Sources

The major sources for this book are the letters and diary of Elizabeth A. Richardson, in possession of Charles Richardson, Jr. Unless otherwise indicated, citations in endnotes are from this collection. Also included in this collection are letters from Margee Main. The records of Milwaukee-Downer College, now deposited at the Lawrence University Archives, Appleton, Wisconsin, provide evidence for Elizabeth Richardson's college years. Also helpful is the university's website about her, which includes selections from her letters and diary: http://www.lawrence.edu/library/archives/richardson/index.htm.

Essential context for the American Red Cross and the Clubmobile work in England and France is provided in documents at three Washington, D.C., area archives. At the National Archives at College Park, Maryland, are Records of the American Red Cross, 1935–1946, Record Group 200. And at the American Red Cross Hazel Braugh Records Center and Archives in Lorton, Virginia, are a variety of sources, including the very helpful manuscript histories prepared in the late 1940s by historians employed by the organization. The Braugh Records Center also has a run of *The Sinker*, the newsletter of the Clubmobile program in Britain. The American University Archives, Washington, D.C., has helpful source materials for the Red Cross wartime training program.

In Cambridge, Massachusetts, the American Red Cross Clubmobile Service Collection at the Arthur and Elizabeth Schlesinger Library on the History of Women in America, Radcliffe Institute, Harvard University, contains a large volume of rich documents from numerous women who served in Clubmobiles during the war. Also helpful were Margaret Morrison's scrapbooks, in possession of her son, Kevin Cornyn.

Oral history interviews with people who knew Elizabeth Richardson and with Clubmobile veterans were essential sources. Unless noted, all were conducted by the author.

Betty Twining Blue
Mary Sullivan O'Driscoll
Ann Bumby Fallon
Kathryn Kirkpatrick Huehl
Mary Haynsworth Mathews, with author and also with Eric Elliott, Women Veterans Historical Collection, University of North Carolina at Greensboro (http://library.uncg.edu/depts/archives/veterans/Mathewstrans.html)

Barbara Pathe, interviews with author and also with Brien R. Williams, Oral History Collection, Hazel Braugh Records Center and Archives, American Red Cross, Lorton, Va.
Rose Policastro
Eloise Reilly
Charles M. Richardson, Jr.
Anne Bodle Schuknecht
Clarissa (Chris) Hanson Watson

Published memoirs and correspondence of Clubmobile women provide good insight into their work. These include:

Bailey, Karon S. "Harriett Engelhardt: A Job Worth Having." *Alabama Heritage* 57 (Summer 2000): 26–35.
Gezzi, Kathleen Havens, ed. *Journey Between Mountains: The Letters and Journal of Mary Hall Baroudi.* Bloomington, Ind., 2006.
Morgan, Marjorie Lee, ed. *The Clubmobile: The ARC in the Storm.* St. Petersburg, Fla., 1982.
Norwalk, Rosemary. *Dearest Ones: A True World War II Love Story.* New York, 1999.
Olewiler, B. J. *A Woman in a Man's War.* n.p., 2003.
Phillips, Edith Steiger. *My World War II Diary.* New York, 1973.
Rexford, Oscar Whitelaw, ed. *Battlestars & Doughnuts: World War II Clubmobile Experiences of Mary Metcalfe Rexford.* New York, 1999.

A good website devoted to Clubmobile history, with some firsthand accounts, is http://www.clubmobile.org/index.html.

Secondary Sources

The secondary literature on World War II is immense and growing rapidly. Among books on combat that provide good context for the Clubmobile work are Gerald F. Linderman, *The World Within War: America's Combat Experience in World War II* (New York, 1997), Peter Schrijvers, *The Crash of Ruin: American Combat Soldiers in Europe during World War II* (New York, 1998), and Max Hastings, *Armageddon: The Battle for Germany 1944–1945* (New York, 2004). The general British context is expertly studied in David Reynolds, *Rich Relations: The American Occupation of Britain, 1942–1945* (London, 1995). Helpful for France is "History of the U. S. Navy in Le Havre, France," typescript [1946?], FCH415.5, City of Le Havre Archives, Le Havre, France; Harvey Levenstein, *We'll Always Have Paris: American Tourists in France since 1930* (Chicago, 2004); and Hilary Footitt, *War and Liberation in France: Living with the Liberators* (New York, 2004).

Books that help understand men and women in war include Leisa D. Meyer, *Creating GI Jane: Sexuality and Power in the Women's Army Corps during World War II* (New York, 1996); Christina S. Jarvis, *The Male Body at War: American Masculinity during World War II* (DeKalb, Ill., 2004); and D'Ann Campbell, *Women at War with America: Private Lives in a Patriotic Era* (Cambridge, Mass., 1984). For a good introduction to wartime correspondence, including several letters from Red Cross women, see Judy Barrett Litoff and David C. Smith, *We're in This War, Too: World War II Letters from American Women in Uniform* (New York, 1994).

Helpful introductions to the American Red Cross are Foster Rhea Dulles, *The American Red Cross: A History* (New York, 1950), and George Korson, *At His Side* (New York, 1945). There is very useful information on the organization's website at http://www.redcross.org/museum/history/.

Acknowledgments

Of the many people who helped in the making of this book I begin with Charles Richardson, Jr., brother of Elizabeth Richardson. He saved the letters and her diary, and he generously made them available for my use and agreed to publication. Twice I visited with Charley in California, where he answered questions and helped in so many other ways. Helpful too in sorting and copying documents at Charley's home was Jane Lesh, a former librarian with an eye for detail. I'm also grateful to Charles Kennard for making photographs of items in the Richardson Collection.

One of the pleasures of this project was getting to know several former Clubmobile women. The qualities in the Red Cross selection process come through today. Those I talked with were all thoughtful and sophisticated about their experience and about larger contexts and meanings of the war years. What I learned from conversations, email, and letters as well as the more structured interviews runs through this book. These special women are listed in the note on sources, but I thank several now for the contributions they made during World War II and for helping me understand: Mary Sullivan O'Driscoll, Kathryn Kirkpatrick Huehl, Mary Haynsworth Mathews, Barbara Pathe, and Eloise Reilly.

Equally enjoyable to know were Liz's friends outside the Red Cross, including Betty Twining Blue, Ann Bumby Fallon, Anne Bodle Schuknecht, and Clarissa (Chris) Hanson Watson (also a Red Cross veteran). Margaret Morrison's son, Kevin Cornyn, lent me his mother's scrapbooks. Rose Policastro shared memories of her husband, Frank.

Archivists and librarians were very helpful, particularly Susan Robbins Watson at the Hazel Braugh Records Center and Archives of the American Red Cross; Tab Lewis at the National Archives in College

Park, Maryland; Susan McElrath at American University; Susan Richards and Julia Stringfellow at Lawrence University; and Sarah Hutcheon, Diana Carey, and Anne Engelhart at the Schlesinger Library, Radcliffe Institute, Harvard University. Other people provided helpful sources and information including Tana Lundahl, Wendy Clark, Joe Culpepper, Jim Gray, and Shelly Jacobs. At the Le Havre Archives in France Sylvie Barot provided sources and guidance.

Several kind people in England answered questions and provide assistance, including Gregory Drozdz, Elaine Heathcote, Glenn Lang, Peter Leach, Bill Myers, and Deryk Wills. Good friend Elizabeth Mattingly helped me find the Imperial Hotel in Barrow-in-Furness. Others who tracked down sources and details closer to home included Elizabeth Blue, Matt Guardino, Jason Lantzer, James Lide, Lori Policastro, Jane Rogan, Roy Shoemaker, and Richard Simons.

I am grateful again to Indiana University, which has long provided me an academic home in which to teach and write about World War II and other subjects. Students in my classes and in the lifelong learning program, Mini University, taught me a great deal about the war. Indiana provided a sabbatical leave that allowed me time to bring the pieces of this book together. In Bloomington I continued to benefit from the resources of the Herman B Wells Library and the superb university librarians who work there, particularly Lou Malcomb and Celestina Wroth. In the history department, Debbie Chase keyboarded the letters and diary, and Nancy Ashley, Becky Bryant, Jo Ellen Fitzgerald, and Deana Hutchins helped in many ways. I owe again great gratitude to Thomas and Kathryn Miller, whose generous gift to Indiana University helps support my research and writing.

I had the benefit of several exceptionally astute readers. Suellen Hoy and Annette Atkins, friends from graduate school days, helped not only in sentence construction but in thinking about subject and audience. Judy Barrett Litoff read an early draft and expertly applied her years of experience working with women's letters from the World War II era. Robert Sloan at Indiana University Press advised me in reshaping important sections of the manuscript. Anne Teillard-Clemmer and Miki Bird at the Press improved the content and appearance of the book while keeping us all on schedule. Paula Corpuz did the hard work of indexing with talent and grace. Jeanne Madison provided the critical eye of a lifetime reader. I am most grateful for this generosity of time and talent.

My family's lives happily intertwine with mine and with my study of the past. As the book dedication indicates, my parents were of the war generation: my mother a nurse on the home front; my father a combat rifleman in Europe. (It's not impossible that Liz Richardson served him a doughnut and a smile in England or France.) My children, John and Julia, have always humored my interests and kept them in perspective. Julie and Adam, daughter-in-law and son-in-law, add new support. Jeanne continues as captain of the family Clubmobile.

Index

James H. Madison is Thomas and Kathryn Miller Professor of History at Indiana University, Bloomington. He is author of *A Lynching in the Heartland: Race and Memory in America* and other books.